THE

RIGHT

TO DIE?

THE RIGHT TO DIE?

CARING ALTERNATIVES TO EUTHANASIA

Mark Blocher

MOODY PRESS
CHICAGO

ISBN: 0-8024-7739-9

1 3 5 7 9 10 8 6 4 2

Printed in the United States of America

To Dr. John White, Jr.,
my pastor, mentor, and friend—
Thank you for teaching me
to love the Savior, teach the Word,
and care about people

CONTENTS

INTRODUCTION

I remember attending my great-grandmother's funeral and seeing, for the first time, an actual dead human being. It was very disturbing to think that someone I knew personally was actually dead. I was traumatized by the thought that someone I loved would no longer be able to speak to me, that I would no longer hear her stories or eat her cookies. I was repulsed by the thought that one day I myself would lie in an open coffin with people milling around it, peering at my lifeless body.

Most people my age (forty-seven) have lived long enough to experience the death of a close friend or family member. For me, some experiences are more vivid than others. My father's death in an automobile collision with a drunk driver is the most difficult death I've had to face. I've also experienced the suicide of a brother-in-law, the sudden death of a high school buddy from a heart attack at age eighteen, the slow death of a grandfather from emphysema, and the long, slow death of a friend from AIDS.

As a pastor and bioethicist, I have stood beside deathbeds many times. In my role as a bioethicist, I have provided counsel to families as they made difficult treatment decisions near the end of a loved one's life. I have held the hands of frightened people moments after they were given a terminal diagnosis. I've held basins for people as they vomited following chemotherapy, tried to comfort people in pain, and designed a church-based hospice program for local churches.

MY GOAL IS TO GIVE . . . SOUND BIBLICAL, MORAL, AND PRACTICAL REASONS FOR REJECTING ASSISTED SUICIDE AND EUTHANASIA.

These experiences motivate me to do what I can to improve the quality of care provided to individuals facing a final illness, being careful to remember that one day I will have to take my own advice. The issues I address in this book deal with real people, and I am well aware that the solutions I offer must work in the real world.

The psalmist called dying the "valley of the shadow of death" (Psalm 23). For many people, death and dying are represented best by darkness and uncertainty. They live in dread of it, fearing the day the "grim reaper" stops at their doorstep.

This book is directed at two primary audiences. First, it is aimed at those who intuitively believe assisted suicide and euthanasia are immoral, but who do not know how to articulate their views. Second, it is aimed at those who believe assisted suicide and euthanasia may be moral, but who remain uncertain. My goal is to give both audiences sound biblical, moral, and practical reasons for rejecting assisted suicide and euthanasia.

WHAT WE OWE THE DYING

What do we owe the dying? The answer to this question is what most distinguishes the "death with dignity" movement from those who oppose it. One thing we owe the dying is the assurance that their worst fears will not come to pass. This book is a contrast between a hospice approach to the end of life and a so-called "death with dignity" approach (what some call Kevorkianism).[1] It is important how each approach responds to the fears expressed by terminally ill individuals and what each promises to do for them. The hospice approach promises the terminally ill that they will not die in pain, they will not die alone, and they will certainly not be a burden to anyone. Those promises are fulfilled through an extensive, inter-disciplinary approach to end-of-life care, an approach I want read-ers to see as the only morally appropriate one.

Killing is not caring. It may be compassionate, it may even seem merciful, but it is not caring. Caring requires commitment, sacrifice, and personal involvement. Euthanasia and assisted suicide are marked by their distinctive lack of commitment, promising only that death will be swift and painless. The hospice approach provides the terminally ill with relief from the symptoms of terminal illness in a life-enhancing manner. It is an approach that provides the terminal-ly ill person with the one thing he has least of—time: time to seek and give forgiveness, to give counsel, to love. Kevorkianism, rooted in a perversion of personal autonomy doctrine, views hastening death as the only solution to terminal illness, believing that nothing good can occur in the midst of it.

What is really at stake in the battle over physician-assisted sui-cide? Certainly not political ideology. The issues transcend any nar-row interest such as politics, evidenced by the fact that there is support for legalized physician-assisted suicide among people in all of the major political parties. The Christian stake really boils down to crucial biblical concerns: concerns about who shall be deemed to belong to the human community with its rights and responsibilities, what we owe the dying among us, and what is to be the significance of death for human beings. In the final analysis, the issues reduce to a question of who will control the exit gates of life. *God* is the One who decides when it's someone's time to die (Job 14:5).

DISTURBING NOTIONS OF CONTROL

Despite the fact that all people do die, many seem to have a stubborn, optimistic faith in modern medicine's ability to do any-thing. The invention of workable medical technologies that extend lives that would otherwise be lost is viewed as a triumph—tanta-mount to human mastery over all medical choices, and, ultimately, mastery over human destiny as well. When this attitude exists among medical practitioners, modern medicine crosses over the line into idolatry, directly pitting the powers of finite, human technologi-cal progress against the pronouncements and power of an infinite, sovereign God: a God who declares that we are really helpless in the face of inevitable demise (Hebrews 9:27; Romans 6:23). Human ingenuity and knowledge clash with the God who urges us to rely upon Him rather than our own inventions (Proverbs 3:5–6). It is a dangerous thing to place one's wholehearted confidence in a scientific endeavor that does not have the humility to know its own limitations.

The emergence of a vocal and vibrant "right to die" movement argues we must not give up control to mindless technologies, but we should expand human control over the end of life, even if it means using death itself as a means of eliminating pain and suffering. Hastening death is seen as a morally appropriate response to the disease, pain, and suffering that medical technologies cannot eliminate.

Even more than death itself, our world fears disability. We have a history of shoving disabled people into the background, treating them as second-class citizens, putting them out of our sight. Americans place a premium on health and strength, and they see no value in suffering or pain. If we sicken and die, too often we do these things alone. Just as hired mourners could not replace the weeping Lord Jesus at the grave of His friend Lazarus (John 11:35), hired caregivers are really no substitute for family and friends during one's time of suffering and death. This is not to suggest that paid caregivers do not care, nor that they only provide care for payment. Fortunately, the caregiving skills of many medical professionals and hospice personnel are extraordinary. However, hired caregivers cannot do what family members and friends can.

THE DEBATE . . . MISSES THE MOST
IMPORTANT ISSUE, HOW TO IMPROVE
CARE FOR DYING INDIVIDUALS.

One aim of this book is to inform and equip the church for the high calling of providing compassionate, caring alternatives to assisted suicide and euthanasia. Rather than seizing upon the present difficulties at the end of life to press for legalization of assisted suicide and euthanasia, we should see them as opportunities to learn more about our own limitations, to be reminded of the limits of medicine, and to press for the "de-medicalization" of life and death.

We should not permit tragic circumstances to become opportunities to shape the concepts of autonomy and human dignity into rationalizations that justify "mercy killing." The fears these scenes create in the public's perception of dying and death are deceptive. The public is led to believe that there are only two options: either dying in the most horrible circumstances imaginable, or dying a "peaceful" death by physician-assisted suicide.[2]

It is unwise to press for legalization of physician-assisted suicide when so few people are aware of alternatives like hospice. In fact, focusing all our effort on the debate whether or not we should legalize the practice misses the most important issue, how to improve care for dying individuals. I am not saying that I oppose efforts to make physician-assisted suicide and euthanasia clearly illegal. Both practices should be illegal. Should we acquiesce to the clarion call to make physicians into killers, we will not only abandon our loved ones and our duty to care for them, but we will have unleashed the worst tendencies of modern life—the tendency to cushion selfishness and inhumanity under the soft pillow of compassion and humanitarianism.

My concern is that too much of our effort will be invested in public policy and courtroom litigation, leaving us with little time, energy, and financial resources to improve care for the dying. If we can effectively resist efforts to plunge society into the darkness of state-sanctioned medical killing, it will not be because we have built the most powerful political coalitions or have proven to be the best litigators in the courts. It will be because we have shown that there is no disgrace in human mortality, that human dignity can be cared for and respected in the midst of life's worst experiences.

NOTES

1. Wesley J. Smith, *Forced Exit: The Slippery Slope from Assisted Suicide to Legalized Murder* (New York: Times Books, 1997).

2. Ibid., 29.

CHAPTER 1

SOCIALLY- ASSISTED DEATH:

Why Physician- Assisted Suicide Is an Issue Today

In February 1998, Roosevelt Dawson, a twenty-one-year-old quadriplegic, became Jack Kevorkian's ninety-first "assisted suicide." Dawson became quadriplegic because of a virus that attacked his spinal cord. He died the same day he was released from a Grand Rapids, Michigan, hospital, where he had been receiving care in one of the state's most sophisticated ventilator units. During those months, Dawson had occasionally expressed a desire to die and had threatened several times to commit suicide (although as a quadriplegic it is doubtful he could have effected his own death without assistance).

After a Grand Rapids circuit court judge ruled that Dawson was competent to make his own medical decisions, Dawson's mother contacted Kevorkian's lead attorney, Geoffrey Fieger, to get her son released from the hospital. Fieger traveled from Detroit to Grand Rapids, demanding Dawson's release, which the hospital reluctantly granted. One hospital official alleges that Fieger, after chasing everyone from Dawson's room, stood beside his bed and was seen arguing with Dawson, presumably over ending his life.[1]

Several hospital employees who had provided care for Dawson during his six-month stay indicated he went back and forth about ending his life. However, it was clear to everyone that when Dawson left Grand Rapids, he intended to return to the Detroit area (his home and Kevorkian's) to meet with Kevorkian. Later that same evening, Dawson was found dead in his mother's Detroit apartment. The cause of death was a lethal injection of poison. The death was ruled a homicide by Oakland County's chief medical examiner, Dr. L. J. Dragovic. Dragovic and others questioned how a quadriplegic man could commit suicide. "Let's put two and two together," Dragovic said. "It's a homicide."[2] Kevorkian complained that he had to "hurry it [Dawson's death] up [because police were outside requesting to be admitted to the apartment] and that wasn't pleasant."[3]

What makes this particular case stand out is the virtual absence of any public outcry of protest and the unwillingness of the prosecutor to press charges against Kevorkian. In fact, the prosecutor had been elected just a few months earlier on the promise that he would not prosecute Kevorkian. Few newspapers denounced Kevorkian's actions. Only one disabilities organization issued a statement condemning him. Public opinion polls and letters to the editor were remarkably supportive. How did the idea of physician-assisted death come to receive such widespread social support?

No one really knows how widespread the secret practice of physician-assisted suicide is in the United States, nor is it known how frequently patients' requests for aid in dying are refused. Some survey data indicate that from 3 to 37 percent of anonymously responding physicians admit taking active steps to hasten a patient's death.[4] Although such survey results may be tainted by low response rates and/or poor design, they indicate that a significant percentage of physicians are willing to risk prosecution to help certain patients die.

Not only are a growing number of physicians willing to assist in a patient's death, but the general public seems more likely to request assistance if circumstances at the end of life are likely to get out of control. According to public opinion polls, a sizable segment of the American people believes physician-assisted suicide should be legal. In 1997, voters in Oregon refused to repeal a law they passed in 1994 making physician-assisted suicide legal. The U.S. Supreme Court has ruled that the Constitution does not contain a personal right to assisted suicide, but the court stopped short of saying it does not contain a right to end one's life and left the whole issue for each state to decide.

Although a majority of people believe assisted suicide should be a legal option, many seem uncertain whether or not they would personally request "aid in dying." Consequently, physician-assisted sui-

cide, like abortion, is couched in the language of personal choice—
"personally, I would never get an abortion, but I support the right of
others to choose."

A tension lies beneath these views that goes to the heart of the
issue. On the one hand, people want to maintain control over circumstances at the end of life, yet they also recognize that those circumstances may not be controllable. Thus, when the course of dying
cannot be controlled by the individual to his or her satisfaction, controlling the timing and circumstances of death is seen as the only
dignified alternative. This can be seen from the actions of Merian
Frederick, one of Jack Kevorkian's first "patients." Frederick suffered
from amyotrophic lateral sclerosis (ALS), a fatal degenerative disease, for more than four years. She died of carbon monoxide poisoning in Kevorkian's presence in 1993 at age seventy-two. Following
her death, her daughter, Carol Poenisch, formed Merian's Friends,
the grassroots organization that succeeded in placing the question
of physician-assisted suicide before voters in Michigan in 1998. Carol recounts her mother's last hours:

> The plans were carefully drawn up. My four brothers and two sis-
> ters gathered together. My sister Linda flew in from California, a
> brother flew in from Texas, and a brother flew in from North Car-
> olina. We had one beautiful week together in the home we'd grown
> up in. We dismissed the round-the-clock nurses and live-in assis-
> tant. Hospice workers and therapists were also asked not to come.
> Mom used a respirator in the last week to give her some comfort
> and to give us more time. She would never have agreed to a respira-
> tor without the knowledge that death was promised to her, since it
> could have meant six months or more of torture. . . .
>
> To avoid turning my mother's house into a crime scene, my
> brother Rick drove mother to Jack Kevorkian's barren apartment in
> the middle of the night. Her minister went too. She didn't want a
> lot of people there. She wanted it to be handled like a routine med-
> ical procedure. She wanted to save us pain. . . . Waiting in Dr.
> Kevorkian's apartment, she listened to a tape about a new theory of
> an 11-dimensional universe. The minister was impressed and said,
> "You're always learning." She scribbled back, "Just distraction, at
> least it won't be on the test." The last words spoken to her were by
> her minister: "Merian, you have passed the test of life with flying
> colors. Be at peace, you deserve it." And the end was peaceful.[5]

Such a highly pragmatic approach to end-of-life issues is consistent with the pattern most people follow in resolving the moral

dilemmas that confront them. Behind moral pragmatism lies the notion that we can solve moral dilemmas by maximizing our options. Since individual choice has become ensconced in culture as the great virtue, whenever we are in doubt about the correctness of a particular course of action we believe it is best to keep a maximum number of options open. People generally want to maintain the option of hastening death if circumstances at the end of life get out of control.

However, expanding the number of options seems to have a reverse effect. First, providing additional options does not make it easier to arrive at a decision. Offering many flavors of ice cream or many different color schemes for a new automobile may be laudable, but increasing the number of options does not make a decision to select one easier.

Second, the use of pragmatism to make moral decisions is akin to nailing Jell-O to the wall. Pragmatism tends to give too much weight to immediate circumstances and too little to the long-term impact of an action. It ignores the question of the results if that action becomes socially accepted and repeated throughout a culture. For example, when a person is in considerable pain and appears to be near death, one may be tempted to hasten death by lethal injection on what appear to be compassionate grounds. However, if compassion for people who experience pain near the end of life constitutes a compelling moral basis for administering a lethal injection, what prevents us from administering a lethal injection *before* a person experiences great pain? Moral pragmatism usually does little to clarify issues for the long term.

SOCIALLY-SUPPORTED ABORTION
AS A MORAL TEACHER

How did this approach to resolving difficult moral problems become so prevalent in a nation whose founding values included the intrinsic value of every human life? One explanation may be the *educational effect* of twenty-five years of legalized abortion and the overall demise of Judeo-Christian influence, particularly the influence of the sanctity of life ethic. Most people today believe that whatever is legal is also moral. An exception may be the moral repugnance toward pornography expressed by large numbers of people. Although pornography is legal and widely available, there are still many who consider it immoral.

Although there may be other factors, the institutionalized practice of aborting preborn children appears to have effectively undermined the sanctity of life ethic in the thinking of many people. Human life is no longer considered to possess intrinsic value. Rather, the value of life is contingent, grounded principally by its quality. Life-and-death decisions are made based on the perceived value of a person. And perceived value is often decided on such flimsy bases as the person's convenience and value to others. Americans have become accustomed to balancing burdens and benefits through an appeal to quality of life concerns like economics, personal career goals, family dynamics, and overall mental and physical health. What is new to this generation is that life itself is balanced on the scale. The U.S. courts have consistently sided with women who believe they possess the right to place their personal interests ahead of the interests of their unborn children. Rather than face inconvenience for nine months, many women rid themselves of this "burden" with the state's blessing.

ABORTION HAS CONDITIONED SOCIETY

TO ACCEPT THE DANGEROUS NOTION

THAT THERE IS SUCH A THING

AS A LIFE NOT WORTHY OF LIVING.

Abortion is viewed as a standard medical practice in obstetrics despite the fact that few physicians actually perform them. Tragically, abortion is used by some states to "solve" the problems of poverty by paying for the abortions of low income pregnant women. This sends a clear message that abortion can be useful in removing personal burdens associated with pregnancy and childbirth, and it is a useful tool in relieving economic burdens on the state. It also is not too far away from forced sterilizations or active killing of a certain unwanted segment of society.

The fact that the U.S. Congress cannot pass a veto-proof law banning so-called *partial-birth* abortion is an indication of how firmly institutionalized abortion has become. Consequently, fewer people are willing to accept the challenges that life sometimes brings, especially when those challenges involve caring for vulnerable and dependent human beings. Abortion has conditioned society to accept the dangerous notion that there is such a thing as a life not worthy of living, that bringing about death can be an act of kindness. Just as it is "cruel" to allow the birth of a severely handicapped newborn when it can be avoided, and it is "kind" to abort one, it is seen as cruel to refuse a person's request to have life ended when pain and suffering are present.[6]

QUALITY OF LIFE

Quality of life receives widespread social support as a factor in decision making. For many, it is the all-important criterion for determining the value of individual human life. An example of how strongly the quality-of-life ethic grips American culture can be observed in a "town hall" discussion of physician-assisted suicide at the 1992 annual meetings of the American Society of Law, Medicine and Ethics. Moderating the discussion was Timothy Johnson, medical editor for *ABC News,* who asked attendees the following question: "If we had a pill that would guarantee perfect health until age 85, but at age 85 you would literally disintegrate, how many of you would take this pill?" In response, all but four individuals (out of more than five hundred) indicated they would take such a pill.

The ensuing discussion revealed that the quality of life was of much greater importance than living longer. Most were willing to sacrifice longevity for quality of life. At the time, I suspected that a majority of Americans would agree with the preeminence of the quality of life. There is nothing inherently wrong with that. Few of us ever make a decision about our lives without some consideration of the impact it will have on our quality of life. We buy a particular brand of automobile, a home, a VCR, clothing, etc., with at least some thought about how an item will affect our quality of life. However, to permit quality of life considerations to *inform* our decision making is one thing; to allow them to *dictate* our decisions is altogether different. It is to elevate a self-centered focus over a God-centered one.

When the quality of life is allowed to dictate our perception of a person's value, a distortion of ethics occurs. A mind-set develops that when an acceptable quality of life is no longer possible it is actually a benefit to bring about death, and to remain alive is burdensome to oneself and to others. In this sense, inducing death becomes a form of medical treatment, the means by which we achieve personal, medical, and even social goals. The logic that supports abortion for severely "defective" fetuses is easily transferred to physician-assisted suicide and euthanasia for others lacking a quality of life. Even the use of words like "defective" in such cases suggests a mechanized view of life: We are machines expected to function efficiently in society, and when we do not function correctly, we can be thrown away without remorse. If death is a suitable solution to unwelcome pregnancies or deformed babies, it is an equally valid response to pain and suffering at the end of life. In both instances, death becomes socially assisted, reinforced by attitudes, policies, and procedures sharply protective of personal interests and social goals and not of life itself.

THE "COAT HANGERS" OF ASSISTED SUICIDE

Nat Hentoff, a columnist for the *Village Voice,* points out that one of the most powerful symbols used in the 1970s by the abortion rights movement to capture public sympathy was the coat hanger.[7] The public repeatedly heard horror stories of women all over America dying because they performed abortions on themselves with coat hangers. These stories were used as evidence of how desperate women were to end unwelcome pregnancies and why abortion needed to be legalized. The coat hanger became the symbol of the movement to make abortion "safe" and legal. Coat hangers appeared on placards at abortion rights rallies and on bumper stickers, and they were often held aloft by picketers at pro-life gatherings.

THE SYMBOLS OF ASSISTED SUICIDE . . . ARE

THE PUBLIC'S PERCEPTIONS OF WHAT HAPPENS

TO PEOPLE AT THE END OF LIFE.

Like those in the abortion rights movement, assisted suicide advocates understand the importance of symbols. Barbara Combs Lee of Oregon Right to Die points to the so-called "Exit Bag" as a symbol of the extremes to which people will go to end a life of pain and suffering. Lee claims that plastic bags are never needed when patients use the right combination of drugs in the proper doses. "The bag is to assisted dying as the coat hanger is to abortion," she says. "When abortions became legal, people didn't need coat hangers."[8] However, most of the symbols of assisted suicide are not inanimate objects like coat hangers. Rather, their symbols are the public's perceptions of what happens to people at the end of life. The movement has been able to exploit popular fears, embodied in the tragic circumstances that befall individuals like Karen Quinlan and Nancy Cruzan.

Karen Quinlan was in her twenties when she overdosed on drugs and alcohol. She was diagnosed as irreversibly brain damaged and in persistent vegetative state. After she spent several years on a ventilator, her parents asked doctors to remove her from the ventilator. They sued the hospital for refusing to allow this. Eventually, the New Jersey Supreme Court ruled that they could remove the ventilator. However, Karen did not die as expected, but continued to breathe on her own and lived another ten years, finally dying from an infection. Karen's case was the first time a court had ruled that family members could withdraw medical treatment from loved ones who could not make their own decisions. Her case was instrumental in drafting legislation that legalized Advance Directives for health care decisions (Living Wills, Durable Power of Attorney for Health Care).[9]

Nancy Cruzan was also in her twenties in 1983 when she lost control of her car on an icy Missouri road and crashed. She was thrown from the vehicle and landed facedown in a water-filled ditch. Nancy's heart and respiration stopped, but she was revived by rescue personnel. She was later transferred to a long-term care facility and diagnosed with irreversible brain damage. Although most media reports about Nancy suggest she was unconscious and unaware of her surroundings, this is disputed by some of her caregivers. Nancy's parents sought to have her feeding tube removed, eventually taking her case all the way to the U.S. Supreme Court, who ruled that there was not "clear and convincing evidence" that Nancy would have wanted her feeding tube removed. Her family later filed another suit against her caregivers seeking to have the feeding tube removed, and they prevailed. Nancy's feeding tube was removed in December 1990. She died the day after Christmas.

Fears of such a fate are magnified by the grandstanding of Jack Kevorkian. It is through the exploitation of these fears that death receives social assistance.

Symbol #1—A Painful Death

People dread pain. Watch any television program and you will likely see at least one commercial for a painkiller. When Americans have a headache, they don't just want an aspirin; they want a CAT scan, and they want extra strength quick relief. Scripture teaches that giving attention to relieving pain is a legitimate goal (Proverbs 31:6). We should take pain seriously and see its relief as consistent with the purpose of medicine. All of us have heard of someone whose final days were lived in severe pain. These experiences fuel our fears. They can challenge the strongest of convictions against assisted suicide and euthanasia. Watching loved ones suffer excruciating pain is second only to actually experiencing such pain personally.

Clinical experience reveals that many physicians do not do a good job of managing the pain of dying patients. Unfortunately, stories of people dying in serious pain are not unusual. Effective management of pain should be a concern for everyone—patients, families, and physicians.

There are three primary reasons physicians fail to provide dying patients with sufficient relief of pain. First, studies indicate that physicians are often not adequately trained in pain management.[10] They rely on outdated training in the use of pain medications, which results in seriously undermedicating patients in pain.

Second, laws designed to prevent the abuse of narcotics are poorly understood by physicians, leading them to undermedicate patients. Physicians fear being fined or having their licenses suspended by the Drug Enforcement Administration (DEA) if they prescribe large dosages of narcotics. This fear is not without some foundation. In 1997, when the state of Oregon began implementing its law that allowed physician-assisted suicide, the U.S. Department of Justice and the DEA announced they would prosecute physicians in Oregon who prescribed large doses of narcotics or other controlled substances to terminally ill patients for the purpose of assisting in their deaths. This threat was later rescinded when the departments learned that their interpretation of drug law might result in physicians undermedicating terminally ill patients who were experiencing severe pain, but who had no intention of seeking physician assistance in dying.[11]

Third, some physicians fear that supplying increasingly larger doses of pain medication will actually hasten a patient's death, which may expose them to criminal prosecution. If a patient receives large quantities of a narcotic such as morphine, there is at least a theoretical possibility that the drug could suppress respiration and even bring about respiratory failure. However, this rarely happens because dosages of pain medications are gradually increased (titrated) as the disease progresses and pain levels change. Physicians do not start patients out with a gram of morphine per hour.

Due to these concerns, there remains a serious discrepancy between what physicians are capable of doing and what they actually do. What can be done about these concerns? Certainly we can supply physicians with better training in pain management. Physicians entering into primary care should be required to do a residency rotation in pain management. Recent research in pain management should receive better treatment in medical journals, and various medical associations should provide more continuing medical education opportunities to their members.

What about those patients whose pain cannot be controlled by current methods? What do we have to offer them? Proponents of assisted suicide contend that it is these patients who make physician-assisted suicide necessary. "Any attempt to argue from the premise that most pain is relievable to the conclusion that all aid-in-dying is unnecessary will be question-begging," says Gregg Kasting, professor of philosophy at Georgia State University.[12]

Timothy Quill, an oncologist who advocates legalizing physician-assisted suicide, suggests that assisted suicide should be a last resort, when all other efforts to relieve pain and suffering prove inadequate.[13] Quill contends that traditional approaches to palliative care will be adequate for the vast majority of patients.

Some believe that if physician-assisted suicide remains a criminal offense, physicians will become even more reluctant to administer pain medication in sufficient dosages to control pain, since the effect of using larger doses of medication may (theoretically) result in the suppression of a patient's respiration, thereby hastening death. A physician does not want to face criminal prosecution when his or her only intention was to make patients more comfortable. Consequently, some physicians will undermedicate patients, resulting in some dying in greater pain. This concern adds fuel to the fears of patients, lending further social support for physician-assisted suicide.

Proponents of physician-assisted suicide argue that animals receive better treatment by society than human beings. If an animal is suffering, most people consider it cruel not to put the animal "out of its misery." If it is merciful to end an animal's suffering by causing its death, how is it criminal to do the same thing for a human being?

Drawing this conclusion requires us to abandon, at least in principle, the societal prohibition against the private killing of human beings. Veterinarian Marco Zancope kills animals on a regular basis in his New York veterinary clinic. However, Zancope extended that expertise to humans when he injected his receptionist, Cara Beigel, with a sedative used to euthanize pets because Beigel was fighting a losing battle with breast cancer. She died later that evening, and Zancope was charged with second-degree manslaughter.

Zancope drew considerable support from the public, including Beigel's father. "This is a nice, wonderful guy," Phillip Beigel said. "Why do you have to die painfully, writhing, kicking and screaming like the doctors and the DA [District Attorney] and the medical examiner would like you to?"[14]

Beigel begs the question. Although anyone who has stood helplessly at the bedside of a loved one dying in pain can understand this father's anguish, the issue is not the motives of the New York district attorney, medical examiner, or doctors, but the act of one person unilaterally taking the life of another. Shall we now endorse the private killing of human beings by others? Shall society now permit animal killers to become people killers? Impugning the motives of those opposed to private acts of killing does nothing to invalidate the basic argument that the state is justified in outlawing private arrangements between two persons to have one of them killed. States outlaw dueling for this reason. We do not want people settling their personal disputes by squaring off in the backyard with guns.

Neither does opposing the private killing of suffering people mean that one is therefore in favor of people suffering in great pain and agony. Such a conclusion is illogical. The prohibition against private killing must be maintained if we are to avoid moral, social, and legal chaos.

Killing a human being is profoundly different from killing an animal. Animals are not created in God's image. Human beings were given dominion over animals, not other humans. Animal rights advocates notwithstanding, the state has a compelling interest in protecting human life, an interest that will be lost if states begin to recognize privately arranged killing. This is particularly pertinent in the doctor-patient relationship.

Symbol #2—The Undignified Death

One of our greatest fears is the specter of being kept alive by artificial life support and being completely unable to experience any sort of meaningful life—the fear of what Philippe Aries calls a "wild death"[15]—a death that follows a lengthy period of "technological brinkmanship."[16] Some call this the "injury of continued existence," claiming that extending such a life is cruel and inhumane and undignified. Remaining dignified in the face of death seems to be important to most people. Being "brain dead," with bodily functions maintained by mechanical means, is distasteful and undignified in most people's minds. No one wants to be a "vegetable,"[17] unable to communicate or experience an acceptable quality of life.

This is particularly true of people who have taken care of loved ones or others whose deaths came after months or even years of nonsentient living.[18] The sights, sounds, and smells associated with taking care of aging, chronically ill, and mentally impaired individuals can be a challenge to the belief that such lives have value and dignity. If they do, by what criteria are value and dignity determined? How do these individuals manifest dignity?

Many people believe that human life, in order to have value, must be a rational human life. No value can be found in living a life without rationality.[19] In fact, according to many, without rationality there really is no human life. There may be a being, *Homo sapiens*, but not a human "person." The organ of rationality is thought to be the brain; therefore, when the cognitive functions of the brain are lost, the person's value as a human being is lost as well.[20]

However, such a conclusion invariably requires us to accept a strongly naturalistic (as opposed to supernatural) orientation in defining the value of human life. It requires a definition of human life that is *physicalist,* reducing human existence to its biological properties and the value of human life to those functions that human beings manifest in accord with biological existence. It produces a view of personhood that is arbitrary and subjective, possessing little capability to explain complex aspects of human psychology. It also means that dignity is undermined when the person is no longer capable of rational conversation or thought. This view of human dignity means it is impossible to retain personal dignity if someone else must meet one's basic needs. To be devoid of rational function renders continued existence at best an injury, and at worst an insult.

I will address the issue of human dignity and suffering in greater detail in chapter 2; however, it is important to state here that such a definition of human dignity makes it unnecessary to care for someone who is incapable of caring for himself or herself. If in fact the loss of rationality translates into a bona fide loss of personal dignity and value, then there can be no justification for investing any resources or effort in the care of such a being. Any act of alleged caring would actually be an insult since we are prolonging undignified existence.

A biblical view of human life is far richer and more comprehensive in its scope. Scripture teaches that the value of human life is not limited to its physical functions, nor is it limited to the span of time one exists here on earth. The resurrection of Jesus Christ (1 Corinthians 15) is one proof of this. Although the loss of rational function in this life is a significant loss, it is a serious error in judgment to conclude that the person who loses it is hopeless. A worldview that reduces the significance of human existence to the function of a single organ (the brain) is a tragically minimalist one. How unfortunate one is to embrace a worldview that has nothing more to offer than the limited functions of human thought.

Symbol #3—Loss of Control

Perhaps no other belief defines modern culture as clearly as the strongly held belief in individual autonomy. It is ironic, however, that the modern individual seems to hold contradictory views simultaneously. When society proposes to restrain a particular behavior or action, we may hear someone say, "No one can tell me what to do." When this same person is asked for an opinion about the actions of others he or she deems harmful, he or she may respond, "There ought to be a law against that." We like autonomy when it comes to our own likes and dislikes, but we are much less magnanimous when someone else's claim to autonomy affects us personally. Many dislike walking into convenience stores that feature displays of pornographic magazines or sitting in a restaurant next to a person smoking a cigarette. We don't like people using their autonomy to play loud music at the beach or in the campground. There are obvious dangers associated with expanding individual autonomy—imagine what would happen if we allowed people to be "free" to drive however they wished or to dump trash or sewage wherever they wanted—but nonetheless we cling tenaciously to our own "right" to almost unlimited autonomy.

The appeal to autonomy as justification for physician-assisted suicide and euthanasia is not unlike using autonomy to justify abortion. Just as a woman asserts autonomy as grounds for ending an unwelcome pregnancy, claiming an absolute right to control of her own body, the person who wishes to die also uses autonomy as justification to control the timing and manner of death. Carol Poenisch, the daughter of Merian Frederick, Kevorkian's seventh "patient," said, "Instead of being pushed off the bridge, she (Merian Frederick) wanted a parachute and a soft landing. She wanted control over her life at a time when every day was a struggle to regain control over a lost function."[21]

Autonomy or self-determination (discussed at length in chapter 6) is embraced by most Americans as one of the premier virtues of modern society. The right to direct one's life, to exercise control over life, is believed to be the paramount feature of a free society. Many proponents of physician-assisted suicide believe autonomy is the only justification needed for the practice. Geoffrey Fieger, the lead attorney for Jack Kevorkian, in a debate on physician-assisted suicide with noted bioethicist Edmund Pellegrino, said, "The only rational basis necessary for physician-assisted suicide is the autonomy of the individual. Just as people do not need the state or the church telling them how or when to go to the bathroom, they do not need the state to tell them how to die."[22] In fact, Fieger and Kevorkian contend that physician-assisted suicide is already a legal, legitimate medical service and does not need any further state involvement.

Fieger ridicules those who suggest that the state or anyone else has grounds for prohibiting the practice. However, Fieger fails to give any rational reason that autonomy should trump all other interests. Are there not other "goods" to be considered, goods equally worthy of protection? Are there not other concerns that justify placing limitations on individual autonomy in order to provide protection against abuses?

Rights and responsibilities cannot be separated, and neither can benefits and costs. A person cannot refuse to go to work for a month because he would rather watch TV, then insist on his "right" to a paycheck. Likewise, a person cannot seek the joys of family relationships, then bail out when his or their health problems make his responsibilities temporarily more evident than his rewards. A society cannot benefit from the talents and hard work of an individual, then abandon that person when he becomes economically unprofitable. Society cannot value an individual based on his productivity, health, or any other criterion without seeing all human relationships lessened to economic categories.

Symbol #4—Becoming a Burden to Others

It is hard to find fault with the desire to possess the resources and ability to care for oneself. Having the physical and financial resources to care for oneself, or to pass on possessions to one's family, is a worthy goal that finds support in Scripture (Job 42:15; Proverbs 19:14; 2 Corinthians 12:14; Ephesians 4:28; 2 Thessalonians 3:10–12). Self-sufficiency is part of the American dream. But because of these values, when people become seriously ill they may come to believe that family members will be inconvenienced beyond any reasonable expectation. This concern, if not dealt with adequately, can lead to patients making treatment decisions that are ill-advised, and, in some instances, dangerous.

IT IS DANGEROUS FOR A SOCIETY TO ENDORSE THE NOTION THAT A PERSON CAN BECOME . . . A PROBLEM TO BE SOLVED BY DEATH.

Although independence and self-sufficiency can be worthy goals, they are not idols to be worshiped or virtues to be acquired at any cost. Jesus cautioned His disciples against assuming an idolatrous degree of self-sufficiency. In teaching them through the parable of the Vine (John 15:1–8), Jesus declared, "Apart from me you can do nothing" (v. 5 NIV). In a similar vein, the apostle Paul taught the Romans that believers are not self-sufficient entities, but each one is part of a larger community of interdependent persons. Paul said, "Just as each of us has one body with many members, and these members do not all have the same function, so in Christ we who are many form one body, and each member belongs to all the others." (Romans 12:4–5 NIV).

Human society is interdependent regardless of the economic, social, or political structures in place. It is dangerous for a society to endorse the notion that a person can become an overwhelming burden to others, a problem to be solved by death, by dying sooner rather than later. One important feature of biblical Christianity is the willingness to accept and bear the burdens of others (Galatians

6:2), to see ourselves as an integral part of a larger community of human beings pledged to care for one another during times of distress and need. The fact that so many people are lonely and disassociated from others is one of the most serious indictments to be made against the hyper-individualization of modern life.

Symbol #5—Being Victimized by Health Care Providers

In the summer of 1973, former fighter pilot and bull rider Don (Dax) Cowart was critically injured near Houston, Texas, in a propane gas explosion that took his father's life and left him with third-degree burns over two-thirds of his own body. The explosion left him blind and without the use of his hands. For more than a year, Dax underwent extraordinarily painful treatments in the acute burn wards of two hospitals. Throughout this ordeal, Dax demanded to be permitted to die by consistently refusing to consent to his disinfectant treatments. Despite repeated declarations of competence by his psychiatrist, all of Dax's pleas were rejected and treatment was provided.

During an initial conversation between Dr. White (his psychiatrist) and Dax several weeks after treatment began, White said to Dax, "From the very beginning, according to what you've told me, and what's been written in your hospital record, you have very strong feelings that you didn't want the doctors to go on with your treatment, that you wanted them to leave you alone and not attempt to sustain your life? How do you feel about that at this point?"

Dax responded, "At this point I feel much the same way. If I felt that I could be rehabilitated to where I could walk and do other things normally, I might have a different feeling about it. I don't know. But being blind itself is one big factor that influences my thinking on the matter. I know that there's no way that I want to go on as a blind and a cripple." Later, a nurse would say that Dax told her, "You know, all I'm going to be able to do is sit on a street corner and sell pencils." Dax didn't end up selling pencils. He was later released from the hospital and received a law degree from Texas Tech University. A financial settlement with the propane gas company paid his medical bills and provided him with a lifetime income, although he now practices law in Houston, Texas. Dax continues to believe the strong paternalism exhibited by his mother and physicians was unethical. "Now I know how it feels to be killed with kindness."[23]

Americans spend nearly $800 billion annually on medical care, more than any other nation in the world. That appetite is unlikely to abate anytime soon, despite the call for reform and the emergence of managed care models of medical services delivery. We like having access to the latest medical gadgetry regardless of how expensive it is.

However, the realities of high-tech medicine are about to come crashing in upon us. An aging population with an average life expectancy of eighty-five years, combined with a high probability of a person's living at least some of those latter years with a serious, chronic (and expensive) condition, means that monumental social, economic, ethical, and legal challenges await us.

WHAT SORT OF PEOPLE EMBRACE THE NOTION

THAT PHYSICIANS HAVE A MORAL OBLIGATION

TO CAUSE THE DEATH OF PATIENTS

THEY CANNOT CURE?

It has been estimated that nearly 90 percent of the medical expenses a person incurs during his lifetime accumulate in the last year of life. Proponents of assisted suicide and euthanasia claim that the "age wave" will make these practices necessary, that the social and economic burdens associated with a large elderly and chronically ill population threaten everyone's quality of life.[24] However, such a conclusion is unwarranted. There is more to a moral society than the financial bottom line. Certainly there must be better solutions to be found among a people who pay movie stars, rock musicians, and professional athletes millions of dollars to entertain them. One look at the homes we live in, the cars we drive, the vacations we enjoy, and the innumerable electronic conveniences we possess should tell us that lack of money is not the problem.

Symbol #6—The Botched Euthanasia

Just as the advocates of abortion exploited the public's fears of women dying in large numbers because of botched abortions, the proponents of assisted suicide and euthanasia claim that legalization is necessary to prevent botched euthanasias. In *Time Lines,* a publication of the Hemlock Society, readers were told that in the Netherlands, "20 percent of those seeking self-deliverance through lethal doses of medications linger in a coma for up to four days!"[25] A worse fear is that some who attempt suicide may not have the "benefit" of lapsing into a coma.

Miles Edwards, a retired lung specialist in Oregon, warns about taking large quantities of barbiturates to end one's life: "The taste is terrible, and anti-nausea medications don't work. The vomit goes halfway up the esophagus and down the windpipe. I've seen patients with dreadful, horribly undignified deaths."[26] Consequently, the Hemlock Society suggests using plastic bags as a backup to barbiturates. An advertisement for the "Exit Bag" on the Hemlock Society's Internet Website says, "This bag is designed to hasten death for the terminally ill in a secure, comfortable manner." Yet the Hemlock Society claims it does not want people to die in this manner. The preferred method is physician-administered lethal injection, which proponents of assisted suicide believe will be permitted once the general public is sufficiently tired of the "yuck" factor associated with back alley, "coat-hanger-type" euthanasias and suicides.

THE DEATH SOCIETY AND
THE FUTURE OF MEDICINE

Social support for assisted suicide and euthanasia is growing. However, the society that embraces death as a medical solution to the burdens of earthly life faces extinction. No civilization that sanctions killing human beings deemed a burden to it has any sort of positive future. What sort of people embrace the notion that physicians have a moral obligation to cause the death of patients they cannot cure? What evidence exists to support the claim that a society that permits physicians to kill suffering patients is a compassionate and morally superior society? What kind of society is it that ignores clear biblical teachings and accepts the elimination of all incurable sufferers by causing or hastening their death? Driven by a poorly defined notion of compassion, a defective mechanistic view of humanity, and a willingness to redefine what constitutes a "benefit" to include inducing death, the future of such a society and its medicine is bleak.

History records examples of nations and civilizations in which abortion, infanticide, and euthanasia were widely practiced and sanctioned by public policy. Greek, Roman, and some Asian societies used death as a means of achieving individual and societal goals. Where are these civilizations today? Where are the nations of the world that have practiced widespread abortion and euthanasia? Do they continue to exist as world superpowers? Is there any nation in the world where physicians are able to kill incurable patients, and whose standards of morality and quality of life we envy?

The Netherlands is the first nation since Nazi Germany to permit euthanasia. What has been the effect of such permissiveness upon the practice of medicine in the Netherlands? Has respect for physicians increased? Are people more or less fearful when visiting their personal physicians?

Although more will be said about the Netherlands in chapter 8, it is important to note that a good number of elderly Dutch citizens carry with them a "Do Not Kill Me" card, much like people in the U.S. carry medical alert cards. Growing numbers of people fear their physicians and are suspicious of their children. There are solid grounds for such concerns. Wesley Smith tells of interviewing a Dutch physician who related the following story:

> A friend of mine, an internist, was asked to see a lady with terminal lung cancer, who had a short time to live and was very short of breath. After the examination, he asked the patient to come to the hospital on Saturday for a few days so that he could alleviate her distress. She refused, being afraid of being euthanized there. My friend assured his patient that he would be on duty and that no such thing would happen. So the lady came. On Sunday night she was breathing normally and feeling much better. The doctor went home. When he came back on Monday afternoon, the patient was dead. The doctor's colleague told him, "What is the sense of having that woman here? It makes no difference whether she dies today or after two weeks. We need the bed for another case."[27]

Of all the nonreligious arguments made in this book against physician-assisted suicide and euthanasia, I believe this argument from history should be the strongest in causing us to reject such practices. Are we willing to stake the survival of Western civilization on a belief that socially-assisted death is a high-water mark of a moral and compassionate society? Are we to accept the double-speak of the new medicine—we show "respect for human life" by ending it; enhance "autonomy" by eliminating the person who is autonomous; celebrate human dignity by injecting humans with lethal drugs? Are we to believe that people will come to trust their physicians more when those physicians are committed to killing them when a cure is not possible? Are we to have greater trust in a government that is willing to pay physicians to end the lives of patients? Are we to think that our family loves us more because they are willing to let a physician inject us with a lethal drug if we run out of money or they run out of patience? If all of this comes to pass, does anyone really believe it will strengthen society, clarify morality, or settle the difficulties at the end of life?

Previous experience in pregnancy care ministry has shown me that fear often motivates a woman to seek an abortion: fear of being rejected by parents, fear of losing a boyfriend or husband, fear of losing a chance at an education or a job, etc. Many fear that carrying a pregnancy to full term will mean the loss of opportunity and hope for the future. These fears provide business-savvy abortion clinic owners with powerful marketing tools to "sell" abortion as the way to avoid having one's fears come true.

Powerful fears also drive the growing public support for assisted suicide and euthanasia, fears that Jack Kevorkian and others exploit to "sell" death as a solution to pain and suffering. People fear dying alone, dying in pain, and being a burden to their families. People fear being overtreated or becoming pawns of an impersonal medical bureaucracy, nervous physicians, or guilt-ridden family members. Consequently, assisted suicide and euthanasia begin to seem the lesser of two evils.

REALITIES AT THE END OF LIFE

Although the Bible speaks of death as an enemy (1 Corinthians 15:25–26), death is also shown to be the inevitable end for every person (Hebrews 9:27), as well as an event that, for Christians, results in being transitioned into God's presence (2 Corinthians 5:1–8). In this sense, we might say that death is the "natural" end of life. Jack McCue writes, "Viewing dying and death as merely a failure of medical diagnosis and therapy is anti-holistic and trivializes the final event in our lives, stripping it of important, non-medical meaning for patients, family, and society."[28]

The naturalness of death does not mean we do not resist it, yet the end of life can be a meaningful time for terminally ill individuals and their loved ones. Being terminally ill does not mean a person is beyond the scope of human caring and interaction. The dying process does not mean a person cannot learn, resolve problems, teach, celebrate achievements, or give wise counsel to others. Being terminally ill does not necessarily mean being set aside from the activity of daily life and interaction with others.

Joyce and Charles Kirk had been married twenty-two years when Charles was diagnosed with liver cancer and told he probably would not last a year. They had two teenage children. Neither they nor their children had given any thought to how they would respond to terminal illness. Charles's personal physician wasn't much help.

A nurse Joyce knew told her about Hospice of Northern Virginia. She liked the idea that choosing hospice care meant she could keep Charles at home to be cared for by his family. Making the call to the hospice was the most difficult thing, however. "It was a defining moment. I was going public and saying, 'My husband is on the road to death.'" However, as soon as she made the call, the hospice began working with her to meet the family's needs. Workers assessed the family's insurance coverage to see what benefits would be covered and spoke with Charles's physician.

"Suddenly, it wasn't only my responsibility anymore," says Joyce. "There was someone who understood exactly what we were facing. We felt like we had a safety net, both practically and psychologically." She says she cannot imagine what it would have been like not to have Charles at home throughout his illness. The children seemingly never left his side. They brought friends over to visit and had long talks with their father. When Charles couldn't sleep because of discomfort, the family would sit around the kitchen table at two in the morning eating peach pies Joyce baked. Joyce says she still bakes a peach pie every August 8, the day Charles died.

When a terminal illness reaches the point where people can no longer do routine things for themselves, and/or when controlling the symptoms of terminal illness require more intensive attention, friends may begin to drift away. Families may begin to experience the hardships brought on by geographic distances, the strains of limited finances, inadequate insurance coverage, and the complexity of providing extended care. Any one of these factors can challenge the strongest of family bonds and cherished values. Together, they can be a formidable challenge to the sanctity of human life principle. In these tough circumstances we must promise to address the dying person's greatest fears.

THREE PROMISES FOR THE TERMINALLY ILL PERSON

Socially-assisted death must receive a potent response from the Christian community. We must not concentrate our efforts exclusively on legislative or courtroom solutions, but we ought to demonstrate in word and deed that we stand with the dying person in his or her final days. Every dying person should be given these three promises:

- *You will not be a burden to us.*
- *You will not die in pain.*
- *You will not die alone.*

You Will Not Be a Burden to Us

Because Americans value self-sufficiency, people tend to believe family members are burdened when they are called upon to care for a seriously ill loved one. In some instances, the fear of being a burden on family members can result in making hasty and inappropriate medical decisions that actually hasten death.

Thinking that one is a burden to others is inaccurate for two reasons. First, the notion that each person is a totally independent entity undermines the very concept of community. What is a community if individualism is overemphasized and an individual in need cannot seek the aid of his or her neighbors, friends, or relatives? Human society is interdependent, a community of people who rely on one another in numerous ways. The privatizing of death has undermined the notion of community substantially, and legalizing assisted suicide just extends this destructive notion of privacy, further eroding any sense of community.

Second, family members cannot be burdens to us. We have a biblical and moral obligation to care for them when they are unable to care for themselves (Galatians 6:2, 10; 1 Timothy 5:2–8). One of my daughters, in the midst of experiencing the consequences of a wrong action, said, "I'm sorry for being such a burden, Dad." I immediately responded that she was not a burden—inconvenient perhaps, but not a burden. Circumstances may become burdensome, but people do not. We ought to pity the person so unfortunate as to have family and friends who regard him or her as a burden.

The significance of the body of Christ is that its members come to the aid of those in need. It is a tragic testimony to the weakened state of body life in many local churches that those in need of assistance at the end of life must turn to strangers in the medical community or government agencies, especially when the Lord Jesus Christ demonstrated throughout His earthly ministry the importance of caring for those who hurt and who were filled with fear (Hebrews 2:14–15). He never regarded people as a burden. Rather, He came to this world that He might lift the burdens of sinfulness and divine condemnation from our shoulders. What other meaning can we find in Jesus' words, "Come unto me, all ye that labour and are heavy laden, and I will give you rest" (Matthew 11:28)? If bearing burdens is not a human responsibility, what shall we read into His condemnation of those in the parable of the Good Samaritan who passed by the man injured in a robbery? Jesus commanded His disciples to show mercy to unfortunate individuals. Thus, believers are obligated to help individuals and families when they struggle with physical, emotional, and spiritual burdens. Others may be needed to come alongside and help us with special skills (e.g., physicians, nurses), but it is we who have the obligation to our own family members by virtue of relationship.

Jesus cared for people's physical, emotional, and spiritual needs, not only to bring attention to His person and message, but because acts of compassion and caring are good in themselves. Jesus healed children, thereby encouraging their parents. He restored some to life, physically as well as spiritually. We, too, as His ambassadors, may imitate these acts of healing and restoration, not necessarily with miracles, but through acts of compassion, kindness, and mercy. (Some ideas will be listed in chapter 11.)

You Will Not Die in Pain

Proverbs 31:6-7 speaks of alleviating pain when it says, "Give strong drink unto him that is ready to perish, and wine unto those that be of heavy hearts. Let him drink, and forget his poverty, and remember his misery no more." We should take the presence of pain seriously and see its relief as consistent with the purpose of medicine. When caring for a terminally ill person, managing pain is of paramount importance.

Fortunately, ongoing pain management research is rapidly removing any medical basis for someone to fear dying in great pain. Data from the British hospice experience and from faithful application of the World Health Organization's basic cancer pain guidelines indicate that more than 80 percent of pain can be controlled with simple drug therapy alone. Data from clinical studies in the U.S. indicate that, with the appropriate application of modern pain management principles using both drug and nondrug therapies, pain can be controlled for 90 percent of patients.[29] There is a considerable amount of data in the medical literature to sustain the claim that pain, for the most part, can be managed.

If this is true, why is there such a widespread fear that pain will not be managed? Because it isn't being managed sufficiently for many patients. The management of pain is a real problem, and the failure to address it aggressively provides proponents of assisted suicide with a powerful public relations weapon.

You Will Not Die Alone

Several national studies of nursing home residents and elderly individuals living in assisted living facilities indicate that loneliness is the leading cause of depression, and depression is blamed for the high rate of suicide among this population. In other words, if more people would regularly visit with elderly individuals we would see a drop in the suicide rate.

Like the elderly, any person given a terminal diagnosis can become lonely as friends and family visit less frequently. This is often due to the fact that people are poorly equipped for visiting a terminally ill person, perhaps because they have not faced up to their own mortality or because the symptoms manifested by the patient are hard to manage. We seem to tolerate the sights and smells of dying less well than was the case earlier this century. We tend to hide such unpleasantries in nursing homes or retirement communities or hospitals. The dying do not live among us, and we tend to forget about them due to our reluctance to face our own mortality and our busyness, independence, and even self-centeredness.

The decrease in visitation may also be attributed in part to the perception that the dying person needs "professional" care, that friends and family should stand aside while the professionals do their thing. Some of the problem is fueled by the common perception that fatal medical problems, including aging itself, will all eventually yield to technological innovation. It can be increasingly difficult for family and friends to feel they are providing beneficial spiritual and emotional care to a loved one with declining willingness to eat and willingness to participate in self-care and social activities, or whose intellectual capability is diminished.

Despite the ravages of a terminal disease, patients are people with needs, ideas, and wisdom, and they need interaction with other people to express them. Dying people have obvious physical and emotional needs, but they also do not cease having spiritual needs. In a 1997 Gallup poll of spiritual beliefs and the dying process, 56 percent said they were concerned about not being forgiven by God. More than half felt their greatest need other than medical care was having someone pray with them, and 44 percent said it was important to have someone help them become spiritually at peace. Interestingly, only 36 percent indicated that such spiritual help could be obtained from a clergyman.[30]

Meeting these needs cannot be done without personal contact. Failing to meet these needs means that individuals will be forced to make medical decisions in isolation from those with whom they have been closest over the years. Often the most effective intervention we can offer is time spent with patients and their families, listening to their concerns and acknowledging their value. The spiritual dimensions of dying bond persons together and can effect dramatic changes in the lives touched by both the life and death of the individual.

Solomon wrote, "It is better to go to the house of mourning, than to go to the house of feasting: for that is the end of all men; and the living will lay it to his heart" (Ecclesiastes 7:2). Most people do not reflect on the meaning of life while attending a New Year's Eve party. Being at the bedside of a dying person or attending a funeral is an environment more likely to provoke serious self-evaluation than the office Christmas party or company picnic. Listening to a dying person's concerns, fears, regrets, and hopes can be a profound learning experience for the caregiver, in addition to being a blessing to the patient.

This does not mean that caregiving is not stressful. Many times it is downright inconvenient and, if undertaken by one individual, exhausting. Thus, not only should our promise be to not allow the terminally ill person to die alone, but we should also promise his or her spouse, family, or other caregivers that they will not provide care alone either. Nothing less than a collaborative effort will unburden distressed individuals and their families.

Fulfilling these three promises is an important antidote to the arguments for assisted suicide. For this reason, I developed a program called Loving Individuals in Final Transition (LIFT), a hospice-type ministry designed to equip laypeople in a local church to meet the physical, emotional, and spiritual needs of terminally ill individuals and their families, whether or not they are members of the church. More will be said about LIFT in chapter 11.

NOTES

1. Hospital employees told me this information and requested anonymity.
2. "Kevorkian Says He Is 'Outraged' by Cops' Behavior," *Grand Rapids Press*, 1 March 1998, A-19.
3. Ibid., A-22.
4. Timothy E. Quill, *Death and Dignity: Making Choices and Taking Charge* (New York: Norton, 1993), 159.
5. Carol Poenisch, "Merian Frederick's Story," *New England Journal of Medicine*, Vol. 339, No. 14, 1 October 1998.
6. This argument is frequently found in the bioethics literature relating to genetic testing and abortion and end-of-life issues. See Phillip Kitcher, *The Lives to Come* (New York: Simon and Schuster, 1996) and James Rachels, *The End of Life* (New York: Oxford Univ. Press, 1986); also James Rachels, "Active and Passive Euthanasia," *New England Journal of Medicine* (Vol. 292, No. 2, 9 January 1975), 79.
7. Nat Hentoff, "The Coat Hanger of Assisted Suicide," *Washington Post*, 6 December 1997, A25.
8. Elizabeth Manning, "What's So Hard About a Painless Death?" www.wweek.com/html/killingpain091797.html
9. Diane Gianelli, "Karen Ann Quinlan's Family Remembers," *American Medical News*, 15 December 1989, 9, 49–50.
10. *Management of Cancer Pain*, 2.
11. "Reno Rejects Intervention in Oregon Suicide Law," *Philadelphia Inquirer*, 6 June 1998, 1D.
12. Gregg Kasting, "The Non-Necessity of Euthanasia," in Robert A. Almeder, et al., editors, *Physician-Assisted Suicide* (Totowa, N.J.: Humana, 1993), 25.
13. Quill, *Death and Dignity*.
14. "When 'Suicide' is Homicide," *New York Daily News*, 16 October 1998.
15. Philippe Aries, *The Hour of Our Death*, trans. Helen Weaver (New York: Knopf, 1981), 5–28.
16. This is a term used frequently by bioethicist Daniel Callahan to describe the overuse of interventionist medical technology in the face of overwhelming illness. See Daniel Callahan, *The Troubled Dream of Life* (New York: Simon and Schuster, 1993).
17. The term "vegetable" is commonly used in reference to individuals who no longer manifest cognitive brain function. However, this is a highly provocative term, one that conjures up negative images of the person to whom it is applied. For that reason, it is unwise for believers to use such a term in reference to individuals the Bible says are created in God's image.
18. Non-sentient is a term that refers to the inability to communicate, express emotion, or experience life in any way. Some use the terms "permanently unconscious" as a synonym. However, a person may be nonsentient, yet not in a closed-eyes state of unconsciousness. Such a person may experience sleep-wake cycles, give an appearance of looking around the room, and manifest other signs of conscious awareness, yet not have the brain function necessary to manifest those traits.

19. The origin of this view can be traced to the philosopher Immanuel Kant. See Immanuel Kant, *Groundwork of the Metaphysic of Morals,* trans. H. J. Paton (New York: Harper & Row, 1964).

20. Peter Singer, *Rethinking Life and Death* (New York: St. Martin, 1996).

21. Carol Poenisch, "Merian Frederick's Story," *New England Journal of Medicine,* Vol. 339, No. 14, 1 October 1998.

22. Geoffrey Fieger and Edmund Pelligrino, *A Public Debate on Physician-Assisted Suicide* (audiotape) Center for Bioethics and Human Dignity, 2065 Half Day Road, Bannockburn, IL 60015.

23. "Confronting Death: Who Chooses, Who Controls?" *Hastings Center Report* (Vol. 28, No. 1, January-February 1998): 14–24.

24. See Ken Dychtwald and Joseph Flower, *Age Wave: The Challenges and Opportunities of an Aging America* (New York: Bantam, 1990). Compare with Daniel Callahan, *Setting Limits: Medical Goals in an Aging Society* (New York: Simon and Schuster, 1987).

25. Hentoff, "The Coat Hanger of Assisted Suicide," A25.

26. Ibid.

27. Wesley J. Smith, *Forced Exit: The Slippery Slope from Assisted Suicide to Legalized Murder* (New York: Times Books, 1997), 100.

28. Jack D. McCue, "The Naturalness of Dying," *Child and Family* (Vol. 21, No. 4, Spring 1998), 304.

29. *Management of Cancer Pain, Clinical Practice Guideline No. 9,* U.S. Department of Health and Human Services, Agency for Health Care Policy and Research (March 1994), 1.

30. The George H. Gallup International Institute, *Spiritual Beliefs and the Dying Process* (Princeton, N.J., October 1997), 1.

CHAPTER 2

DEATH

AND

DIGNITY:

Toward a
Christian View
of Death

Centuries ago Hippocrates wrote, "Young men fear death, old men fear dying." For the young, death is an enemy that comes too soon, robbing them of their dreams, destroying plans of seeing their children grow up, and dashing hopes that they will make a difference in the world. For older people it is not the event of death that is feared; it is the process of dying. There is fear of what dying might entail, the suffering they may experience, and the loss of usefulness to others.

What do dying people want? By paying attention to what they want to talk about we may gather some clues. Rarely do terminally ill people speak of death itself. Rather, they talk about how tired they are, how frustrating it is to be so dependent upon others, or how they still long to be needed by a world that is often too quick to forget about and continue on without them. Will they be remembered? Will their life have made any lasting difference in the world? Sometimes they ask questions they have never had before—thoughts about life and its meaning and questions about God, the value of the life behind them, and what lies ahead. In some instances, they will confess long-held secret sins or reveal tightly held family secrets. It is important for caregivers, whether physicians, nurses, family members, or friends, to understand this. When you care for a dying person, the frail, deteriorating body is not all that needs attention.[1]

Although modern culture has become comfortable discussing other formerly taboo subjects (e.g., human sexuality), most people are still reluctant to talk openly about death. Death remains mysterious, untamed, and chilling to the modern mind, which is accustomed to being in total control. Consequently, there is a tendency to treat death as an exclusively biological event, one to be concealed and sanitized.

There is something about machines, tests, and images on full-color computer screens that gives otherwise subjective information an objective quality. Perhaps this is our way of getting a handle on death, a way of putting it into objective terms. It is hard to be subjective about statistics, test results, CAT scans, and other diagnostic techniques.

But this "medicalization" of death over the last two decades has created the illusion that death is something to be controlled and managed. No longer do we experience a "natural death." This has been replaced with the "managed death," and this kind of death requires us to move it out of the home and into facilities where medical personnel feel most comfortable—hospitals and other medical facilities. It is here that far too many people die, often separated from family and friends by the "necessities" of hospital efficiency and administration. According to government statistics, nearly two-thirds of deaths occur in the hospital setting.

A Christian approach to the end of life must include an appreciation for the complexity of needs experienced by those in the last stages of life.[2] A biblical view of death need not leave people fearful, anxious, and uncertain. It need not become a horror-filled sequence of painful and degrading technological attenuation. However, that does not mean that death can be dignified, depicted as a *friend* that one can embrace without qualification.

Most people, especially Christians, idealize death as the end of a long and full life, an end that comes once they have "made their peace" with God and mankind. It is the kind of death that is relatively free of pain, and though it means a sorrowful separation from the loved and known, it ushers one into the presence of God in a glorious home-going. Is this ideal anything close to what the Bible teaches about death?

Fortunately, most people do not experience a death preceded by immense pain, suffering, and grave, gut-wrenching decision making.

Most people do quite well in the last year of life, and for many death comes quickly. However, achieving the goal of a well-managed death, a death that is quick and painless, does not bring us any closer to seeing death for what it really is. There is much about death that remains "in the closet."

DEATH AND MODERN SCIENCE

Much of the language about death these days gives the impression that this event can somehow be shaped to one's individual specifications, or at least it should be. There is a strong movement, both inside and outside the medical community, to control death, even eliminate it. The scientific quest to unlock the secrets of aging is in high gear, pursued mainly through genetic research. The search for the "fountain of youth" now seems to be a molecular one, with regular news updates touting the most recent discovery of clues that may "cure" aging and render death obsolete.

I see this wholesale dispensing of scientific hope, not biblical hope, as the most profound demonstration of the growing stranglehold that scientism has over western culture.[3] Modern science has largely succeeded in eliminating God as even part of the equation for many people, despite recent claims that medical schools will now train physicians how to integrate spirituality with physical care.

Nor does modern medicine exhibit a supernatural orientation in its pursuit of truth. For the most part, modern science surrounds itself with theories and methodologies that reflect a *this-world-only* perspective, and if one is to maintain any hope for further career advancement in science, he or she had better maintain that perspective. This does not mean that all scientists embrace naturalism. Fortunately, there are a number of Christians in various scientific fields. However, reason, not revelation, dominates modern science and rules supreme in the modern world. Faith in divine revelation is seen as the opposite of reason.

Consequently, a highly secularized version of modern medicine, despite its pretense of dealing with "whole persons," is reduced to dealing only with physical bodies, using finite man-made tools. Despite the presence of many believers in the scientific research and medical establishment, there is a naive but dangerous optimism that science will ultimately prevail over nature.

However, the Christian, by definition, embraces a supernatural orientation toward the visible world. This mind-set is informed by the special revelation of God in Scripture and sustained through the ministry of the Holy Spirit. Consequently, in the midst of this flurry of scientific activity and the secular quest for immortality, Christians find themselves living with a paradox. They do not want to live on this earth any longer than the Lord intends, yet they understand that life is precious and they have a growing arsenal of life-extending medical technologies at their disposal.

Being able to aggressively intervene to prevent death makes it harder to know when someone is really dying. When a person's life is extended, it is frequently medical technologies and the physicians who use them that receive the credit, not God. We immediately see a causal relationship between the injection of a medication and improved physical well-being, but we often do not even look for a causal connection between prayer and improved health.

Consider the state of mind most people are in when a physician tells them there remains nothing more to be done to alleviate their chronic or terminal condition. Most people experience a significant emotional letdown. Through a voice that reflects dejection and defeat, they say, "All we can do is pray!" Does that sound like the voice of optimistic faith? Does this sound like a person who is thinking "Christianly"? Well, if the Food and Drug Administration has not approved prayer, perhaps we can't really rely on it. Certainly I'm being facetious, perhaps even absurd, but do we not think this way at times? Prayer often is an afterthought, not a priority.

BIBLICAL DOMINION AND TECHNOLOGY

How much technology is a Christian obligated to use in resisting death? Where do we draw the line on efforts to extend earthly existence? These issues will remain murky to us as long as we do not have a clear understanding of the place death has within a Christian worldview. Frequently, the charge is leveled at scientists that they "play God," taking on powers and prerogatives that belong only to God. Is it "playing God" to develop and use technologies that give us greater knowledge about ourselves and the power to eliminate existing or potential diseases? Are we overstepping natural biological barriers, or merely exercising over creation the dominion God has given to us? (Genesis 1:26–28).

One's assessment depends, in part, upon one's disposition toward nature and the legitimacy of human control over it by technological means. Are we to pursue control to whatever extent our technology permits? Shall we view all of our scientific capability as progress, as obedience to God by exercising maximum dominion over creation?

Those who celebrate new medical technologies often welcome the added control over nature. For some, such knowledge is a legitimate application of biblical dominion, a valid use of God-given abilities and talents. Others, however, go to the opposite extreme, saying all technologies are unwarranted encroachments upon the natural order created by God.

Maximum Dominion

The view that humans are to exercise maximum control over nature began with the work of the seventeenth-century philosopher Francis Bacon.[4] He argued that all earthly dignity belongs to human beings, who were given dominion over nature by God. In his view, the natural order and natural processes have no dignity of their own; therefore, they can be mastered by humans.

According to this perspective, technology is simply society's toolbox, introducing new tools as options for individuals, or entire societies, to use for their own ends. How the tool will be used depends on the values and beliefs of those who use it. Thus, some will use it for good, whereas others will not, but the technology itself is values-neutral.

However, technologies are often applications of specific theories, which themselves emerge from the theorist's personal worldview and values. Believing they are neutral is a scientifically and philosophically naive position. Technologies represent not only what we *can* do, but what we *want* to do. They not only satisfy wants; they stimulate them. For example, procreation technologies enable some to have children who otherwise could not. When these technologies are coupled with genetic testing, they stimulate the desire for a particular kind of child. In this sense, procreation and genetic technology act as shapers of life and values, not just functions of them. They shape what it means to be a person, and what it means to be a parent.[5] Television promotes the idea that life's primary purposes are entertainment (the programs) and acquiring material possessions (the advertisements). Medical technology changes the meaning of life and death.

Bacon's position—"maximum dominion"—says that technologies merely provide options where none existed before. Yet, if technologies instead reflect a specific worldview, and are values-laden, then the options they produce are equally values-laden.

Although Bacon's idea contributed to human well-being, technology does not always work out that well. The benefits of technology also bring undesired effects like water and air pollution and other socioeconomic challenges.

One of the problems with Bacon's view of dominion is that it invariably led to the technological imperative—what can be done must be done; if it works, it must be moral to use it. It is relatively easy to see the implications of this in the modern intensive care unit. Although intensivists are motivated by compassion and a desire to care for people in the most effective way, there tends to be a mindset of all-out warfare against death in the ICU. It is generally a good thing that ICU personnel have this perspective, that they are reluctant to surrender easily. However, it does have a downside.

Minimal Manipulation

In contrast to Bacon's view of dominion is a "back to nature," or minimalist position. Its central tenet is the *principle of minimal manipulation*. This position holds that natural systems—although corrupted by sin—were nonetheless created by an omniscient God. As a general rule, finite human beings should use caution before supervening natural systems with technology, and people should be committed to minimal manipulation.

Scripture reminds us that God's ways are not ours. Solomon admonished that we not rely upon our own understanding, not trust in our own wisdom (Proverbs 3:5–8). Scripture records numerous examples of people relying upon their own wisdom and heeding the counsel of fellow humans, only to find that their plans failed to produce the desired results because they had not sought divine guidance. Israel's desire for a king led to difficult days for the young nation. My wise grandfather once said, "There are two kinds of disappointment in the world: the disappointment of not getting what we want, and the disappointment of getting what we want." Humans push natural biological limits at their own risk.

Sometimes what we regard as a tragedy may ultimately turn out to be merciful. Notable examples from science support "minimal manipulation" as well. The overuse of antibiotics in the twentieth century produced a wave of superviruses far stronger than existing antibiotics were designed to conquer. The result is the dangerous possibility of unleashing devastating plagues upon the world.[6] Another example is the recent discovery that the genetic mutation that causes cystic fibrosis may also protect the carrier from typhoid fever.[7] Thus, eliminating genes in order to prevent death from one disease may sentence a person to die from another.

The principle of minimal manipulation suggests that the issues facing us are more than just questions about what individual users do with technology. Bacon took "dominion" too far, placing too much control in human hands. Before fundamental biological processes are supervened with technological solutions, we should ask how much new power it will place into human hands. Nothing in the history of science suggests that scientists are any more immune to abuses of power than anyone else.

Minimal manipulation, as an interpretation of the biblical concept of dominion, is useful in restraining the human propensity to "play God." God introduced the "natural" event of death in Genesis 3 to prevent disobedient humanity from living forever. In a fallen universe, "natural" processes like aging constrain human dominion, and attempts to restrain them should be kept to a minimum. The universality of death (Hebrews 9:27) is not a contingency to be eliminated by technological means; it is a reality to be recognized as inevitable. Although we may briefly restrain its onslaught, we are powerless to eradicate death—it is not a strictly biological event subject to human control.

It is dangerous to make conclusions about what is best for human beings solely on the basis of naturalistic science. A science that refuses to recognize the sovereignty of God over nature lacks the humility and wisdom to recognize its own limitations, and we should hold this kind of science up to close biblical scrutiny.

Minimal manipulation questions the motives and purposes behind invasive technologies that appear to treat death as something that can be avoided. It challenges humanity's utopian pretenses and resists scientific paternalism that insists everyone else "just trust us." The purpose of biblical dominion is not to re-create what God has created, nor to improve upon the divine engineering of human beings. Instead, it exercises an imperfect stewardship over a fallen world—alleviating pain and suffering where it can while recognizing that it is impossible to eliminate them completely.

Dominion, like every aspect of human function, is a divine-human cooperative. All must be done to the glory of God (1 Corinthians 6:20) and with God's enablement (James 4:13–15). If one's eating and life planning are to be done for God's glory and with His counsel, shouldn't we think about His plan with regard to the use of genetic knowledge? Natural processes exist because they are created by God to function within a specific design, and finite human beings should not be casual when interfering with them. Rather than impose our own purposes on nature, we should first seek God's purposes as revealed in nature.

DEATH IN THE CHRISTIAN WORLDVIEW

The management of dying is somewhat dependent on what we take death to be. What medical interventions we employ, the intensity with which we use them, and what we do for dying people when medical intervention is no longer possible are influenced by our overall view of death and its place in the context of relations between God and man.

Many nonbelievers treat death in purely physical terms, believing that the end of life represents the complete cessation of individual existence. This is the dominant view within the scientific community, which should itself serve as a warning to the believer about embracing the judgments scientists make about human life. It is not that all the judgments of modern science are wrong when it comes to definitions of personhood and quality of life; it's just that its judgments start from the wrong place and use the wrong instruments for measurement, so they are more likely to be wrong than right.

For the most part, care for the dying person is directed toward physical symptoms. Much of the care provided at the end of life does not reflect a recognition of a life in the hereafter. Medicine orients itself to the care of the body (hospice being a notable exception) and demonstrates little understanding about caring for the spirit. We most certainly want what physicians and other medical personnel have to offer, but dying people need more than that. They need to be treated as whole people, as complete beings. The scientific, this-world-only orientation cannot provide this.

A BIBLICAL DEFINITION OF DEATH

Whatever may be said about death biologically, sociologically, legally, or philosophically, death strikes human beings in their totality. Death possesses both a physical and spiritual reality. From a physical standpoint, death means the end of earthly temporal existence. From the spiritual perspective, death means a transition to another realm of existence, though not the end of conscious existence.

Despite an overwhelming fear of death, people remain irrepressibly curious about it and continue to ask hard questions: *How much technology is too much in resisting death? Is it wrong to not want to become a burden to my family? Do people have a right to die with dignity? Am I morally obligated to accept every medical intervention that might extend my earthly, bodily existence?* These are reasonable questions. An even more important question is, *What is death according to the Word of God?* For the Christian, is death a friend or a foe? Is it a tragic, unwelcome stranger that robs us of our future, or is it the friend that rescues us from a fate worse than death itself—the indignity of pain and suffering? Or is it a combination of the two?

Death as a Foe

In Genesis 2:16–17 we have the record of the Lord's warning to Adam against eating from the tree of the knowledge of good and evil. He explicitly states, "In the day that thou eatest thereof thou shalt surely die." There can be no misunderstanding that this was a warning of certain judgment if Adam disobeyed God. Interestingly, this warning was given at a time when Adam had never seen death. He had never seen a dead animal. No plants had withered; no bird had fallen from the sky. What must Adam have thought when God warned him against eating from that one tree in the Garden?

Tragically, Adam disobeyed God's command, and he subsequently died (Genesis 5:5). Death was the means God used to demonstrate the seriousness with which He regards all manner of sin. Death is not based on a biological necessity, but on a spiritual reality—God is holy, and He has declared that "the soul that sinneth, it shall die" (Ezekiel 18:4). All human beings are sinners (Romans 3:23); therefore, all human beings die.

Although we may not be able to provide a specific biological explanation for every death, we do know that the universality of sin is the only proper biblical explanation for the universality of death. Despite the fact that specific causes for specific deaths can be traced through natural processes (e.g., cancer, cardiac arrest), the death of all created beings has an ultimate, special cause—death is a divine judgment against sin.

The apostle Paul reinforced this view of death as a judgment in Romans 5:12 when he said, "Wherefore, as by one man sin entered into the world, and death by sin; and so death passed upon all men, for that all have sinned." In Romans 6:23 Paul said, "For the wages of sin is death." In 1 Corinthians 15:26, Paul stated, "The last enemy that shall be destroyed is death." There can be no theology of death without seeing it as an enemy—a divine judgment for sin against a holy God (Hebrews 9:27). With death comes *despair* (Psalm 88:15 NIV), *anguish* (Psalm 116:3 NIV), and *fear* (Hebrews 2:15). At its worst, death is a separation from God. Death is antithetical to God's original intention for man. In this sense, death is an affront to human dignity. It is ugly and unsightly.

Death is the reminder that this is a sinful world and men are alienated from God because of sin. Every time we read of a death in the obituaries, hear of a death on the news, experience the death of a friend or family member, or even see a dead animal in the road, we should be reminded of the horrible price to be paid for sin. In light of the Cross, there can be no denying the reality of death or the terrible power the fear of death can hold over the dying.

In Gethsemane, Jesus asked that the cup of death might be removed from Him (Matthew 26:39). On the cross, Jesus cried out, "My God, my God, why hast thou forsaken me?" (Matthew 27:46). The death of Jesus Christ on the cross was marked by pain, betrayal, abandonment, and anguish. His death was not only horrible because of its cruelty, but because it separated Him from the Father. Jesus knew death as an enemy. Death is real, and it is evil (Deuteronomy 30:15). It threatens all of humanity, instilling the fear of separation from relationships, communities, and God.

Death also threatens us with the fear of being separated from our bodies, for we are not immortal spirits awaiting liberation from the tomb of the soul. We are creatures of flesh and blood. We walk, talk, eat, work, worship, and play in our flesh. It is in the body of flesh that we experience color, shape, sound, scent, taste, and the revelation of one human self to another through gestures, words, smiles, tears, and touches.

Death threatens us, and never is this more real than when the dying begin to feel alienated from their own bodies. Immense pain may cause people to regard their bodies as enemies. Weakness may rob them of the capacity to act or to exercise control of themselves and their world. All too often, medical technology reduces the dying person's body to manipulable flesh. Worse, the power of death is felt when the experience of dying reduces the marvels of God's creation to something barren, colorless, tasteless, inhospitable, and alien. Most of all, death makes its power felt in loneliness at the end of life.[8]

Fortunately for us, Jesus Christ has destroyed the ultimate victory of this enemy. Through His own death, burial, and resurrection, believers experience victory over death (1 Corinthians 15:55–58). Because Jesus has been raised from the dead, faith in Him gives us hope (1 Thessalonians 4:13–14). Since Jesus has risen from the dead, God promises to raise others from the dead, to restore wholeness and well-being to human beings.

Death as a Friend

Although referring to death as a "friend" may overstate the case, death is portrayed in much of the Bible as the natural end of life in a fallen state. It is certainly viewed as inevitable.[9] Genesis 25:8 records the death of Abraham and says, "Then Abraham gave up the ghost, and died in a good old age, an old man, and full of years; and was gathered to his people." Although we are not told the exact circumstances of Abraham's death, the Bible portrays it as natural and expected. It is recorded in peaceful terms.

In one sense, Abraham's death may be seen as "death with dignity." It was not a premature death, but came following a long and fruitful life. It likely permitted Abraham to bring closure to his relationships with family members.

DEATH MAY BE A NECESSARY WAKE-UP CALL,

NOT ONLY FOR THE DYING PERSON, BUT FOR

THOSE WHO LOVE AND CARE FOR HIM OR HER.

Paradoxically, most people would like time at the end of life to say good-bye to family and friends and to tie up loose ends in business or personal matters, but they also want death to be quick and painless. We believe that time is required to bring closure to the areas of life most important to people, but we don't always get the time we need. Death can be sudden and unexpected, leaving family members with regrets—perhaps with an "if only" mentality: "If only I had not canceled that lunch appointment." "If only I had asked for his forgiveness." "If only I had visited her one last time." A quick, sudden death can leave loved ones bewildered, stunned, and groping with feelings of guilt.

We have a tendency to believe that the best death is the quick one. If we can't prevent it, then we should get it over with as quickly and painlessly as possible. The advocates of assisted suicide believe this. What good can come from extending a person's pain or suffering? It is considered merciful to end a life filled with pain and cruel not to end it. However, pain at the end of life is not the only issue to address. Certainly we should treat intense pain as an emergency, doing all we can to control it, but we must also give attention to the spiritual care of the individual. Many terminally ill patients indicate that their pain is reduced when an individual prays with them.

As the pastor of a small church in Montana during the late 1970s, I spent many hours at the bedside of a highly respected church leader who was dying from cancer. For several weeks, he had received regular morphine injections to control his pain, but in the last few days of his life, when physicians were quite sure that death was imminent, he asked to have the morphine injections removed so he could be as alert and lucid as possible. He had things to say to his family and friends, and he wanted to say them with as clear a mind as possible. Without the pain medication he had to endure excruciating pain and severe nausea, but he accepted them in order to accomplish his goal of saying farewell to loved ones. Every time someone prayed in his room, the pain diminished and the nausea ceased. His final hours were spent alternating between prayer and engaging in conversation with those most important to him.

Unfortunately, in the accelerated pace of modern life, it is often only at the time of death that some people really get around to talking about the things that matter most. Like the friend who occasionally has to get in our face to get our attention about an issue of considerable importance, death may be a necessary wake-up call, not only for the dying person, but for those who love and care for him or her. Euthanasia thus short-circuits the entire process, cheating it of its usefulness as well as its pain. Solomon wrote, "It is better to go to the house of mourning, than to go to the house of feasting: for that is the end of all men; and the living will lay it to his heart" (Ecclesiastes 7:2). If it takes a terminal illness for a person to accept the Lord Jesus Christ as Savior, then death can be a friend, albeit a brutally honest one.

The apostle Paul spoke of his own impending death when he said, "For I am now ready to be offered, and the time of my departure is at hand. I have fought a good fight, I have finished my course, I have kept the faith" (2 Timothy 4:6–7). Paul knew that his death would be that of a martyr and that it was imminent. However, while his death would mean a significant loss to the church, his death could also be celebrated as a victory for Christ. "Precious in the sight of the Lord is the death of his saints" (Psalm 116:15). Paul looked forward to being with his Lord, face-to-face.

It is clear that Paul struggled with his feelings about death in his writing to the Philippians. In this letter Paul declared, "For to me, to live is Christ and to die is gain. If I am to go on living in the body, this will mean fruitful labor for me. Yet what shall I choose? I do not know! I am torn between the two: I desire to depart and be with Christ, which is better by far; but it is more necessary for you that I remain in the body" (Philippians 1:21–24 NIV). Paul's perception of death as the "friend" that would usher him into the presence of his Lord should not be construed as a death wish, as though some painful physical condition overwhelmed him. Paul was not longing for death because he was suffering. Rather, here was a veteran missionary whose body had endured enormous hardship, who was imprisoned for his faith and longed to be with his Lord. He was perfectly willing to remain alive if that was God's will, but his own desire was to be with Christ. Paul and the other martyrs of the early church learned to live triumphantly with both the tragedy and the victory of death. Peter David writes, "The death of martyrs could be celebrated and the death of the faithful, while sorrowful, could be spoken of with confidence and joy. . . . Death was not denied nor sorrow suppressed, but death was seen as hopeful, an event in Christ, an event for which one could prepare."[10]

In the final analysis, resisting death at all costs is not the ultimate calling for the child of God; obeying and trusting God is. We are to "walk worthy of the vocation wherewith [we] are called" (Ephesians 4:1). The day of one's death is a calling; there is an appointed time for it (Hebrews 9:27). Whether we live or die, we belong to the Lord, and it is important to be as faithful in death as we are in life. Acknowledging that it may be time to die is not incompatible with a respect for the sanctity of human life. Scripture does not compel us to value physical life above all other considerations.[11]

Death with Dignity

Those who argue in favor of euthanasia and assisted suicide cite the relief of suffering as a central goal. These practices are also said to acknowledge that people are entitled to die with dignity. In this sense, euthanasia is not only a matter of mercy but respect. However, one need not practice euthanasia or assisted suicide to desire that people die with dignity.[12]

What is human dignity in the face of death? What would a dignified death look like? Would the painless death of a three-year-old be dignified? Is the absence of pain one of the essential criteria for a dignified death? How are we to make the ugliness of death "dignified," or, more important, how are we to make an event "good" when it is part of God's judgment on rebellious human beings? It appears that many things can occur that make life seemingly undignified. Christopher Coope writes,

> Not everything we can do can be done with dignity. Would we understand what is meant by "birth with dignity"? Could one ask what is more dignified: a cesarean or a normal delivery? And would it matter? A child cannot be said to grow with dignity [slobbering on everything in sight, vomiting at inopportune times, requiring diapers, etc.]. And it is not at all clear what breathing with dignity would mean. Perhaps breathing one's last with dignity is similarly empty.[13]

It is clear to most people that the phrase "death with dignity" is intended to define a particular way of dying. But "death with dignity" is not something we find in television news broadcasts. We come away from these with the impression that death cannot be dignified. On television, people die in all sorts of undignified ways. Convicted murderers are executed by a variety of methods, innocent people are shot to death in drive-by shootings, and commercial airliners fall from the sky, spreading human bodies around in all sorts of undignified ways. We watch graphic television footage of the shattered bodies of victims from bombings, automobile crashes, and natural disasters, all of which present death in a dramatically undignified light. We read about Jack Kevorkian dropping off the bodies of his "patients" at hospital emergency rooms and still do not find dignity.

When a commercial airplane crashes, the public is curious about how much people may have suffered before dying. The first images of the tragic circumstances surrounding the death of Princess Diana were of the shattered automobile sitting in the middle of a highway tunnel in Paris. Millions watched as cameras zoomed in as close as possible to get a look at where the Princess of Wales spent the final moments of her life. The curiosity over how someone dies is overpowering for most people, whether the victim is famous or not.

For some morbid reason, the public is transfixed by the specter of brutal deaths, yet people insist on a "dignified death" for themselves. Brutal, sudden deaths do not lend themselves easily to the label "death with dignity." Neither do the slow deaths of modern medical technology. It is the painless and mercifully quick "managed" death or the quick death in one's sleep that earns such a label. Yet is it dignified to die of poison? Why do many find execution "cruel," yet consider such a death to be appropriate if chosen for medical reasons?

During the same week Princess Diana died, an elderly unglamorous nun, whose life was spent serving the poor and dying in Calcutta, India, also died. No one was shocked by Mother Teresa's death. I do not recall one news report calling her death "undignified," though she had been dying for several years from multiple causes and she died penniless. No one sent camera crews to Calcutta to obtain footage of the ragged mattress upon which she spent her final earthly moments. No one sought a medical examiner's report on the cause of her death. No public outrage erupted over the circumstances of her demise. Yet Mother Teresa was given a state funeral by the Indian government, a first in that nation's history for someone other than a state official. Her death was not considered a tragedy, as was Diana's. Like Diana's death, the loss of Mother Teresa was felt by millions, but, unlike Diana's, Mother Teresa's death had an air of quiet dignity about it. It did not incite the same sense of outrage as the death of Diana.

DEATH NEED NOT BE DIGNIFIED
BECAUSE IT CANNOT BE DIGNIFIED.

Indeed, the circumstances of these two deaths were different. But what difference does it make if they were dignified or not? Would the world be a better place if Diana had died of breast cancer instead of lethal injuries from a car crash? Would she be any less dead if death came in her sleep? The world is not the same place without these two women; the human community has been diminished by their loss. In that sense, both deaths are offensive and undignified. But whatever dignity these two women demonstrated was not diminished in the least by the kind of death they experienced, nor could that dignity have been enhanced if each had died in a different manner. The circumstances surrounding death have nothing to do with the dignity that is intrinsic to every human being.

The Lord Jesus, most of the apostles, and an innumerable host of Christian martyrs throughout the history of Christianity have died brutal deaths. Many would describe these deaths as "undignified." Yet circumstances have nothing to do with a person's dignity. Dignity is something that human beings have, irrespective of circumstances. In the end, the kind of dignity we all long for in the moment of our death is grounded in the quiet dignity of the life that precedes it, being secured by the relationship we have with God as beings created in His image. One of the underlying teachings of the parable of the Prodigal Son (Luke 15:11–32) seems to be that even a lad whose quality of life has sunk to such a low level that he envies the food supply of pigs possesses intrinsic dignity as a human being.

Death need not be dignified because it cannot be dignified. Death is an event, an occurrence that takes place in the normal course of human events. Death shows no partiality. It is not a "thing" to be tamed because it has no being; it has no characteristics to be shaped or reformed. It is a privation of good, a lack in something. In particular, death demonstrates the privation of good in human beings, a privation that exists because of sin. Since death has no being, it does not "think" about the person it kills; it just kills, and it kills everyone equally. Since it has no being, it cannot be made "good." Horrendous circumstances take the lives of rich and poor, male and female, all of us from all cultures.

However, this does not mean that caregivers need not pay attention to the circumstances surrounding the dying process. Virtually all of the circumstances we consider negative can be alleviated to some degree. We need not stand by and permit pain, disfigurement, disability, and despair to dominate a dying person's remaining time on earth. Imitating the example of God as our Comforter (2 Corinthians 1:3–4), we are called to comfort others. Being part of the body of Christ involves bearing burdens (Galatians 6:2). James admonishes believers to show that their religion is "pure" by visiting the widows and orphans in their distress (James 1:27).

The problem for many people who speak of "death with dignity" is not how people die, but the fact that some people do not die in a manner to their liking. The position of the person who requires twenty-four-hour care because of a massive stroke, the elderly person with severe Alzheimer's dementia, or the individual whose condition is described as "persistent vegetative state" is viewed by those at the bedside as an insult to the individual experiencing them. The proponents of assisted suicide and euthanasia view these circumstances as so undignified that continued existence is regarded an insult. For them, it is undignified to be helpless and require others to provide care.

If this perception is accepted as morally legitimate, then any claim I might make on others to meet needs I cannot meet for myself is suspect—potentially unreasonable and onerous. Perhaps it is irrational for me to want my life continued, but I do not have the capacity to appreciate how continued existence is harming me and others. This is a seriously flawed and mischievous way of viewing individuals who cannot take care of themselves! There is a significant danger in linking indignity with incapacity.[14]

MUCH OF THE TALK CONCERNING
"DEATH WITH DIGNITY" IS LADEN
WITH FALSE ASSUMPTIONS ABOUT
WHAT GIVES HUMAN BEINGS VALUE.

Does anyone really consider changing a baby's soiled diaper to be an insult to the baby? Does it diminish the child's dignity? Of course not! Everyone knows that babies lack the capacity to meet this need on their own. How is it different when the person whose diaper needs changing is an older person rendered helpless by a massive stroke or a degenerating disease, who must rely on temporarily able-bodied individuals to meet such basic needs? (I say "temporarily able-bodied" because all of us will experience some form of disability at some point in life.) Is it morally inappropriate and undignified because that person used to be capable of meeting such needs for himself? Indeed, it is unfortunate that a formerly competent individual now requires others to take care of his or her basic hygiene needs. Concern for privacy and independence are genuine. However, the fact that someone needs assistance is not an insult to his or her value as a person. It is an insult to all human beings to presume that a major disability or medical catastrophe renders one "undignified."

Jean-Dominique Bauby, the former editor of *Elle* magazine, suffered a massive stroke that left him completely paralyzed except for the use of his left eyelid. Trapped "like a mind in a jar," Bauby struggled for escape until finally devising a blinking scheme for selecting letters of the alphabet as they were recited to him. Using this as his only outlet for expression, he "dictated" his memoirs into a book entitled *The Diving Bell and the Butterfly*, which aired in November 1996 as an HBO documentary. "There is so much to do," he wrote in his book. "You can wander off in space or in time, set out for Tierra del Fuego or King Midas' court." He died in March 1997 from heart failure.

Much of the talk concerning "death with dignity" is laden with false assumptions about what gives human beings value. Among these assumptions is that the manner of death one experiences is all that loved ones, family, and friends will remember about his or her death. Although a person's death can affect loved ones' memories of him, an entire life, with all of its contributions and meaning, cannot be dismissed and discounted even if the last days are spent tethered to a ventilator, tube-fed, diapered, or unable to recognize visitors. And will giving a person a lethal injection or having him inhale carbon monoxide in the back of Kevorkian's van enhance our memories of the person?

How can it be thought to be "undignified" to be comatose? Do any of us consider sleep intrinsically undignified? How can unconsciousness be considered an embarrassment or an insult to the person? How can it be indecent to remain alive? There is already far too much contempt for the weak, the infirm, the enfeebled, and those too many regard as the inferior. "Death with dignity" is intended to conjure up positive images, but, as Christopher Miles Coope points out, "these thoughts are romantic; and romanticism . . . is an invitation to disaster: it is the substitution of what appears impressive for what is true."[15]

The Finality of Death

Death is physiologically final in that it brings to an end one's earthly, bodily existence, and it is spiritually final in the sense that it renders one's decision for or against Christ final and unalterable (Luke 16:26; 2 Corinthians 5:10). What happens in life on earth becomes history in death.

However, physiological death of the human body is not the final chapter in the individual's life. Heaven awaits the child of God, and it is death that transports us from the temporal state to the eternal (1 Corinthians 15:51–58). The tension between earthly existence, with all of its problems, compared to the bliss, wonder, and glory of heaven, might lead one to think it foolish for any believer to willingly remain on earth. If heaven is such a wonderful place, why be reluctant to go there? Who would choose to remain here on earth and endure immense pain and suffering when he or she has the assurance of a better life in heaven?

There is one compelling reason why in such a circumstance the child of God should not choose assisted suicide: Assisted suicide is unjustified killing and God prohibits it (Exodus 20:13). The advocates of euthanasia and assisted suicide are far too quick to lose sight of death as an enemy, and they too readily embrace death as merely the natural end of life.[16]

The Bible teaches that divine judgment awaits those who die without confessing and knowing Christ as Lord and Savior (John 3:16; 14:6; Romans 10:9–10; Revelation 20:11–15). Such a death is a tragedy—the tragedy of opportunity lost forever. According to the Scriptures, death for them does not mean the end of pain and suffering—only the beginning. For them, death is not a friend. It is a deceiver and betrayer, holding out the promise of relief from the sufferings of this life, but in reality it becomes the thief that robs men of their souls. It ushers them into the second death—the death that for all of eternity separates people from God and leaves them in a perpetual torment in hell that is the most undignified death of all.

TOWARD A THEOLOGY OF PAIN AND SUFFERING

Is suffering a necessary part of human experience? Most people, including some Christians, might respond with a resounding no. Pain and suffering are associated with evil by definition; therefore, they are experiences to avoid at all cost. We've often seen pain and suffering transform a normally thoughtful, compassionate person into an angry, irrational, and demanding one. The pain and suffering an individual experiences can be excruciating for everyone involved, the patient most of all.

It is hard to defend God's goodness (although He really does not need our defense) when terrible things happen to people. However, it is possible to understand how such evil can exist in a universe ruled by a sovereign God who is also good. God certainly could have created a world where even the capacity for evil—with the consequence of pain and suffering—was removed. However, God is interested in a particular kind of goodness, a goodness that can only be achieved through the free choice of beings living in a world where evil choices are possible.[17]

Since we live in a fallen, sinful world, pain and suffering are realities in human experience. Children are seldom born into this world without some pain associated with their entrance. Child rearing is often painful, although with a different type of pain. It is painful to stand by while a child suffers through making mistakes, injuries, illnesses, and the trials of life. Marriage partners may find themselves suffering through painful misunderstandings, distress arising from ill health, job loss, or a host of problems life can throw at them. Of course, suffering through the difficulties that marriage invariably presents sounds a little quaint in the age of easy no-fault divorce. Nonetheless, we applaud those who "stick it out" and emerge all the stronger for it.

The promises contained in Romans 8:28, 2 Corinthians 12:9, and other biblical texts are not that all pain and suffering will be eliminated for the child of God, but that God will not abandon him in the midst of pain and suffering. We know that "all things work together for good to them that love God, to them who are the called according to his purpose." What is that purpose? Paul tells us in Romans 8:29 that it is to be "conformed to the image of his Son." If pain and suffering were necessary in the experience of the Lord Jesus Christ to secure our redemption, we can be certain that pain and suffering will be an integral part of becoming like Him.

One cannot read the New Testament without seeing that pain and suffering are inherent properties of life on earth. To be human in this world includes pain and suffering, a reality that should cause the child of God to long for release from this temporal existence, not cling to it. The tools of modern medicine may potently and rightly be used to alleviate some of that pain, but those tools are not omnipotent.

Human pain and suffering can only truly be understood within a biblical/theological context. It is hard, if not impossible, to comprehend what purposeful suffering would be within a purely naturalistic, nontheistic system, a worldview that reduces all explanations for human experience and action to interactions between elementary physical particles. However, for the child of God, suffering that God sovereignly and, yes, lovingly permits into His children's lives al-

ways serves a greater good, a good that only prayer, faith, and biblical encouragement from fellow believers can help one understand
and embrace. Yet temporary relief from overwhelming pain and suffering may be sought using medical tools, enabling the sufferer to reflect on God and His workings in the midst of the suffering. Paul
said, "For I reckon that the sufferings of this present time are not
worthy to be compared with the glory which shall be revealed in us"
(Romans 8:18).

Quite often, however, the individual is unable to concentrate on
the spiritual significance of his or her disease and its complications,
especially if pain is not being managed sufficiently. Physical pain
and general overall malaise is debilitating, undermining one's ability
to focus on even minor mental tasks. In such a condition, the only
spiritual discipline one may exhibit is prayer expressed as single-
word groans. This provides us with a powerful reason to pursue improvements in pain management. However, choosing death as the
means of eliminating suffering takes one beyond what is legitimate.

NOTES

1. I commend to the reader Sherwin B. Nuland's fine book, *How We Die: Reflections on Life's Final Chapter* (New York: Vintage, 1995) for further in-
sights on how individuals view death and dying.

2. The George H. Gallup International Institute, *Spiritual Beliefs and the Dying
Process* (Princeton, N.J., October 1997), 2.

3. Scientism is the belief that all claims to truth must meet the methodological
standards of scientific verification, that science provides the foundational
principles for defining ultimate reality.

4. For an excellent discussion of Bacon's impact on modern science and technology, see Hessel Bouma, Douglas Diekema, et al., *Christian Faith, Health,
and Medical Practice* (Grand Rapids: Eerdmans, 1989), 189–95.

5. Bouma, Diekema, et al., *Christian Faith*, 191.

6. Jeffrey A. Fisher, *The Plaguemakers: How We Are Creating Catastrophic New
Epidemics and What We Must Do to Avert Them* (New York: Simon and
Schuster, 1994).

7. Josie Clausiusz, "Hidden Benefits," *Discover Magazine*, March 1998.

8. Adapted from Foundational Affirmations, Program of Christian Hospice
Care, Hospice of Greater Grand Rapids. Used by permission.

9. I am indebted to Dennis Hollinger for his fine treatment of this subject in
"Theological Foundations for Death and Dying Issues," *Ethics and Medicine*
(Vol. 12, No. 3, 1996): 62.

10. Peter H. David, "Death," *The Evangelical Dictionary of Theology*, ed. Walter
Elwell (Grand Rapids: Baker, 1984), 300.

11. C. Christopher Hook, "Medical Futility," in John F. Kilner, et al., ed., *Dignity
and Dying: A Christian Appraisal* (Grand Rapids: Eerdmans, 1996), 93.

12. Christopher Miles Coope, "Death with Dignity," *Hastings Center Report*, September-October, 1997: 37.

13. Ibid., 37.

14. Ibid., 38.

15. Ibid.

16. Dennis Hollinger, "Theological Foundations for Death and Dying Issues," 62.

17. An excellent discussion of the problem of evil can be found in Norman Geisler's *The Philosophy of Religion* (Grand Rapids: Zondervan, 1985); also C. S. Lewis, *The Problem of Pain* (New York: Macmillan, 1978) and Peter Kreeft and Ronald K. Tacelli, *Handbook of Christian Apologetics* (Downers Grove, Ill.: InterVarsity, 1994), 120–44.

CHAPTER 3

DEATH
BECOMES
HIM:

Jack Kevorkian's
Goals for America

The person most Americans associate with physician-assisted suicide is Jack Kevorkian, the unemployed pathologist known as "Dr. Death." Kevorkian has admitted to "attending" more than 130 suicides.

It is worth noting that Kevorkian was dubbed "Dr. Death" long before he invented his bizarre "Mercitron" suicide device. As a resident at Detroit Receiving Hospital, Kevorkian engaged in "research" by examining how eyes change at the moment of death. He believed doctors could know precisely when to cease resuscitation efforts on patients if it could be shown that there is a perceptible change in a person's eyes immediately following death. He dubbed his research the "Death Rounds," as he moved from one terminally ill patient to another. On some occasions, he even wore a black armband so everyone would know what he was doing. His "Death Rounds," and retrieving body parts from operating rooms for experimentation in the pathology lab, led Kevorkian's colleagues to tag him with the moniker "Dr. Death." Little did they realize how well it would describe him later in life.[1]

In March 1990, a Detroit newspaper carried the following advertisement:

Applications are being accepted. Oppressed by a fatal disease, a severe handicap, a crippling deformity? Write Box 261, Royal Oak,

MI 48068-0261. Show him proper, compelling medical evidence that you should die, and Dr. Jack Kevorkian will help you kill yourself, free of charge.[2]

On Monday, June 4, 1990, at approximately 2:30 P.M., Jack Kevorkian telephoned the Oakland County Medical Examiner's Office to tell them that he had just assisted a woman in committing suicide in the back of his 1968 Volkswagen van at a campsite lot in the Groveland Oaks County Park, Groveland Township, in the county of Oakland, Michigan.[3] Kevorkian admitted to investigators from the Michigan State Police that he attached his "Mercitron I" suicide machine to a fifty-four-year-old Portland, Oregon, woman, Janet Adkins, and that she had killed herself by lethal injection.[4]

KEVORKIAN'S LICENSES TO PRACTICE MEDICINE WERE REVOKED BY BOTH MICHIGAN AND CALIFORNIA.

Kevorkian claimed Adkins wanted to die because she had Alzheimer's disease and was afraid of suffering. He was less forthcoming about the fact that it was Adkins's husband, not Janet herself, who had first made contact with him and made all of the arrangements for Janet to meet Kevorkian. Prior to the events of June 4, Kevorkian had met with Adkins only once, a visit that consisted of an interview, not a medical examination. At a *show cause* hearing on June 8, 1990 (in which a person is expected to show why he should not be put under an injunction or a temporary or permanent restraining order), before Oakland County Circuit Judge Alice Gilbert, Kevorkian admitted:

- He was only certified in anatomic and clinical pathology, that he had been unemployed in medicine since 1982, and that he had no special training in Alzheimer's disease, geriatric diseases, or neurology. His main work with live patients was during his internship and while in the Army from 1953 to 1955;
- He had to "make up" his own ethics rules;

• The use of his "Thanatron" or "Mercitron" device was not a medically accepted or recognized medical procedure approved by the FDA;
• Helping individuals with physical diseases to die was only a first stage until society matured a bit.[5]

KEVORKIAN AS PHYSICIAN

A lifelong bachelor and nonconformist, Kevorkian lives alone in a small apartment in the Detroit suburb of Southfield. Although he is the most visible and vocal advocate for physician-assisted suicide, Jack Kevorkian possesses meager credentials.

Kevorkian's licenses to practice medicine were revoked by both Michigan and California, and all efforts to get them reinstated have failed. His medical experience (with the exception of his internship following graduation from medical school) is exclusively in pathology, a branch of medicine that studies the functional and structural manifestations of disease. Other than his internship, Kevorkian has no clinical experience with patients in a caregiving capacity. He has never been certified by a medical board in any area of medicine other than pathology.

His professional writing is equally unimpressive. The few articles he has published deal with pathology, medical experimentation, and subjects unrelated to curative medicine or improving care for terminally ill individuals. Prior to his involvement with assisted suicide, Kevorkian had no experience in the care of terminally or chronically ill individuals. He has no prior experience in pain management, no experience in psychiatry, nor any training in palliative care. Neither has he ever associated himself with any organization whose purpose is to provide or improve care for terminally ill or chronically ill individuals.

KEVORKIAN AND RELIGION

Kevorkian claims to be an agnostic. He believes religion does not have any legitimate role to play in making medical decisions, including decisions at the end of life. "Any religion ought to be irrelevant to the strictly secular doctor-patient relationship. . . . The religious or philosophical orientation of either the patient or the doctor is absolutely irrelevant to the latter's professional duty to the patient's health problem. . . . Medicine is a purely secular profession, like engineering and many others."[6] Kevorkian has such disdain for Christianity that he assisted a suicide inside a Detroit-area Roman Catholic Church in 1997.

Kevorkian accuses Christians of keeping medicine in a moral stranglehold by their opposition to abortion, infanticide, euthanasia, and assisted suicide.[7] He calls the Judeo-Christian sanctity of human life principle "inflexible, punitive dogma."[8] He goes on to say, "It's [Christianity] all made up. Every religion is concocted myth. It's made up out of the human mind. It offends me that people want me to adhere to a law based on such beliefs. . . . What we need in this state is a reverse inquisition. We need to burn the religious kooks at the stake. That's what we need. Clean up this society and get down to a secular reality."[9]

Kevorkian believes physicians alone should determine the true morality of actions associated with euthanasia. "It is the primary obligation of the medical profession, no matter how soul-wrenching and disagreeable. And until doctors tackle the problem vigorously and with unshackled ratiocination [reasoned thinking], the validity of moral judgment as well as the law will always be in doubt."[10] Who, then, is permitted to scrutinize the work physicians do? Will self-policing be enough?

Kevorkian's contention that medicine is a purely secular profession that must not be influenced by nonmedical or nonscientific disciplines is deficient. First, it is a view that fails to take into account the complexities of human psychology. In their vocations, people find it difficult to disassociate themselves from their values, beliefs, and past experiences. Those things are an important part of what makes a person who he or she is. People simply do not jettison strongly held beliefs in order to think in a particular way. Neither do they compartmentalize their lives into the professional and personal as easily as Kevorkian seems to think they do. Second, a completely secular practice of medicine means abandoning the treatment of patients as persons who also have beliefs, values, preferences, etc. Family relationships, personal goals, and a sense of obligation are important considerations in our notions of caring and compassion. Medical decisions are not made solely on the basis of medical or scientific criteria. We do not want physicians to function as robots, consulting with computers and other technologies instead of patients about the correct course of action to take.

The essence of medicine is caring for persons, and what counts as caring depends to some extent on what we take the term "person" to mean. Neither medicine nor any other scientific discipline can by itself supply a suitable description of personhood. It is the very concept of the patient as person that "humanizes" medicine, setting it apart from mere scientific experimentation. If human medicine is to be practiced without regard to how the concept of the person is interpreted by religion and psychology, by what objective criteria are we to determine that physicians have actually met a person's needs?

KEVORKIAN THE OBITIATRIST

Obitiatry is a term Kevorkian devised by combining the Latin word *obitus* meaning "to go to meet death," and the Greek work *iatros* meaning "doctor." "Obitiatry is the name of the medical specialty concerned with the treatment or doctoring of death to achieve some sort of beneficial result, in the same way that psychiatry is the name of the medical specialty concerned with the treatment or doctoring of the psyche for the beneficial result of mental health."[11]

Once it is legalized, Kevorkian believes the practice of obitiatry will become an accepted part of the medical establishment, with its own specialized training and board certification in obitiatry. He even goes so far as to advocate suicide centers called *obitoriums,* which sounds as innocuous as abortion clinics being called "Women's Health Centers." In this way, voluntary death can be "validated in official 'suicide centers' created specifically for the good of moribund subjects by affording them a serene, dignified death as well as a proper atmosphere for completely ethical manipulations [removing organs, medical experimentation]."[12]

THE RULES OF KEVORKIAN OBITIATRY

Kevorkian claims that obitiatry must be practiced in accord with strict guidelines in order to protect patients from abuse. Those guidelines, published in a 1992 article in the *American Journal of Forensic Psychiatry,* include:

1. Every assisted suicide candidate undergoes extensive counseling.
2. Every candidate for assisted suicide must be examined by a psychiatrist.
3. Patients who complain of chronic pain should be examined by a pain specialist.
4. Every candidate for assisted suicide must have his or her medical records thoroughly examined to assure the diagnosis.
5. Every candidate for assisted suicide must have a confirmed diagnosis that he or she suffers from afflictions that are incurable or cannot be treated without intolerable side effects.

6. Death should not take place sooner than twenty-four hours·
after a patient has made a final request.

Does Kevorkian follow his own rules? Kevorkian's attorney,
Geoffrey Fieger, admits that it has been hard for Kevorkian to follow
these rules in an atmosphere of "persecution and prosecution."[13]
The circus atmosphere Kevorkian and Fieger create doesn't help.
But how well did Kevorkian follow his own rules before all of the
publicity and criminal prosecution began?

How well did the death of Janet Adkins, his first "patient," which
came long before his notoriety, comply with Kevorkian's rules? In
his 1992 article setting out the rules of obitiatry, Kevorkian wrote it
is *mandatory* to bring in a psychiatrist because a person's "mental
state is of paramount importance."[14] Yet Adkins's own psychiatrist,
Murray Raskind, told Kevorkian in a telephone conversation that
she was not competent to make an end-of-life decision.

Dr. Kalman Kaplan, a psychologist and head of the Suicide Research Center at Chicago's Michael Reese Hospital, reviewed four-
teen videotapes made by Kevorkian of conversations with twelve
people seeking his assistance. He expresses serious doubts about the
"counseling" Kevorkian offers people before they die. Kevorkian
claims, "If a person seeks help committing suicide and then mani-
fests any degree of ambivalence, hesitancy, or outright doubt with
regard to her original decision [to commit suicide], the process is
stopped."[15] Yet, when Marjorie Wantz expressed some ambivalence
Kevorkian never noticed.

In remarking about the videotapes he reviewed Kaplan said,
·"There are aspects of counseling in some of them. But in many of
the tapes, it's difficult to see." I fully agree. The "counseling" interview videotapes I've viewed have not shown any counseling taking
place. Kevorkian accepted Janet Adkins as his first patient without
talking directly to her, nor did he make any real effort to discover
whether she really wished to end her life.[16]

The fact that Kevorkian carries out assisted suicides in the absence of psychiatric evaluations reveals just how important evaluation by independent professionals is to him. In at least five cases, the
people who died had histories of depression, and one was scheduled
to be admitted to a mental health facility the day after she died. This
demonstrates Kevorkian's cavalier attitude toward the issue of competent, informed consent.

Margaret Garrish suffered from pain due to severe rheumatoid arthritis, pain that her own doctor apparently was unable to control. In a videotape played by Kevorkian's lawyers at a press conference, Garrish threatened that if she did not receive relief from her pain she would obtain Kevorkian's help in ending her life. Seven pain control specialists responded, offering to assist the woman without charge. However, Garrish never learned of the offer, dying from carbon monoxide poisoning a few days later with Kevorkian at her side. Kevorkian's lawyers did not tell Garrish that doctors had offered to treat her pain because Fieger considered them "publicity seekers."[17]

What of the rule that patients must have a confirmed diagnosis of an incurable affliction? Rebecca Badger, a thirty-nine-year-old single mother of two from Goleta, California, was told she "might" have multiple sclerosis. She had a history of drug and alcohol abuse, as well as psychiatric and emotional problems. An autopsy by Oakland County Medical Examiner Ljubisa Dragovic found no sign of any disease whatsoever.[18] California police believe Badger's mother encouraged her to seek Kevorkian's help after she assisted her daughter in two previous failed suicide attempts.

IN ONLY FORTY-TWO OF THE

ONE HUNDRED PLUS SUICIDES ASSISTED

BY KEVORKIAN WAS THERE SOME

ANATOMICAL EVIDENCE OF SERIOUS DISEASE.

Even in his first assisted suicide (Janet Adkins), Kevorkian stretched medical terminology in order to "qualify" a patient for death. Just two weeks before her death, Adkins had defeated her adult son in tennis. When later confronted with this Kevorkian said, "Yeah, she beat him, but she couldn't remember the score."[19] Kevorkian said, "Even though from a physical standpoint Janet [Adkins] was not imminently terminal, there seemed little doubt that mentally she was—and, after all, it is one's mental status that determines the essence of one's existence."[20]

In only forty-two of the one hundred plus suicides assisted by

Kevorkian was there some anatomical evidence of serious disease, with only eleven that could be considered terminal—which is defined a disease or condition expected to result in death within six months with or without medical treatment. What if only a small percentage of all people with nonterminal conditions similar to Kevorkian's "patients" were to seek and obtain assistance in ending their lives? It would not be long before the reasons a person might have for ending his or her life would be considered irrelevant.

Does Kevorkian observe his own rule of a twenty-four-hour waiting period? In seventeen of forty-three cases, the person's first meeting with Kevorkian was his or her last because he or she died during the visit. In at least five cases, less than three hours passed from the signing of the request to the moment of death. In one case, the "waiting period" was one hour.[21]

KEVORKIAN'S "FINAL SOLUTION"

What is Kevorkian's ultimate goal? In a 1986 article published in a German journal entitled "A Comprehensive Bioethical Code for Medical Exploitation of Humans Facing Imminent and Unavoidable Death," Kevorkian extols the virtues of being able to experiment on a broad range of human subjects.[22] His book, *Prescription: Medicide —the Goodness of Planned Death,* is preoccupied with this goal, including experimentation on death row inmates.

From the earliest days of his career in pathology, Kevorkian consistently demonstrated an almost fanatical passion and fascination with the experimental side of medicine. Recently, Kevorkian announced that he would begin harvesting the organs from individuals whose suicides he "attends." Roosevelt Dawson, Kevorkian's ninety-ninth "patient," claimed that his death would give life to others because he planned to donate his organs. He didn't. People who die from lethal injections of poison don't make good organ donors.

During research on medical experimentation, Kevorkian found that ancient Greek and Roman civilizations performed anatomical experiments on condemned criminals as the method of execution.[23] From this information, from his career as a pathologist, and his involvement in assisted suicide and euthanasia, Kevorkian concludes, "The time has come to smash the last irrational and most fearsome taboo of planned death and thereby to open the floodgates of equally momentous benefit for humankind."[24] What is the "momentous benefit"? "The positive euthanasia of obitiatry would expand enormously the amplitude and intensity of the ordinary 'visible spectrum' [of medicine], allowing doctors for the first time to carry out on living human beings otherwise impossible trials of new and untested drugs, devices, or operations."[25] In other words, his real goal is not helping dying persons experience "death with dignity."

BEYOND KEVORKIAN

Difficult though it may be, the issue of physician-assisted suicide must be separated from Kevorkian. Many who support the practice dislike him and his tactics. Kevorkian's recent move into actively administering lethal injections further inflames his critics. Thomas Youk, a 50-year-old Waterford, Michigan man dying from Lou Gehrig's Disease, was killed by Kevorkian on September 17, 1998. A segment of the videotape Kevorkian made of the death was aired on CBS's "60 Minutes" on November 22, 1998. During his interview with Mike Wallace of "60 Minutes" Kevorkian challenged prosecutors to charge him with murder. "I've got to force them [Waterford Township legal authorities] to act," Kevorkian told Wallace. "They must charge me. Because if they do not, that means they don't think it's a crime." As of this writing, Oakland County Prosecutor David Gorcyca has filed charges of first degree murder, assisting a suicide (a violation of Michigan's assisted suicide law that took effect September 1, 1998), and delivering a controlled substance as an unlicensed physician. Kevorkian was arraigned on the charges in late November and ordered to stand trial. He declared to the presiding judge his intention to act as his own attorney and has vowed to starve himself to death in prison if convicted.

Because we live in a day when public discussions about hard moral issues get reduced to ten-second soundbites, bumper stickers, and slogans, we should give careful and thoughtful attention to the issues associated with end-of-life decisions. We should not casually dismiss the arguments proposed by thoughtful, well-meaning people who believe physician-assisted suicide is morally defensible. Christians especially must resist the temptation to dismiss these arguments by substituting clever slogans for thoughtful, biblical reflection and analysis.

Oregon already has a "death with dignity" law in place, and as many as a dozen states are poised to follow. Although efforts to legalize physian-assisted suicide in Michigan failed, other states are expected to face similar attempts in the next election cycle. A task force in Oregon drafted a set of guidelines for implementing the law, including a recommendation that assisted suicide be covered under medical insurance. Perhaps we're closer to realizing Kevorkian's dream than any of us care to acknowledge.

NOTES

1. Michael Betzold, *Appointment with Dr. Death* (Troy, Mich.: Momentum Books, 1993), 1.

2. "In Royal Oak: The Death Machine," *Detroit Free Press Magazine*, 18 March 1990, 24.

3. Richard Thompson, *The Legal Case Against Assisted Suicide in Michigan*, unpublished notes from the Office of the Prosecuting Attorney, County of Oakland, n.d., 38.

4. According to Forensic Toxicologist Fredric Reiders, Janet Adkins died from the suppression of her breathing from the succinylcholine, not from the potassium chloride as Kevorkian claimed would occur by way of a heart attack. This reveals Kevorkian is not only a poor bedside physician but a poor anesthetist.

5. Thompson, *Legal Case*, 40

6. Jack Kevorkian, "A Fail-Safe Model for Justifiable Medically-Assisted Suicide," in Michael M. Uhlmann, ed., *Last Rights: Assisted Suicide and Euthanasia Debated* (Grand Rapids: Eerdmans, 1998), 265.

7. Jack Kevorkian, *Prescription: Medicide—the Goodness of Planned Death* (New York: Prometheus, 1991), 240ff.

8. Ibid., 240.

9. Brian Harmon, "The Many Faces of Jack Kevorkian," *The Detroit News*, 23 February 1997.

10. Kevorkian, *Prescription: Medicide*, 201.

11. Ibid., 203.

12. Ibid., 202.

13. Kirk Cheyfitz, "The Suicide Machine," *Detroit Free Press*, 3 March 1997, 7A.

14. Jack Kevorkian, "A Fail-Safe Model for Justifiable Medically-Assisted Suicide," *Journal of Forensic Psychiatry*, Vol. 13, No. 1, 1992.

15. Kirk Cheyfitz, "The Suicide Machine," *Detroit Free Press*, 3 March 1997, 7A.

16. This was the statement of the Michigan Court of Appeals upholding in a 1995 ruling a court order against Kevorkian's assisted suicide activity.

17. Emilia Askari and Mike Williams, "Doctors Wanted to Help," *Detroit Free Press*, 29 November 1994.

18. "Medical Chief Takes to Task Jack Kevorkian," *Akron Beacon Journal*, 19 October 1997.

19. A videotaped interview between Jack Kevorkian and Janet Adkins was played as part of an HBO special on Kevorkian.

20. Kevorkian, *Prescription: Medicide*, 222.

21. This information is gleaned from court transcripts, press reports, and unpublished notes.

22. In *Law and Medicine*, Vol. 5: 181–89.

23. Kevorkian, *Prescription: Medicide*, 28–29.

24. Ibid., 241.

25. Ibid.

CHAPTER 4

DISSECTING THE LANGUAGE OF DEATH:

The Abuse of Language to Justify Assisted Suicide

The success of a social movement largely depends on its ability to marshal language to its advantage. Abortion rights activists are good examples of how language can be used in the pursuit of specific social ends. Abortion proponents gained an advantage by framing the abortion question in terms of personal freedom (privacy, right to one's own body). Making the issue a question of who makes the decision to end a pregnancy took the focus off the humanity of the unborn. Opposing abortion today means one risks being accused of being antiwomen and antifreedom. The common accusation against those who oppose abortion is that they are antichoice.

Similar tactics are used by the proponents of physician-assisted suicide and euthanasia. They try to turn the debate to their advantage by using terms designed to disguise rather than disclose. By using terms like "the right to die" and "death with dignity," it is relatively easy to paint those who oppose assisted suicide as cruel and lacking compassion. Thus, the debate about physician-assisted suicide and euthanasia, like other dubious attempts to expand individual freedom, is confused by the imprecise use of language. In some instances, the terms used are dishonest.

SUICIDE DEFINED

Suicide is an intentional act of self-destruction. Generally, suicide involves both an intention and an action to carry out that intention. J. P. Moreland provides a working definition of suicide: "An act is a suicide if and only if a person intentionally and/or directly causes his or her own death as an ultimate end in itself or as a means to another end (e.g., pain relief), through acting (e.g., taking a pill) or refraining from acting (e.g., refusing to eat) when that act is not coerced and is not done sacrificially for the lives of other persons or in obedience to God."[1]

Such a definition excludes actions we may view as morally justified, those acts we regard as heroic (e.g., the soldier who falls on a live grenade to spare his comrades' lives) and acts of martyrdom (e.g., Christians who die because they refuse to renounce their faith in Christ). Martyrdom normally implies that the death can only be avoided if the person disobeys God (e.g., Christians who faced death if they did not accept the deity of Caesar). Suicide is a self-directed act. Heroism and martyrdom differ in that: (1) they are responses to the needs of others or to divine commands; (2) the means of death are not under the individual's control; and (3) death is a consequence of the objective to protect others or obey God; it is not the principal objective.

Some try to give a definition of suicide that does not include a moral judgment about the rightness or wrongness of the act. Is self-destruction for the purpose of avoiding pain, or to spare family members considerable financial expense, an immoral act? Some argue that the second reason is like that of the person falling on a live grenade to spare the lives of his comrades in battle. On its face, there may appear to be little difference between the two actions. Even Moreland's definition may be seen as leaving the door open to assisted suicide when death is sought for the benefit of others. Perhaps a person seeks death in order to spare his or her family the financial expense or emotional and physical burdens associated with end-of-life care. But this suggests that families should be able to protect financial interests at the expense of vulnerable, needy loved ones. The right to life supersedes a right to financial security.

EUTHANASIA DEFINED

Euthanasia may be defined as an intentional, direct act of causing the death of another person for supposedly merciful or compassionate reasons, either by a deliberate direct act (e.g., the administration of a drug, suffocation, carbon monoxide poisoning, bullet), or by a deliberate direct neglect (e.g., withholding or withdrawing medical therapies). To use the word *killing* is technically correct since both action and neglect in particular contexts result in a death that is intended. Euthanasia is allegedly killing for merciful reasons, for reasons of compassion. This is "humane" killing, even "dignified" killing. Killing in the context of an overwhelming end-stage illness that entails immense pain and can only end in death is considered to have a different meaning than a drive-by shooting. Yet both involve killing that is intentional. While the randomness of the drive-by shooting underscores the senselessness of the act, the victim is not "deader" than the patient with multiple sclerosis whose doctor gives her a lethal injection of poison. The absence of malice associated with acts of euthanasia tends to soften our reaction to it. We are less inclined to label these acts "killing." Yet they are.

ASSISTED SUICIDE DEFINED

Assisted suicide is defined as providing lethal assistance to an individual who initiates and desires his or her own death. Proponents of physician-assisted suicide emphasize the role of the physician as a mere "assistant" to an act initiated by the patient.[2] It is the patient who decides when and if to use the means provided.

During a radio exchange I had with Jack Kevorkian following the death of Janet Adkins, he was outraged when I referred to his role in Adkins's death as "killing." He vehemently argued that all he did was provide the means for her to take her own life. "She pushed the button, not me" was his response to my contention that he was engaging in euthanasia.

However, Kevorkian was not a reluctant or passive partner in Janet Adkins's death. In fact, one could make a case that his role in assisted suicide is predatory. It was Kevorkian who advertised his willingness to "assist" people with their death. It was Kevorkian who designed the apparatus that provided the means by which Janet Adkins killed herself. Kevorkian purchased the chemicals, picked her up at the airport, and transported her to the park in his van. Kevorkian inserted the intravenous line into her arm through which the deadly chemicals entered her body and snuffed out her life. It may be that the only direct actions Adkins performed on her own were flying to Detroit and pushing the button. Kevorkian is no innocent bystander. He cannot play such an active role and then claim that the death is solely the patient's own action.

Common definitions of euthanasia mean someone other than the patient is the agent who brings about death, whether this be a physician, a family member, a friend, or a Mafia hit man. In assisted suicide, it is the patient who acts to bring about his or her own death, although the means of death may be provided by someone else and that person may be present to "assist" with any necessary setup or application of delivery apparatus.

REMOVAL OF LEGAL SANCTIONS AGAINST ASSISTED SUICIDE UNDERMINES THE STATE'S COMPELLING INTEREST IN PROTECTING HUMAN LIFE.

Advocates of physician-assisted suicide argue that providing or assisting with the means of death does not compromise the physician morally or legally, since the action is initiated by and carried out by the patient. Kevorkian insists he merely provides the means —he simply "attends" the suicide—thereby avoiding moral and legal culpability. However, this does not exonerate him.

First, Kevorkian's claim can only be true *if* suicide can be a competent, rational choice and *if* deliberately and knowingly providing the lethal means to a person who fully intends to take his own life is morally and legally consistent with a caring, private, contractual relationship between a physician and his patient. This latter point was addressed in chapter 2. Removal of legal sanctions against assisted suicide undermines the state's compelling interest in protecting human life. This interest is justified both constitutionally and scripturally. Scripture teaches that after the Flood, God instituted civil government to protect human life (Genesis 9:6). Throughout the Old Testament, civil government is seen as the entity that justly addresses crimes against persons. Romans 13 reiterates this, stating that civil authorities do not bear the sword in vain. In other words, civil authorities are delegated the authority to carry out justice against those who do evil to other human beings.

This principle is reflected in the United States Constitution, particularly through the Due Process clause of the Fifth Amendment. In the interest of protecting human life, the state is justified in establishing laws against unwanted touching. Laws prohibiting assault and battery reflect this interest. However, when a person is threatening to kill himself, the laws against unwanted touching (assault and battery) are set aside by the state's compelling interest in protecting human life. Police and fire department personnel, as well as private citizens, are justified in using nonlethal force to prevent a person from taking his own life, under the state's compelling interest doctrine. Legalizing assisted suicide will undermine this interest. Further, it suggests that certain people may be excluded from the state's protective interest based upon subjective classifications of illness or disability.

Physician-assisted suicide does not appear to be the usual "evil of malicious intent or overt violence" that we associate with homicide. Kevorkian clearly uses this public perception to his advantage. To many people, Kevorkian appears compassionate and caring, with his only interest being in meeting the expressed needs and desires of his "patients." It is what ethicist Leon Kass calls "evil with a smile: well-meaning, gentle, and rational, especially rational."[3] He argues that assisted suicide is both harder to recognize as evil and harder to combat because of the appearance of humaneness. "Yet, also for this reason, it deserves our most vigilant attention, for it is an exquisite model of modern rationalism gone wrong, while looking oh so right."[4]

NAZI DOCTORS USED THE TERM

"MERCY DEATH" TO DISGUISE THEIR

MURDER OF THE HANDICAPPED.

The subtlety and seduction of language that champions patient empowerment and compassionate, caring altruism cannot be fully appreciated in a culture flooded with competing claims of rights and freedoms. Proponents of assisted suicide argue that the practice is a right that a pluralistic society must respect. However, as Daniel Callahan eloquently states:

It is a mistake to classify active euthanasia and assisted suicide as acts solely expressive of individual autonomy, as is now common. On the contrary, because they entail the assistance of another (someone who will kill us in the case of active euthanasia, or help us kill ourselves in the case of assisted suicide), they are essentially a form of concerted communal action, even though the community in question may only be two people. That ceases to make them individual acts; they become a form of social action. Second, we have never allowed killing as a form of a contractual relationship between two consenting adults. The killing of another is now justified only in cases of self-defense, capital punishment, and just war. In none of those cases is the killing for the benefit of the person killed, but allowed only to protect the lives or welfare of others, even if that life is our own (as in self-defense). There must, in short, be a public interest at stake in the taking of life. We have otherwise considered it too great a power to be given to individuals to serve their private ends, even if they are good ends. . . . It is to create the wrong kind of relationship between people, the creation of a community that sanctions private killings between its members. . . . It would be to make the killing of another a matter of individual choice or personal contract rather than societal judgment and (rarely invoked) social necessity.[5]

Some advocates of assisted suicide prefer the euphemism "aid in dying" to describe how physicians may help patients end their lives. Of course, the use of soft-sounding terms to deflect attention from the reality of one's actions is a common device. The leaders of the Third Reich were particularly good at using pleasant-sounding terms to hide the grisly realities of their actions from the public. The Nazi doctors used the term "mercy death" to disguise their murder of the handicapped, but the handicapped were killed to achieve racial and eugenic ends, not for merciful reasons. Henry Frielander writes, "Their [Nazis'] killing operation was a secret government program and not an act of individual mercy. It was not applied against people suffering from common physical diseases like cancer but only against those considered 'life unworthy of life.'"[6]

Abortionists employ a similar tactic, using (or abusing) language to their advantage, by calling abortion "pregnancy termination" and the person being aborted merely a "fetus" or "product of conception." The general public becomes desensitized to the reality of abortion by such terminology. Regardless of the terms used to describe assisted suicide and euthanasia, there can be no mistaking the end result—death.

SUICIDE IN HISTORICAL PERSPECTIVE

Acts of self-destruction have always mystified us. We wonder why a person would end his or her life. Suicides usually leave us confused, even angry. They generally involve deaths thought to be senseless, lives ended prematurely and unnecessarily.

I know this from personal experience. When my brother-in-law took his own life while in his early twenties, it spawned an enormous wake of emotions—anger, feelings of betrayal and abandonment within the rest of the family. How could he do such a thing to us? What drove him to it? Some family members felt anger at him for leaving us without any explanation for his actions. Some were overwhelmed with guilt because we did not respond to his needs, or we failed to see warning signs of trouble brewing.

A consideration of the entire psychology of suicide lies outside of this current discussion. However, in order to address the psychology of suicide under medical auspices it is necessary to include a general consideration of self-destruction. Unlike the so-called "senseless suicide" of a young person seriously depressed over a failed romantic relationship or a drug addiction, the case of the terminally ill older adult who ends his or her life in the final stages of an incurable and painful degenerative disease does not appear senseless and premature.

Suicide in the face of a debilitating disease that cannot be cured makes a great deal of sense to many people. It has an appearance of reasonableness, but can suicide, even in the midst of immense pain and suffering, truly be a rational choice? (I deal with this issue later in this chapter.) Can such a suicide be morally justified? Do pain and suffering warrant a choice to end one's life?

Numerous societies throughout history (Greece, Rome, Japan, and some Arab nations excluded) have considered self-destruction a vice, not a virtue. Philosophers from Seneca to David Hume defended the right of suicide. Friedrich Nietzsche, the German philosopher, claimed, "There is a certain right by which we may deprive a man of life, but none by which we may deprive him of death."[7]

For the most part, Western civilization, whose moral underpinnings have largely been Judeo-Christian, has treated suicide as aberrant behavior, an action undertaken by irrational and disturbed individuals. In the 1800s, some jurisdictions of the U.S. made attempting suicide and assisting a suicide criminal offenses. In some jurisdictions, if a person attempted suicide and succeeded, he or she was denied burial and all property was seized. If one attempted suicide and failed, he or she could be imprisoned or even hung!

In modern society suicide has been decriminalized, considering punishment or confiscation of property as unfair to relatives. More important, suicide came to be regarded as a mental health issue. Individuals who threaten suicide are now likely to be viewed as irrational and in need of counseling, not jail. However, assisting a suicide remains a criminal offense in most states.[8]

Ironically, according to Herbert Hendin, executive director of the American Suicide Foundation and professor of psychiatry at New York Medical College, studies indicate that nearly three-fourths of suicides communicate their intentions, often with the hope that something will be done to prevent it.[9] According to Hendin, most people who attempt suicide are ambivalent about it. Several individuals who survived jumps from tall buildings indicated they wanted to survive as soon as they jumped. We will never know how many more had similar desires but whose actions were irrevocable and fatal.

SUICIDE IN BIBLICAL PERSPECTIVE

Can there be moral justification for self-destruction, or is every act of self-destruction immoral?[10] In Scripture there are at least seven individuals whose lives ended by their own hand: Abimelech—Judges 9:50–57; Samson—Judges 16:23–31; Saul and his armor bearer—First Samuel 31; Ahithophel—Second Samuel 17; Zimri—First Kings 16; Judas Iscariot—Matthew 27.

Arthur Droge and James Tabor argue in their book, *A Noble Death: Suicide and Martyrdom Among Christians and Jews in Antiquity,* that "the Bible nowhere proscribes suicide."[11] They claim that since there is no biblical reference to suggest that the acts of self-destruction recorded in Scripture were condemned, suicide itself is not a violation of biblical moral law. In addition, they claim the Bible is not neutral about self-destruction but actually promulgates the view that voluntary death is acceptable and, in some instances, even noble. Droge and Tabor contend that the record of Old Testament acts of self-destruction were scarcely commented on, leading one to conclude that voluntary death, given the proper circumstances, was understood as honorable and even routine.[12] "Despite the claim of Augustine and later theologians, the New Testament expresses no condemnation of voluntary death."[13]

Is this true? Shall we adopt this argument from silence, making a normative moral judgment concerning suicide solely on the basis of what Scripture does not say? Shall we conclude that the silence of Scripture on the morality of a specific practice constitutes an endorsement of it? The Bible does not explicitly condemn polygamy or slavery. Does this mean these practices have God's blessing?

It is true that we do not have a biblical text that explicitly condemns self-destruction, but acts of self-destruction do contradict other clear biblical teachings. I believe Droge and Tabor's argument fails for several reasons. First, the prohibition against killing contained in the Decalogue (Exodus 20:13) is sufficiently broad to include the prohibition of self-destruction. The burden of proof rests with those who argue that the killing prohibited in Exodus 20:13 does not include self-killing. Droge and Tabor do not strengthen their claim by arguing from silence. Just because Scripture does not record an explicit condemnation of Old Testament characters who caused their own deaths does not justify the claim that the deaths were noble. Biblical commentators throughout church history have not held Saul and Judas Iscariot in very high regard.

Droge and Tabor claim, "One person's martyr was another person's suicide, and vice versa. It is our contention, moreover, that no distinction can be made philosophically between 'suicide' and 'martyrdom.' In the final analysis, the distinction devolves upon personal commitment."[14]

Biblically speaking, suicide is immoral, just as all murder is immoral and a violation of God's moral law. In the Ten Commandments given to Moses on Mount Sinai (Exodus 20), the sixth commandment states, "Thou shalt not kill." The preponderance of biblical scholars agree that this refers to murder, the unjustifiable taking of a human life, which means it would exclude justifiable war, self-defense, the death penalty, etc. This prohibition especially applies to what might be termed "private killing." Justifiable killing in Scripture is linked to specific divine commands to be carried out by specific individuals (Genesis 9:6; Romans 13:1ff). Scripture does not support "private killing," the killing of one person for the benefit of one or both parties.

Suicide represents an abandonment of God as loving, caring, powerful, and just. Suicide in the midst of great pain and suffering is blameworthy not so much because it is wrong to take actions to relieve one's own suffering, but because it is wrong to take ultimate authority that belongs only to God. It is blameworthy because it deliberately takes the life of one who is made in God's image (Genesis 9:6).

In Scripture, suicide is cast in a negative light each time it is encountered. King Saul's death came from his own sword (1 Samuel 31:4) in the face of a devastating military defeat that followed a lengthy period of rebellion against God, a rebellion that included such spiritual defection as consulting with the Witch of Endor (1 Samuel 28:7). Judas hung himself following the betrayal of the Lord Jesus. The Scriptures need not give lengthy commentary in depicting the actions of those who take their own lives as being the fruit of a life of moral and spiritual failure.

THE DEATH OF JESUS: SACRIFICIAL DEATH

The Bible does teach the virtue of a sacrificial death. Jesus Himself gave His life on the cross as a sacrifice for mankind. Jesus said, "Greater love has no one than this, that a man lay down his life for his friends" (John 15:13). Self-destruction to avoid pain, suffering, or captivity is never presented in Scripture as a noble or heroic act, and such acts are to be distinguished from the nobility of martyrdom. Dying for the cause of Christ is not the same as dying to avoid one's own suffering, to save money, or to exercise personal control over one's death.

Throughout the history of the church, deliberate self-destruction has been viewed as moral and spiritual failure. As Moreland contends, intentionally ending one's life denies its intrinsic value and dignity. The suicidal person wrongly assumes that he is the originator and controller of his own life.[15] A biblically correct view of human life cannot coincide with a notion that humans are morally free to destroy themselves. A biblical view of life and death does not tolerate humans being their own judge, jury, and executioner.

THE MYTH OF RATIONAL SUICIDE

The Hemlock Society contends there are two forms of suicide. One is "emotional suicide," or irrational self-murder, and the other is rational, justifiable suicide or "autoeuthanasia."[16] In order for the advocates of physician-assisted suicide to make a case for rational suicide, they must show how suicide in general can be the act of a rational person. They cannot limit the notion of rational suicide to those deaths chosen under medical auspices, attended only by physicians. It makes no sense to say that if a person kills himself the act is irrational, but if he asks a physician to help him the act somehow becomes rational.

If physician-assisted suicide can be rational, by what criteria is it deemed rational? The current model of mental health regards suicidal desires to be symptomatic of mental illness requiring treatment. Police and fire department personnel are allowed to use nonlethal force to stop people from killing themselves, and they may force such people into treatment against their will.

However, if physicians are permitted to honor patients' requests for assistance in ending their lives on the grounds that such a request is rational, under what circumstances and by what criteria would any desire to kill oneself be considered irrational? If suicide under medical auspices can be a rational choice, by what criteria is any suicide irrational?

Our first instinct may be to wonder how we can judge as irrational the wish for an end to immense, intolerable suffering that can only be ended with death. Among the general public, there is the perception that death brings about the end of pain and suffering, and many find it entirely rational to seek death under such circumstances.

Following major surgery in 1995 to remove a portion of my colon, I experienced a small sample of what some must experience in the midst of terminal or chronic illness. It was about three o'clock in the morning. I had been out of surgery for about forty-eight hours, and to say I was feeling miserable is to put it mildly. Despite the fact that my physical pain was managed quite well, the nasogastric tube caused my nasal passages to continually drain, the Foley catheter hurt, the staples that held my incision together seemed to tear every time I moved, and the combination of everything made sleep impossible. I remember thinking, *What if this feeling were all I had to look forward to every day? What if it would never improve as long as I was alive? How would I endure it?* I actually began to have some empathy for those who have sought Kevorkian's help. There, in the middle of the night, I began to question my own convictions about the value of living under such miserable circumstances.

I'm certain that my experience is not uncommon. In fact, I believe mine was quite benign compared to many. When morning came, and people began to stir around me, such thoughts left me. However, when I was alone, and all I could do was focus on my predicament, my thinking was skewed.

The conditions that provoke one's wish for death are the same ones that may render him or her clinically depressed, thereby distorting his or her decision-making capabilities. "Psychological autopsy" studies have documented that up to 90 percent of completed suicides had some psychiatric disorder at the time of death.[17] A 1990 study revealed that 90 percent of the 30,000 people who committed suicide that year suffered from depression.[18] "Treatment studies have shown that identification and treatment of psychiatric disorders can result in a substantial decrease in risk of suicide. Depression, and to a lesser extent medical illness, have been identified as the primary risk factors for suicide in the elderly."[19] One particular study of forty-five terminally ill patients revealed that only three seriously considered suicide and, upon psychiatric exam, they were found to be undergoing major clinical depression.[20]

One of the serious hurdles to be overcome by the proponents of physician-assisted suicide is the dismal record physicians have in diagnosing minor and major clinical depression. According to some studies, the failure to accurately diagnose such depression ranges from 45 to 90 percent.[21] Given such a discrepancy, shall we entrust physicians with the task of distinguishing between those requests for assisted suicide that are rational and those that are not? Should it not be the role of physicians to ascertain more than whether a given patient is "competent" to make his or her own medical decisions? Is society asking too much to require that those who request physician assistance in dying be given an independent psychiatric evaluation to not only consider the patient's competence, but to look for pressures and anxieties that may lie behind the request?

THE PRINCIPAL MISSION FOR A PSYCHIATRIST
IS NOT TO . . . CONFIRM THE PATIENT'S
WORST FEARS ABOUT LIFE,
BUT TO ALLEVIATE THOSE FEARS.

If a person can be "talked out of" ending his or her life, shouldn't he or she be talked out of it? The refusal to deal with the fears and anxieties of such individuals while ending their lives is an assault upon their dignity, something proponents of assisted suicide and euthanasia claim to be most interested in preserving.[22]

Yet, requiring an independent psychiatric examination of every patient who requests assisted suicide is itself problematic. First, it suggests that responsibility for such a troubling moral decision can be shifted to an outside specialist.[23] By requiring this of psychiatrists, we grant them a level of social control over the exit gates of life for which their training and the standards of the psychiatric profession do not qualify them. The principal mission for a psychiatrist is not to open the exit gate, not to confirm the patient's worst fears about life, but to alleviate those fears and to diminish the anguish of the dying process.

Second, there exist no truly scientific or completely objective criteria for judging competence. "Indeed, competence is not well measured by standardized instruments, but is 'a malleable entity that is inevitably molded to fit the particular interpersonal emotional, clinical, and cultural context.'"[24]

Third, if suicide attempts or completions are to be considered acts of harm perpetrated by incompetent persons, how can a request for assisted suicide be treated as the choice of a competent person? Shall psychiatrists make this final determination? If they shall, does it not undermine the notion that individuals are exercising control over their own lives? How can one claim to be acting autonomously if the premiere act of self-determination must pass an examination by a psychiatrist? Ultimately, it is the psychiatrist who possesses the power in this relationship, not the patient.

Not surprisingly, one study of psychiatrists indicated that their support for legalized physician-assisted suicide was related to a desire for assisted suicide for themselves in case of terminal illness.[25] This indicates that although psychiatrists have specialized skills relevant to assessing patients' wishes and options, we should not treat them as the final authority on when or if it is right for a person to obtain physician assistance in dying.

Psychiatric problems are common among the terminally ill, and assessing the nature of these problems is complex. Delirium has been noted in 25 to 40 percent of hospitalized cancer patients and up to 85 percent when patients are in the final stages of cancer. Depression has been diagnosed in up to 58 percent of hospitalized cancer patients, and up to 77 percent among patients with advanced cancer. Interestingly, while the rates of psychiatric disorder increase as a patient's medical severity worsens, the accuracy of diagnosis of those psychiatric disorders by primary care physicians diminishes. Psychiatric disorders are the most common cause of a patient's inability to make clear medical decisions.[26]

NOTES

1. J. P. Moreland, "The Morality of Suicide: Issues and Options" in Roy Zuck, ed., *Vital Contemporary Issues* (Grand Rapids: Kregel, 1992), 78.

2. Timothy E. Quill, *Death and Dignity: Making Choices and Taking Charge* (New York: Norton, 1993), 139.

3. Leon Kass, "Suicide Made Easy: The Evil of 'Rational' Humaneness," *Commentary*, December 1991, 19.

4. Ibid.

5. Daniel Callahan, *What Kind of Life: The Limits of Medical Progress* (New York: Simon & Schuster, 1990), 230–31.

6. Henry Frielander, *The Origins of Nazi Genocide: From Euthanasia to the Final Solution* (Chapel Hill, N.C.: Univ. of North Carolina Press, 1995), xxi.

7. Friedrich Nietzsche, *Human, All-Too-Human*, trans. H. Zimmern (Edinburgh: Foulis, 1909), 88.

8. *On June 26, 1997, the U.S. Supreme Court ruled in two separate cases (*Washington v. Glucksberg *and* Vacco v. Quill*) that there exists no constitutional right to die by means of lethal medication prescribed by a patient's physician. In this way, the Court upheld state laws that prohibit assisting a suicide. See appendix for additional pertinent case summaries.*

9. Herbert Hendin, *Seduced by Death: Doctors, Patients and the Dutch Cure* (New York: Norton, 1997), 156.

10. The term "self-destruction" denotes an action or omission by an individual with the intention that death will be the result. There are many actions an individual may take where a probability of death exists, but death is not intended (e.g., heroic actions to rescue individuals from a burning building, participating in a military invasion where the probability of being wounded or killed is high). When death is an unintended result of an action or omission, it is not a suicide.

11. Arthur J. Droge and James D. Tabor, *A Noble Death: Suicide and Martyrdom among Christians and Jews in Antiquity* (San Francisco: HarperCollins, 1992), xi.

12. Ibid., 113.

13. Ibid., 125.

14. Ibid., 188.

15. Moreland, "The Morality of Suicide," 85.

16. Derek Humphry, *Dying with Dignity: Understanding Euthanasia* (New York: Birch Lane Press, 1992), 79.

17. Gabrielle A. Carlson, Charles L. Rich, Patricia Grayson, and Richard C. Fowler, "Secular Trends in Psychiatric Diagnoses of Suicide Victims," *Journal of Affective Disorders* 21 (1991): 127–32, as cited in Mark D. Sullivan, Linda Ganzini, and Stuart J. Younger, "Should Psychiatrists Serve as Gatekeepers for Physician-Assisted Suicide?" *Hastings Center Report* (Vol. 28, No. 4, July-August 1998): 25.

18. Yeates Conwell and Eric D. Caine, "Rational Suicide and the Right to Die," *New England Journal of Medicine* 325 (1991): 1105.

19. Robert L. Frierson, "Suicide Attempts by the Old and the Very Old," *Archives of Internal Medicine* 151 (1991): 141–44; Thomas B. Mackenzie and Michael K. Popkin, "Medical Illness and Suicide." In *Suicide Over the Life Cycle: Risk*

Factors, Assessment, and Treatment of Suicidal Patients, ed. Susan J. Blumenthal and David J. Kupfer (Washington, D.C.: American Psychiatric Press, 1990), 205–32. Cited in Mark D. Sullivan, et al., "Should Psychiatrists Serve as Gatekeepers," 25.

20. Conwell and Caine, "Rational Suicide and the Right to Die," 1106.

21. Leon Eisenberg, "Treating Depression and Anxiety in Primary Care," *New England Journal of Medicine* 326 (1992): 1080–84.

22. Herbert Hendin, *Seduced by Death,* 131.

23. Mark D. Sullivan, et al., "Should Psychiatrists Serve as Gatekeepers," 24.

24. Ibid., 26.

25. Linda Ganzini, Darien S. Fenn, Melinda A Lee, et al., "Attitudes of Oregon Psychiatrists Toward Physician-Assisted Suicide," *American Journal of Psychiatry* 153 (1996): 1469–75.

26. Judith B. Bukberg, Doris T. Penman, and Jimmie C. Holland, "Depression in Hospitalized Cancer Patients," *Psychosomatic Medicine* (Vol. 46, 1984): 199–212. Also see H. C. Schulberg, M. Saul, and M. N. McClelland, "Assessing Depression in Primary Medical and Psychiatric Practices," *Archives of General Psychiatry* (Vol. 42, 1985): 1164–70.

CHAPTER 5

THE
RIGHT
TO DIE:

Is Death a Right, a Duty, or an Inevitability?

The phrase "right to die" is used both by those who support the right of terminally ill individuals to refuse unwanted medical treatment and by the proponents of physician-assisted suicide and euthanasia. For the former, it is a phrase that shows respect for an individual's right to die of natural causes without having to fear overtreatment. For the latter, it is a clever slogan designed to sell euthanasia and physician-assisted suicide to an ambivalent public.

What is most intriguing is that anyone would consider death a personal right in light of the fact that death is inevitable—and usually considered undesirable. "The notion of the right to die has a preposterous quality, conjuring up images of the state denying us that right and granting us immortality," says Herbert Hendin, M.D.[1] It is as though we need someone's permission to die, that death is somehow not a biological fact.

Much of the public debate over physician-assisted suicide is focused on whether individuals possess a "right to die." Recent U.S. Supreme Court decisions have not given as clear an answer as we might like, further complicating the matter. In its most recent rulings (*Quill v. Vacco*, 1997, and *Washington v. Glucksberg*, 1997), the Court ruled that the Constitution, under the due process clause of the Fourteenth Amendment, contains a right to die, but it does not contain a right to assisted suicide. However, Chief Justice William

Rehnquist wrote in *Washington v. Glucksberg*, "Throughout the nation, Americans are engaged in an earnest and profound debate about the morality, legality, and practicality of physician-assisted suicide. Our holding [in Glucksberg] permits this debate to continue, as it should in a democratic society."[2] This debate is only in its beginning stages. Reversing judgments from the Second and Ninth Circuits, the Court held that neither the equal protection nor the due process clauses of the Fourteenth Amendment prevent states from making it a crime to aid a suicide, even when such assistance takes the form of a physician prescribing lethal medication to a competent, terminally ill adult who voluntarily requests the physician's help.[3]

LEGAL FOUNDATIONS FOR A RIGHT TO DIE

Legal experts contend that the right to die is rooted in three strains of American law: the right to control one's own body, the right to privacy, and the due process liberty interest.[4] In its recent decisions involving "right to die" questions the U.S. Supreme Court, and many lower courts, relied on these three principles to establish that individuals have some liberty interest at the end of life.

The rights to control one's own body against unwanted intrusion (governmental, institutional, or personal) and to protect one's self from unwanted touching have a long history in American law. The courts have consistently applied these principles to medical care as well.[5] The principles of self-determination, control, and protection against unwanted touching are crucial to the concept of informed consent, which entails the right of a competent adult to refuse medical treatment, including medical treatment that is lifesaving. A number of states have based a right to die on such a principle.

The right to refuse medical treatment has been interpreted by some state and federal courts to be broad enough to encompass a "right to die." This means that the law does not require people to remain alive as long as possible, that individuals have a right to die a "natural death." The right of individuals to refuse unwanted medical treatment exists, in part, as a recognition of each individual's right to die without being subjected to all manner of unwanted, futile medical intervention. A physician cannot force a competent adult to accept medical treatment, even if that treatment would save his or her life. Forced treatments violate laws against battery—against unwanted touching.

Just how broad is this right to die? It is relatively easy to recognize an individual's right to forego life-extending medical intervention when that individual is a conscious, competent adult who is terminally ill and in severe pain. What of those who do not meet one or more of these stipulations? What do we do in those situations where the individual is unable to participate in the decisions that affect him or her? Do children or teenagers have a right to demand death? (Do parents have the right to make such a decision for them?) What of a mother or father with small children who depend on him or her? What of a person who is not terminally ill, but has an incurable, debilitating condition? If the right to die exists, in what ways might it be limited?

Nancy Cruzan and Karen Ann Quinlan are examples of unconscious, formerly competent adults who could not participate in their own medical decision making. Their cases represent the worst-case scenarios that proponents of assisted suicide and euthanasia like to use to their advantage. Both of these women were in their twenties when catastrophic events left them severely brain damaged. Cruzan experienced an automobile crash, whereas Quinlan overdosed on drugs. After several years, families of both women petitioned courts in their respective states (Missouri and New Jersey) for a court injunction that would allow the removal of life support from their daughters. Quinlan's parents wanted to remove her ventilator, and Cruzan's wanted to withdraw their daughter from tube feeding.

The courts face several problems in dealing with such cases. First, they have to determine if any evidence exists to support the belief that the patient would not want his or her life continued under such circumstances. Second, the courts must determine how much discretion to give to families in making decisions to terminate life-sustaining treatment. Third, if surrogate decision-making authority is given to a patient's family, what would ensure that they acted in the best interests of the patient?[6]

In the Quinlan case, the New Jersey Supreme Court ruled that Karen's parents could have her ventilator removed, allowing her to die.[7] The Cruzan case was decided by the U.S. Supreme Court in 1990, allowing the withdrawal of life-extending medical treatment by surrogate decision makers when "clear and convincing evidence exists . . . that the individual would decide to forego further treatment in such circumstances."[8] The Cruzans went back to court in late 1990 with new witnesses to meet the "clear and convincing" standard. Cruzan died the day before Christmas after the withdrawal of her feeding tube.

In neither case did the parents argue for assisted suicide, and at least two federal court decisions since have maintained that the right to withdraw life-sustaining medical treatment does not constitute a right to assisted suicide. However, both the Cruzan and Quinlan cases failed to clarify the limits of substituted judgment in instances where treatment is withdrawn.

The advocates of physician-assisted suicide and euthanasia maintain that the right to die, though not unlimited, is broad enough to not only encompass the right of a competent, conscious adult to decide to have his or her life ended, but the right of a formerly competent, conscious adult (now unconscious, incompetent) to have his or her life ended as well, using substituted judgment (decisions made by a surrogate). Substituted judgment is already used to make medical decisions for patients when they are unable to participate in making them. The courts recognize the rights of family members (particularly spouses and children) to make these decisions on behalf of loved ones.

THAT WHICH IS IMMORAL CANNOT BE A "RIGHT" IN ANY MORAL SENSE.

Proponents of assisted suicide and euthanasia want to expand the use of substituted judgment beyond permitting a natural death. They are interested in advancing the claim that individuals have a "right to die with dignity," that people not only have a right to die, but a right to die a particular kind of death. Their interest is not a passive one, just "allowing nature to take its course." Rather, they insist on expanding the use of the right to die to permit direct actions to end the lives of individuals, whether competent to make such a decision or not. The danger posed by such a proposal should be obvious.

THE LIMITS OF LAW IN A PLURALISTIC SOCIETY

Can we (or should we) adopt a legal approach to death and dying that respects the right of the individual to control his or her own body, without creating a right to self-killing under medical auspices?

Are we able to make both a moral and legal distinction between harms inflicted on others and harms inflicted on oneself? How are we to resolve the issues surrounding the end of life in a society that celebrates individual freedom and celebrates diversity, but lacks a consensus on morality?

Suggestions that there is a substantial moral difference between harming others and harming oneself are troubling. They suggest that the reasons for restraining a person from killing others may be set aside when the issue is a person killing himself or herself; killing others is one thing, but taking your own life is an act of self-sovereignty, an action that requires no justification to others.[9]

This is the view expressed or implied by proponents of assisted suicide and euthanasia. When confronted by those who disagree, they simply reassert the right to die, as though such a right is a self-evident fact. Merely asserting that something is true has the same rational advantage as asserting that theft is preferable to work. Just because one stipulates something to be true does not make it true. Neither does asserting something as a right make it "right." That which is immoral cannot be a "right" in any moral sense.[10]

Anyone observing American culture for the last thirty years understands the boundless ingenuity people exhibit in inventing the most morally incoherent rights claims. In order for something to be a right, it should at least be expected to meet the minimal standards of the laws of reason. A right to assisted suicide does not meet those standards.

When there is a lack of consensus about the moral issues surrounding life and death, there are bound to be problems developing a consistent and enforceable public policy. I am deeply troubled by efforts to enact legislation that legalizes physician-assisted suicide without giving sufficient attention to improving care at the end of life. The legal history of abortion should teach us that simply legalizing something does not establish its morality. In fact, legalizing physician-assisted suicide undermines the reasons for acting to make improvements to end-of-life care, which should certainly be considered a moral issue.

Oregon's hospice organizations have expressed their willingness to cooperate with patients who intend to seek physician assistance in dying. Since hospice positions itself as being patient-driven care, this is not surprising. However, when an easier form of assistance is available, the motivation to improve comfort care for those who do not choose assisted suicide seems less compelling. Perhaps patients should be "educated" about the advantages of assisted suicide over the standard palliative care approach: It is quick, painless, and cheap, and it demands less from caregivers.

Just as some organizations dedicated to preventing birth defects have been distracted from finding actual cures by legalized abortion, so the pursuit of improved pain management and other palliative methods can be supplanted to give physicians the option of writing lethal prescriptions for patients. The courts, legislators, and voters appear confused over these issues, making attempts to expand the practice of legalized physician-assisted suicide precarious and ill-advised. Legalized abortion by judicial fiat already divides this nation, so we should question the wisdom of instituting another form of privatized killing.

FICKLE PUBLIC OPINION

Although public opinion polls consistently show that a majority of Americans support physician-assisted suicide, support evaporates quickly when people begin to seriously consider the ethical and practical implications of such a public policy. Both Washington and California rejected assisted suicide, while Oregon became the first jurisdiction since the Nazis to overtly legalize physicians providing lethal medications to patients. In 1998, Michigan voters overwhelmingly rejected physician-assisted suicide in a ballot referendum, with 71 percent of voters voting no on Proposal B.

LIFE IS A STEWARDSHIP FROM GOD.

Before assisted suicide was placed on the state ballot, opinion polls consistently showed widespread public support for physician-assisted suicide or "aid in dying." In Washington and Oregon, nearly two-thirds of the voters believed physician-assisted suicide should be legal. In Michigan, early polls indicated a majority favored legalizing assisted suicide. Benchmark polls immediately prior to the campaign in September 1998 showed the voters were equally split, with only 10 percent undecided.

In Washington, California, and Michigan, once voters were informed about the issues and the gaping holes in the so-called "safeguards," they refused by significant margins to legalize physician-assisted suicide. Oregon's initial physician-assisted law passed by a small margin and was affirmed in 1997 by a slightly smaller margin. In each case, once voters began to understand the enormous problems associated with regulating and implementing such a practice, and when they understood the subtle nuances of decision making at the end of life, support for the practice diminished.

The one issue that resonates with voters is control. A national poll taken in July 1998 of 1,000 people by GILS Research of Los Angeles revealed that 72 percent of Americans want to remain in control of their end-of-life care. Seventy-six percent believe it is not appropriate for Congress or any other legislative body to get involved in regulating drugs prescribed by doctors for their patients. Sixty-six percent would support a law like Oregon's Death with Dignity Act in their state.[11] Ironically, laws such as Oregon's have failed in Washington, California, and Michigan.

The right to die actually becomes the right to demand death. However, the ideal of controlling the circumstances of one's own death is an illusion. Kevorkian's practice of assisted suicide demonstrates this to be true. He decides which patients will be assisted, the timing, the methods, the setting, and the disposal of the body. Kevorkian-style assisted suicide shows that the control remains in the hands of the physician, not the patient.

Life is a stewardship from God. As stewards, we do have something to say about how we will be treated during the dying process. For example, we make the decision to seek medical attention when we become ill. We make choices about the types of treatment to be used, the physician who will provide those treatments, and, in some instances, what the duration of treatment will be. We make decisions concerning accepting or rejecting certain medications. However, we lack the authority to choose the exact moment of death.

A BIBLICAL RIGHT TO DIE?

So far, we have been discussing the legal right to die. From a legal standpoint, the right to make decisions concerning management of the dying process properly belongs to individuals, not the state. We do not want statism, where the state decides how all treatment should be managed at the end of a person's life. We do not want the state making judgments about an individual's worth and quality of life. Fear of such state control is what led to the defeat of the Clinton health-care reform plan in 1994. However, this does not mean the state has no interest in what individuals decide. It does have a compelling interest in protecting human life (Romans 13:1–4).

The right to refuse medical treatment does not supersede all other obligations. One may have the legal right to refuse medical treatment but have a moral obligation to accept it. For example, the father of small children is not legally required to submit to surgical removal of a ruptured appendix, but most would agree he has a moral obligation not to leave his children fatherless when it is relatively easy to prevent. A right to refuse medical treatment, grounded in the right of individuals to make their own decisions, is not an absolute right. One may clearly have other obligations. In this sense, we cannot resolve the issue of a "right to die" without a consideration of the moral significance of human life.

There is a difference between having the power or means to do something and the moral authority to justify it. Most people have the physical power to break into a neighbor's home and take the homeowner's possessions, but not the moral or legal authority to justify such an action. A judge may have the legal power to release a convicted murderer, but not the moral authority to do so. Rights, in order to be basic human rights, must comport to the laws of reason. Even if a judge has the means to hand down a jail sentence to a person proven innocent by a jury, such a decision defies the laws of reason.

THE BIBLICAL AUTHORITY FOR ENDING A LIFE BELONGS ONLY TO GOD.

Likewise, we possess the power or means to cause our own deaths, but we lack the moral authority to justify such killing. Although we would like our laws to conform to moral principles, the reality is that many do not. It is legal to operate a pornography shop in some communities, but this does not mean it is moral to sell pornography.

Being free moral agents means that God permits us to make decisions for ourselves, and He allows us to live with the consequences of those decisions. When God created us, He gave us stewardship over all of creation. He also gave us what many theologians and moral philosophers call "moral agency"—the ability or "power" to make moral choices. Some call this "free will."

Adam was a free moral agent who used his moral agency to make the terrible choice to eat from the forbidden tree (Genesis 3:1ff). Adam could make choices because he was made in God's image, but not all choices are morally justified. Having the means to make choices does not in itself justify the choices one makes.

A man may take action to end his own life, but he does not have authority from God to do so. He cannot be commended by God for doing it. Like stealing the property of another, causing one's death is morally blameworthy because it steals what belongs solely to God. The biblical authority for ending a life belongs only to God.

A DUTY TO DIE

Some have argued that people not only have a right to die but, under certain circumstances, a duty to die. John Hardwig, professor of ethics at East Tennessee State University, writes, "I feel strongly that I may very well some day have a duty to die."[12] He cites the example of Captain Oates, a member of Admiral Scott's expedition to the South Pole. Oates became too ill to continue. If the rest of the expedition team stayed with him, they would all perish. When this became clear to everyone, Oates left his tent one evening, walked out into a blizzard, and was never seen again.[13]

Hardwig admits that such lifeboat ethics produces bad ethics, yet he tries to justify a duty to die on grounds that each of us has an obligation to avoid burdening others by our continued existence. "The impact of my decisions upon my family and loved ones is the source of my strongest obligations and also the most plausible and likeliest basis of a duty to die."[14]

Hardwig's reasoning represents a challenge to the strong autonomy asserted by most advocates of the right to die. He comes right out and says that once continued existence becomes not only burdensome to oneself, but to his or her family, there is an obligation to die. The right to die becomes the duty to die.

Even if death were the *greatest* burden, serious questions would remain about the moral justifiability of choosing to *impose crushing burdens* on loved ones in order to *avoid* having to bear this burden oneself. The fact that I suffer greater burdens than others in my family does not license me simply to choose what I want for myself, nor does it necessarily release me from the responsibility to try to protect the quality of their lives. I can readily imagine that, through *cowardice, rationalization, or failure of resolve,* I will fail this obligation to protect my loved ones. . . . I cannot imagine it would be morally permissible for me to *ruin* the rest of my partner's life to sustain mine or to cut off my sons' careers, *impoverish* them, or compromise the quality of their children's lives simply because I wish to live a little longer. This is what leads me to believe in a duty to die.[15] (italics added)

Notice the strong language Hardwig uses—"greatest burden," "choosing to impose crushing burdens on loved ones," "cowardice," etc.—language that suggests the patient is somehow acting irresponsibly by remaining alive. It is as if the only valid alternatives are a self-inflicted death or selfish imposition of monumental burdens on family members. Hardwig lists nine features of one's illness, history, or circumstances that make it more likely a person has a duty to die:

1. A duty to die is more likely when continuing to live will impose significant burdens on family and loved ones.
2. A duty to die becomes greater as you grow older. As we age, we are giving up less by giving up our lives.
3. A duty to die is more likely when you have already lived a full and rich life. Hardwig says, "To have reached the age of, say, seventy-five or eighty years without being ready to die is itself a moral failing, the sign of a life out of touch with life's basic realities."
4. There is a greater duty to die if your loved ones' lives have already been difficult or impoverished, if they have had only a small share of the good things that life has to offer.
5. A duty to die is more likely when your loved ones have already made great contributions to make your life a good one. Especially if you have not made similar sacrifices for their well-being or for the well-being of other members of your family.
6. To the extent that you can make a good adjustment to your illness or handicapping condition, there is less likely to be a duty to die. A good adjustment means that smaller sacrifices will be required of loved ones and there is more compensating interaction for them.
7. There is less likely to be a duty to die if you can still make significant contributions to the lives of others.

8. A duty to die is more likely when the part of you that is loved will soon be gone or seriously compromised. Or when you soon will no longer be capable of giving love.

9. There is a greater duty to die to the extent that you have lived a relatively lavish lifestyle instead of saving for illness or old age. It is a greater wrong to come to your family for assistance if your need is the result of having chosen leisure or a spend-thrift lifestyle.[16]

My visceral reaction to Hardwig's proposal is to ask who could be so unfortunate as to have him for a relative. Unfortunately, although few are as crass as Hardwig, a growing number of people suggest there is a duty to die. This is a dangerous proposition for a society increasingly accustomed to using death as a solution to social and personal problems. A "duty" can easily become an enforceable obligation. Child support is a duty in a legal as well as a moral sense. Thus, the ominous next step beyond a duty to die is a right to kill.

The extensive use of patient autonomy as a justification for assisted suicide suggests that the practice can be justified solely on autonomy. However, the individualism and autonomy that justify one's right to control the circumstances of his or her death, independent of the wishes of others, only work as long as continued existence is only considered a burden to oneself. Once an individual becomes a "burden" to others, autonomy ceases, and an obligation to die takes over. In this sense, Hardwig tries to have his cake and eat it too. Like many advocates of assisted suicide and euthanasia, Hardwig sets up an erroneous scenario consisting of two unappealing options, illustrated by the following example:

Consider the following case: An 87-year-old woman was dying of congestive heart failure. Her APACHE score predicted that she had less than a 50 percent chance to live another six months. She was lucid, assertive, and terrified of death. She very much wanted to live and kept opting for rehospitalization and the most aggressive life-prolonging treatment possible. That treatment successfully prolonged her life (though with increasing debility) for nearly two years. Her 55-year-old daughter was her only remaining family, her caregiver, and the main source of her financial support. The daughter duly cared for her mother. But before her mother died, her illness had cost the daughter all of her savings, her home, her job, and her career. Now ask yourself which is the greater burden: a) To lose a 50 percent chance of six more months of life at age 87? b) To lose all your savings, your home, and your career at age 55? Which burden would you prefer to bear?[17]

At first glance, this scenario tugs at our heartstrings. However, embedded in it are flawed assumptions, including an erroneous view concerning the value of human life, a view held by nearly all proponents of assisted suicide. The first assumption is that elderly people experiencing multiple medical problems do not have a right to receive care from members of their families. Evidently, family members are only expected to provide care when it is economically and practically convenient for them. Indigenous to this belief is the notion that the right to life is subordinate to family members' quality of life, that with advancing age and declining health comes a corresponding decline in the person's value. There comes a time when a person's age and health status completely obliterate his right to remain alive, and an obligation to die takes its place.

The second assumption is that the desire to remain alive can be unreasonable, especially when remaining alive requires loved ones to alter their lives in order to provide care. This assumption represents the lethal logic seen so often in the abortion debate, where the rights of the mother are pitted against the rights and interests of the unborn child. Here the right of the elderly woman to choose life is undermined by pitting the value of her continued existence against the immediate and long-term interests of her fifty-five-year-old daughter. Hardwig clearly indicates that the elderly woman has a duty to die in order to protect the daughter's quality of life.

IF PHYSICIAN-ASSISTED SUICIDE
AND EUTHANASIA BECOME LEGAL,
OTHER OPTIONS WILL EVAPORATE.

What he does not factor into this equation are the personal sacrifices the elderly woman has made over the years for her daughter. Hardwig's views challenge the very meaning of family, implying that age and health factors can dissolve the obligations family members have for one another. He says nothing about respect for the elderly. Rather, he reinforces the stereotype that when elderly people need our help most, they are little more than a burden to the rest of us.

Perhaps this woman clings to life much more strongly than we consider necessary. People do not have an obligation to remain alive at any cost. The mother's continued existence may involve expense and investments of time that could be used elsewhere, but are we as a society so devoid of options that the only solution is death?

Hardwig asks us which burden we would rather bear: (a) To lose a 50 percent chance of six more months of life at age eighty-seven? (b) To lose all your savings, your home, and your career at age fifty-five? He believes these are the only two options. In real life, there are seldom either/or situations such as this.

For one thing, the elderly woman can be certified under hospice guidelines, allowing much of the intensive caregiving to be provided by hospice personnel. This would allow the daughter to continue working while assisting in her mother's care, thereby averting the impending financial disaster Hardwig believes the mother's continued existence would provoke. The woman's terror over death can also be addressed by improving the quality of her care through the holistic model of care provided by a hospice. In short, we are not forced to choose between the mother's death and the daughter's financial future. We have other options.

Eleanor Nielson, a single mother of a daughter engaged to be married, was diagnosed with breast cancer in 1989. When faced with her own death and all of the fears surrounding dying, it was little, tiny things that gave her hope—like the word "mother" in the term "chemotherapy." Now sixty, remarried, and healthy, Nielsen says, "Nobody notices 'mother' embedded in the word. Many might assume that hope and terminal illness are mutually exclusive, that they can't co-exist. But they can."[18]

If physician-assisted suicide and euthanasia become legal, other options will evaporate. There will be little incentive for family members to forego certain luxuries and conveniences to care for a dying loved one. And when these options disappear, any genuine notion of individual choice will disappear with them. The right to die will have given way to the duty to die.

NOTES

1. Herbert Hendin, *Seduced by Death: Doctors, Patients and the Dutch Cure* (New York: Norton, 1997), 157.

2. *Washington v. Glucksberg*, U.S. Supreme Court, 26 June 1997.

3. Alexander M. Capron, "Death and the Court," *Hastings Center Report* (Vol. 27, No. 5, September-October 1997): 26.

4. John A. Powell and Adam S. Cohen, "The Right to Die," *Issues in Law and Medicine* (Vol. 10, No. 2, Fall 1994): 170.

5. *Quinlan*—1976; *John F. Kennedy Hospital v. Heston*—1971; *Maine Medical Center v. Houle*—1974; *Superintendent of Belchertown State School v. Saikewicz*—1977; *Bouvia v. County of Riverside*—1983. See appendix for discussion of some of these cases.

6. Powell and Cohen, "The Right to Die," 171.

7. *Quinlan*, 355 A.2d 647, 651 (N.J. 1973).

8. *Cruzan v. Director, Missouri Department of Health*, 110 S. Ct. 2841 (1990).

9. Hadley V. Arkes, "The Right to Die—Again," in Michael M. Uhlmann, ed., *Last Rights: Assisted Suicide and Euthanasia Debated* (Grand Rapids: Eerdmans, 1998), 98.

10. Ibid., 101.

11. "Death with Dignity: National Poll; Americans Overwhelmingly Opposed to Congressional Action," *PRNewswire*, 30 July 1998.

12. John Hardwig, "Is There a Duty to Die?" *Hastings Center Report* (Vol. 27, No. 2, March-April 1997): 34.

13. See Tom L. Beauchamp, "What Is Suicide?" in *Ethical Issues in Death and Dying*, ed. Tom L. Beauchamp and Seymour Perlin (Englewood Cliffs, N.J.: Prentice Hall, 1978).

14. Hardwig, "Duty to Die?" 36.

15. Ibid., 38.

16. Ibid., 39.

17. Ibid., 37.

18. "Even Terminally Ill Maintain Hope, New Study Shows," *Canadian News*, 25 June 1998.

CHAPTER 6

ABUSING AUTONOMY TO DEATH:

Natural Limits on Personal Freedom

Among the social forces behind the dangerous turn of public opinion toward accepting euthanasia and physician-assisted suicide is the excessive cultural emphasis upon freedom of choice and self-determination (autonomy). Such an emphasis upon autonomy is the universal trait of all social movements whose goal is to morally justify and legalize actions previously prohibited or scorned. The abortion rights movement and the movement to legalize drugs are two of the more recent examples. Another example is the push to change the image of prostitution to that of a freely chosen career. A large number of recent movies have shown prostitutes in sympathetic roles, communities are beginning to decide whether to legalize the practice, and attempts have been made to legitimize it by getting rid of the negative term "prostitute" and instead using the term "sex worker." The appeal to individual autonomy also characterizes the "right to die" movement.

There is nothing inherently wrong with self-determination. All of us exercise a certain level of self-determination, making most decisions for ourselves. We like being in control, being able to make our own choices, going where we please, and doing what we wish. On its face, autonomy is an important part of humanness. The term autonomy comes from two Greek words, *autos* meaning self, and *nomos* meaning law or rule. Thus, autonomy literally means self-law or rule.

The notion of individuals as autonomous has its theological roots in the doctrine of human creation in the image of God (Genesis 1:26) and its philosophical roots in the writings of German philosopher Immanuel Kant, who taught that autonomy is central to the concept of human beings as rational, free moral agents.

> If morality is to be derived from freedom (autonomy), and if—as we have maintained—morality must be valid for all rational beings as such, it looks as if we have got to prove that the will of a rational being as such is necessarily free. . . . This must be equally true of practical reason: a rational agent must regard himself capable of acting on his own rational principles and only so can he regard his will as his own. That is to say, from a practical point of view every rational agent must presuppose his will to be free. Freedom is a necessary presupposition of all action as well as of all thinking.[1]

It is human beings who have the unique capacity to rationally choose their own ends, to choose their own course, and to will their own acts. Kant attempted to ground his notion of autonomy solely on the basis of reason, without reference to religion. Wesley Smith is correct in saying that autonomy, properly understood, is a liberating virtue when balanced with other social virtues such as communitarianism, which promotes interdependence, mutual support, and mutual concern. However, Smith also cautions us about the abuse of autonomy:

> Individualism is an inherent American trait, as natural to us as building dams is to beavers. But unbridled, near-absolute individualism leads to social anarchy that asphyxiates true freedom. That is why self-determination . . . is but one of the several equally important and sometimes conflicting values that add up to the dynamic concept the Founders called "ordered liberty."[2]

In a fallen world, abuse of autonomy is to be expected. One way it can be abused is to use it as the sole justification for acts that are themselves immoral, to apply autonomy to morally incoherent claims. The woman who sells her body into prostitution, the person who injects heroin into his or her body, or the father who sells himself and his family into slavery may all be said to be exercising their autonomy, but it is autonomy run amok.

Autonomy—our right to control our own lives free from the influence or coercion of others—is considered the core value of American life. As I stated earlier, Kant considered autonomy central to the idea of humans as moral agents. He believed that a fully rational person is one who is free to choose his or her own course. However, Kant also considered it essential to the character of a moral agent that he or she have access to the laws of reason in order to determine the rightness or wrongness of those choices. He argued that animals do not reason, and consequently they do not reflect on the rightness or wrongness of their actions.

MODERN SOCIETY RESISTS THE NOTION OF OBLIGATION AND MAKES AUTONOMY INTO AN IDOL.

In order to be free, an agent must have access to the laws of reason in judging whether the choices being made are moral or immoral, rational or irrational, justified or unjustified. Animals may be free to roam where they wish, to eat what they wish, etc., but they cannot be regarded as moral agents because they lack access to the laws of reason, and they lack the capacity for moral understanding that is necessary to judge whether an action is justified or not. My cat does not reflect on the moral pros and cons of killing a mouse (though he is free to kill as many as he can eat as far as I am concerned). Therefore, animals are not rational moral agents. Autonomy is a right that arises only for a rational, moral being capable of understanding that there are actions he or she is not free to choose.[3]

Autonomous, rational, moral agents also understand the need for authority within society. Without it, society loses order. Although we celebrate individualism, we also recognize that human beings are part of a larger community and that each person has certain obligations to fulfill. Yet modern society resists the notion of obligation and makes autonomy into an idol. For instance, the doctrine of autonomy has become so absurd that an entire social problem was created as mental institutions were emptied of their residents and closed because to keep people institutionalized was a violation of their autonomy. Today, society cannot even force mentally impaired homeless people into shelters in the dead of winter because they have an autonomous right to freeze to death on a sewer grate!

ABUSE OF AUTONOMY

In a society whose moral guidance system is constructed largely upon purely secular notions of equality, justice, and rugged individualism, the individual is not seen as subject to any authority beyond that of the "public interest." As long as a person does not harm others, he is free to do as he pleases, even though he may harm himself.

Kant regards this an abuse of autonomy. For example, suppose a respected surgeon develops a serious nerve problem that affects his hands, rendering him incapable of performing surgery. He concludes that life is not worth living if he cannot do surgery, and he decides to end his life. Would the nature of his condition make the choice to end his life a coherent choice? If life is really not worth living if a person loses the ability to perform surgery, should we end the lives of all other physicians when they no longer can perform surgery?

Kant's "categorical imperative" approach to ethics means that whatever action an individual chooses, its rightness can be determined by the agent's willingness to make it a universal law. Thus, for the doctor to be justified in killing himself because he could no longer do surgery, such an action would have to be universalized and applied to all future doctors in a similar situation. The doctor's decision to end his life because of his disability cannot be universalized; therefore, within the Kantian moral system, the action is immoral. If it cannot be universalized, the action cannot be right for the individual. Robert Bork, in commenting about modern liberalism's emphasis on rights without a corresponding emphasis upon obligations, says, "Modern liberalism employs the rhetoric of 'rights' incessantly to delegitimize restraints on individuals by communities. It is a pernicious rhetoric because it asserts a right without giving reasons."[4]

In the case of physician-assisted suicide, the person requesting the lethal medication is said to be acting as an autonomous moral agent. However, within the Kantian tradition at least, such a claim is incoherent, for the action cannot be universalized. It is a misuse of autonomy because it does not conform to the laws of reason, and it undermines the idea of community.

This is illustrated by some of the reasoning behind a string of court cases dealing with end-of-life matters. Hard cases (e.g., *Quin-*

lan—1976; *Cruzan v. Director, Missouri Department of Health*—1990) represent what many people fear: individuals in the midst of a serious, overwhelming condition not being allowed to die, forcing their families to seek relief in the courts, or good, compassionate physicians having to sue the state in order to provide patients with relief from suffering (*Quill v. Vacco,* 1997). The relief sought in such circumstances is usually grounded in the right of individuals to make their own decisions. When a patient requests that a physician provide her a lethal medication with which to end her life, she is certainly exercising her autonomy. However, Hadley Arkes is correct that individuals do not possess a "free floating" autonomy, an autonomy grounded only in its assertion. A right to die does not exist simply because someone asserts it.[5]

We can understand the difficulty and anguish experienced by a suffering person and his or her family. A serious chronic or terminal condition can be quite burdensome, and some people will request and receive help in hastening their deaths even when it is illegal to do so. All of this may occur under the umbrella of autonomy; however, using autonomy in this way is an excuse, not a justification. The mere exercise of autonomy is not its own justification.

Advocates for euthanasia consistently use hard cases to pressure society into recognizing a right to assisted suicide. These hard cases are employed to illustrate what happens when individuals are not given the right to make their own decisions at the end of life. From them, many people erroneously conclude that if they ever become permanently unconscious, they will likely have their life extended past the point any reasonable person would want to endure. Thus, the proponents of euthanasia tutor the public to demand total control over their destiny, even to demand death if necessary. It seems perfectly reasonable within the context of great suffering and pain.

GETTING PAST THE RHETORIC

We should not ignore the rhetoric of assisted suicide and euthanasia proponents. Although they claim that the principal motivation is to eliminate pain and suffering, it is hard to believe this is the real goal. If it were, they would not argue for laws that restrict a right to assisted suicide just to competent, conscious, terminally ill adults. Any advocate of assisted suicide who claims the practice will be limited to individuals who meet those criteria is being disingenuous. If Kevorkian's victims give us any indication, there are plenty of chronically ill and disabled people willing to end their lives. Proponents of assisted suicide know that it will be impossible for the state to restrict the practice to terminally ill adults.

Using the public's fear of pain and suffering as a battering ram to expand public notions of individual autonomy is a dangerous gambit. Such a misuse of autonomy invariably paves the way for society to include the practice of active *nonvoluntary* euthanasia, through the use of substituted judgment. More will be said about this in chapter 9.

By connecting autonomy and compassion, advocates of assisted suicide drive a wedge between human dignity and the sanctity of life. It is as if we are forced to abandon one or the other; either we forfeit human dignity or the sanctity of human life. If we do not legalize assisted suicide or euthanasia, we are accused of lacking compassion and imposing our morality on others. Peter Singer, a longtime advocate of abandoning the sanctity of human life ethic, states,

> The desire for control over how we die marks a sharp turning away from the sanctity of human life ethics. It will not be satisfied by the concessions to patient autonomy within the framework of that ethic —a right to refuse "extraordinary means" of medical treatment, or to employ drugs like morphine that are "intended" to relieve pain, but have the "unintended but foreseen side-effect" of shortening life. . . . Most cancer patients . . . are more likely to be helped by liberal injections of morphine, but even that is not a solution for people like Janet Adkins. . . . She did not want to die by a continuous infusion of morphine . . . which would most likely have put her into a state of drowsy confusion for some days before death came. She preferred to die at a time of her own choosing. . . . That is why the traditional ethic will be unable to accommodate the present demand for control over how we die.[6]

However, if it is permissible to kill the competent, conscious adult on grounds that such an action respects his autonomy and is compassionate, there is no reason to refrain from killing the incompetent, unconscious adult. If the action is justified because it is assumed that the action is a reasonable extension of the autonomy principle in the quest to alleviate pain and suffering, what justification can be offered for restricting this benefit from the incompetent, unconscious adult? If it is rational for the competent, it is reasonable for the incompetent.

Once there is a consensus that killing a terminally ill person who requests it is a proper extension of autonomy, especially on grounds that it is merciful and compassionate, using death as a treatment to eliminate pain and suffering will come to be viewed as that which "reasonable persons" would choose for themselves. Thus, since a "reasonable person" standard is used to make medical decisions for patients who have never been competent, there is no doubt in my mind that civil libertarians will petition the courts to expand the application of assisted suicide laws to such patients on grounds that to deny them the benefit of assisted death is a violation of their due process and equal protection rights under the Constitution. This reasoning is how never-competent retarded women, impregnated through sexual assault, are granted the right to an abortion. These women do not consent to abortion; it is simply stipulated that a "reasonable person" would abort under similar circumstances. The case law is already in place, just waiting for an enterprising lawyer to use it once assisted suicide is legalized.

EXPANDING "FREEDOM" TOO FAR

Proponents argue that we are merely responding to these dismal circumstances by expanding options for people. No one is being forced to choose death. Yet ethicist Allen Verhey is right that expanding personal freedom is not morally innocent. What begins as an option may ultimately be socially enforced.[7] Social Security began as an option for taxpayers. It is no longer optional. Automobile insurance began as an option, but virtually all states now require it.

EXPANDING PERSONAL FREEDOM TO INCLUDE

ASSISTED SUICIDE UNDERMINES ANOTHER

RIGHT—TO REMAIN ALIVE WITHOUT

HAVING TO JUSTIFY ONE'S EXISTENCE.

Abortion began as an option; however, increasing social pressures are now brought to bear upon parents to abort preborn children suspected of having genetic defects. Although there are a number of organizations that serve as strong advocates for the disabled and the medically vulnerable, aborting preborn children with "preexisting" genetic defects is commonplace. Despite laws such as the Americans with Disabilities Act (ADA), there is still a strong movement within society to discover in the womb and destroy children with conditions society finds expensive and burdensome. These acts are done, of course, in the "best interests" of the children and their families, but there is also a "benefit" to the rest of society as well—fewer people who do not fit the desired design. Although parents are not yet required to abort their "defective" children, genetic counselors are often aggressive in outlining for parents the enormous problems associated with caring for these children. Consequently, the majority of preborn children with handicaps (found through prenatal genetic testing) are aborted. What begins as an option can ultimately become socially, if not legally, enforced. In fact, in some cases parents who choose not to abort then have to fight with medical personnel after the baby is born about treatment issues, because the "option" of abortion has lessened the willingness to treat handicapped newborns. Sometimes it is minor surgery (like surgery to enable an infant to swallow) that doctors are reluctant to perform on such infants.[8]

It is also true that expanding freedom may be accomplished at the expense of the vulnerable. One means of protecting convenience store clerks is to not give them a key to the store's safe. Usually, a sign is posted alerting would-be robbers that the clerk does not have access to the safe, presumably to prevent them from harming the store clerk. Suppose we decide that this policy is an infringement on the freedom of store clerks, and we provide them with the key to the safe. Have we expanded their freedom—yes. But we have also made them more vulnerable.[9]

Expanding one freedom often limits another. It does more than simply provide options. The invention of the automobile expanded transportation options by giving people an alternative form of travel. However, the option of travel by automobile ultimately led to socially enforcing the diminishment of another option—travel by horseback or horse-drawn carriage. Although society makes some accommodation for those who still travel by horseback (e.g., the Amish), a person does not have the option of riding a horse down an interstate highway. Likewise, expanding personal freedom to include assisted suicide undermines another right—to remain alive without having to justify one's existence.

Autonomy is abused when it is used to assert one's autonomy or "self-sovereignty" in relation to God—to act as though one is completely independent of God. Of course, it is quite silly to assert that a person is completely self-sovereign just because he or she issues a "declaration of independence" from God. If the universe was created and is superintended by an infinite, sovereign God, there is no room for created, finite, mortal beings to be self-sovereign.[10] Sovereignty cannot apply to both God and people simultaneously. The very concept of God makes human sovereignty impossible. Even if there were no God, only one person could be sovereign. Although Christian theologians owe the world a rational account for the goodness of God in a less-than-perfect world where suffering exists, the difficulties in providing such an account should not strengthen the call of the agnostic to abandon all such effort and permit individuals to seize control for themselves.[11]

WHO HAS THE POWER?

Ironically, by resting so much of their case upon individual autonomy, the proponents of physician-assisted suicide and euthanasia have sown the seeds of their own destruction. It has already been shown that an appeal to personal autonomy as the foundational principle for assisted suicide or voluntary euthanasia is a contradiction of the autonomy principle. A person cannot use his or her autonomy to end that autonomy.

The appeal to autonomy, both in relation to other people and to God, demonstrates that the real issue is not how badly people suffer, nor is it how ineffective medical technology is in managing pain. The real issue is control—human control.

Highly emotional hard cases effectively distract us from these real issues. Just as an artillery salvo from a Navy battleship softens up coastline defenses before an all-out infantry assault, the proponents of assisted suicide throw a steady stream of heart-wrenching tragedies in the public's face to soften people up for the real assault. The real issue is not how we can better manage the suffering of the dying, but who will rule over the individual—the individual himself, the state, or God. Ultimately, the central issue in the assisted suicide/euthanasia debate is theological, not medical. The contest is really between worldviews. It is a theological debate that travels well beyond questions of medical techniques and therapies.

The notion of unfettered individual freedom gives patients a false sense of personal power over their situations. The present emphasis upon human moral autonomy by the major culture shapers in society—law, education, the arts, economics, the media—provides the proponents of euthanasia and assisted suicide with a powerful, popular appeal.

The pragmatism of this way of life is quite appealing to the masses, mainly because it does not require the existence of a transcendent divine being. God can easily be excluded, and arguments that invoke His name can easily be dismissed as religious and, therefore, irrelevant. In this sense, the dispute over assisted suicide is not just a question of how to help suffering, dying people deal with their misery, but a question of who owns us, who is in control of life. Who controls traffic at the entrance and exit gates of life?

WHO HAS THE MORAL RIGHT TO KILL?

However, there are other aspects of the debate to consider. It is no coincidence that the advocacy of euthanasia and assisted suicide comes at a time when the number of elderly, permanently unconscious, and AIDS patients is increasing, and when there is growing concern over the rising cost of health care. The cost of medical care in one's latter years is becoming a more frequent topic of discussion among health care administrators and government bureaucrats. Today, people live longer lives, but they tend to die "sicker," costlier deaths.

Art Caplan, Director of the Center for Biomedical Ethics at the University of Pittsburgh, was a member of President Clinton's 1993 commission to reform health care. Caplan reported that in the course of deliberations the subject of euthanasia as a cost control measure was not directly discussed, but "it [euthanasia] was waiting at the door to be invited in." The introduction of managed care and open discussions about the need to ration medical resources suggest that the altruism that characterized Western medicine is increasingly being tainted by the nature of political and economic pressures. The history of medicine suggests that physicians tend to follow the predominant social and political pressures of the day.

It is interesting to note that Oregon instituted a health care rationing program just a few years before the state legalized physician-assisted suicide. It appears that Caplan's warning about euthanasia being part of overt rationing of medical resources is a valid one. A fair amount of implicit rationing already exists in the U.S. For example, individuals older than seventy are not considered candidates for heart transplants. Some other surgeries are limited to people below a certain age.

If any conception of community is to exist, euthanasia and assisted suicide cannot be regarded as private matters for individuals to decide. For either euthanasia or assisted suicide to be effected, the aid and assistance of someone else is required, presumably one who also has a right to self-determination. In this context, assisted suicide and euthanasia are mutual social decisions between two people, one of which will do the killing. Granting such a liberty represents a startling and confusing expansion of individual autonomy. "It [assisted suicide, euthanasia] is the killing of one person by another in the name of their mutual right to be killer and killed if·they freely agree to play those roles. This turn flies in the face of a long-standing effort to limit the circumstances under which one person can take the life of another," says Daniel Callahan.[12]

Callahan asks, "How are we to make the moral move from my right to self-determination to some doctor's right to kill me—from *my* right to *his* right? Where does this doctor's moral warrant to kill come from?"[13] If physicians are to be considered responsible moral agents, they must have their own independent moral grounds for killing patients who request assistance. They cannot simply be amoral "hired guns" who mindlessly carry out the wishes of patients. Callahan is correct when he says:

> The doctor will have a problem at this point. The degree and intensity to which people suffer from their diseases and their dying, and whether they find life more of a burden than a benefit, has very little directly to do with the nature or extent of their actual physical condition. Three people can have the same condition, but only one will find the suffering unbearable. People suffer, but suffering is as much a function of the values of individuals as it is of the physical causes of that suffering. Inevitably in that circumstance, the doctor will in effect be treating the patient's values. To be responsible, the doctor would have to share those values. The doctor would have to decide, on her own, whether the patient's life was "no longer worth living."[14]

How would any doctor know this? There is no objective way to measure or judge the claim that suffering is unbearable. If gauging suffering is difficult, how much more difficult is it to make the judgment that life itself is not worth living? Some might respond that the subjective nature of these assessments is what requires us to maintain them as private decisions. However, it has already been shown that these are not private acts, but acts requiring at least two people to make them possible and a cooperative society to make them acceptable.[15] In the end, these decisions require communal complicity.

NOTES

1. Immanuel Kant, *The Groundwork of the Metaphysic of Morals*, trans. H. J. Paton (New York: Harper & Row, 1964), 42.

2. Wesley J. Smith, *Forced Exit: The Slippery Slope from Assisted Suicide to Legalized Murder* (New York: Times Books, 1997), 6.

3. Hadley V. Arkes, "The Right to Die—Again," in *Last Rights: Assisted Suicide and Euthanasia Debated* (Grand Rapids: Eerdmans, 1998), 104.

4. Robert H. Bork, "Hard Truths About the Culture War," *First Things,* June/July 1995: 20.

5. Arkes, "The Right to Die," 101.

6. Peter Singer, *Rethinking Life and Death* (New York: St. Martin's, 1994), 147.

7. I am indebted to Allen Verhey, professor of ethics at Hope College in Holland, Michigan for his excellent analysis of autonomy given during a panel discussion of current issues in medical ethics—Mark B. Blocher, Allen Verhey, and James Grier, "Medical Ethics Issues in the 21st Century," Evangelical Press Association Spring Meetings, Amway Grand Plaza Hotel, May 4–7, 1997, Grand Rapids, Michigan.

8. One example of reluctance to treat is Baby Doe in Bloomington, Indiana, in 1982, an infant born with Down's Syndrome and a tracheo-esophageal fistula (blocked esophagus), preventing the child from taking nourishment by mouth. Baby Doe's parents refused to give consent for surgery, arguing that Doe would not attain a "minimally acceptable quality of life" (In *re Infant Doe,* 1982). Although in this case the decision was made by the parents, this case has given physicians legal precedent to provide less than aggressive care for impaired infants. See Mark Blocher, *Vital Signs: Decisions that Determine the Quality of Life and Health* (Chicago: Moody, 1992), 84, 85.

9. Verhey, "Medical Ethics Issues in the 21st Century."

10. For an excellent treatment of this subject see R. C. Sproul, *The Invisible Hand: Do All Things Really Work for Good?* (Dallas: Word, 1996).

11. I commend to the reader C. S. Lewis's *The Problem of Pain* (New York: Macmillan, 1978) and Philip Yancey, *Where Is God When It Hurts?* (Grand Rapids: Zondervan, 1977).

12. Daniel Callahan, "When Autonomy Runs Amok," *Hastings Center Report* 22 (March/April 1992): 52.

13. Ibid., 53.

14. Ibid., 54.

15. Ibid., 55.

CHAPTER 7

THE MYTH OF REGULATING ASSISTED SUICIDE:

Increasing Physician Burdens Without Protecting Patients

Can physician-assisted suicide be carried out within the confines of rigorous guidelines that effectively prevent abuses, or will there be a subtle slide into active, involuntary euthanasia? Some proponents claim that physician-assisted suicide will be carefully regulated to ensure that only those terminally ill individuals who are experiencing great pain and suffering and who request it will receive "aid-in-dying." I have no doubt that physicians, acting under laws like the Oregon "Death with Dignity" Act, will initially observe legal guidelines. Assisted suicides will be carried out according to the letter of the law to show that these laws work. But do they?

A LOOK AT THE OREGON LAW

The Oregon "Death with Dignity" Act stipulates that a person requesting physician assistance in dying must traverse a number of legal hurdles. According to the law:

1. The person requesting physician assistance in dying must be a resident of Oregon. Furthermore, he or she must make a written request to a licensed physician. The initial request may be oral, but fifteen days must elapse between the initial request and the written request for a prescription to end life.

2. The attending physician must:
   a. Certify that the illness is terminal (meaning the illness is likely to cause death within six months).
   b. Make an initial determination that the patient's request was made voluntarily.
   c. Inform the patient of his or her medical diagnosis, prognosis, potential risks associated with taking the prescribed medication, probable result of taking the prescribed medication (death), and feasible alternatives, including, but not limited to, comfort care (palliative care), hospice care, and pain control.
   d. Refer the patient to a consulting physician for confirmation of the diagnosis, and to a psychiatrist to confirm that the patient is competent and acting voluntarily.
   e. Refer the patient for counseling when appropriate.
   f. Request that the patient notify his or her next of kin.
   g. Inform the patient that he or she may rescind the request at any time, verbally or in writing.
   h. Verify immediately prior to writing the prescription for medication that the patient is making an informed, voluntary decision.
   i. Fulfill the medical documentation required of the Act.
   j. Ensure that all appropriate steps are carried out in accordance with the Act prior to writing a prescription for medication.
3. A waiting period of fifteen (15) days must transpire between the initial oral request to an attending physician and the writing of the prescription for medication to end the patient's life. No less than forty-eight (48) hours shall elapse between the patient's written request and the writing of the prescription under the Act.
4. Insurance policies will not be affected by the patient's act of ingesting medication to end his or her life.

LEGAL LOOPHOLES IN THE LAW

Although these provisions appear to give sufficient protection from abuses, they are full of unenforceable loopholes, and ultimately, they undermine the very arguments used to justify legalizing assisted suicide. Let's look at the legal loopholes.

1. *A patient must be a resident of the state to be eligible.* The Oregon "Death with Dignity" Act only permits physicians to assist residents of the state in dying. Presumably, this is to prevent people from other states from flocking to Oregon. However, how long will it take before this provision faces a legal challenge from civil liberties organizations? Civil libertarians have challenged state laws lim-

iting education and medical care to U.S. citizens, so it is highly probable they will challenge Oregon's residency requirement in the Act.

It is not hard to see what their line of reasoning will be. If physician-assisted suicide is a legitimate medical procedure that licensed physicians may perform in the state, how can the state prevent nonresidents from receiving that treatment? Are state residents the only ones allowed to receive medical treatment in the state of Oregon (or whatever other state legalizes physician-assisted suicide)? Are physicians in Oregon only licensed to provide medical treatment to state residents?

Furthermore, if the state recognizes a right to physician-assisted suicide, how does the state justify discriminating against nonresidents who wish to exercise that right? Does it prevent nonresidents from purchasing vacation property in the state? Does it prevent nonresidents from getting married in the state? Are nonresidents barred from obtaining fishing or hunting licenses? Are they prevented from driving on the state's roads, using the state's parks, or attending the state's colleges?

Although nonresidents of a state have the same rights as residents, greater restrictions may be placed on nonresidents. For example, nonresidents may be required to pay more tuition to attend state colleges or universities or to use parks, museums, etc. Likewise, they may be required to pay more for medical care in the state's medical facilities, but the law will not allow a state to refuse to treat nonresidents. Thus, in regard to physician-assisted suicide, if this practice is recognized as a right under a state's constitution, it is unlikely that assisted suicide can be restricted to residents.

Even assuming that the residency requirement stands up in court, how hard is it to establish residency in a state? In most states, a person can establish residency by having a permanent address and obtaining a state driver license.

2. *There must be one oral request and one written request made to the patient's attending physician over a fifteen-day period.* The patient must also confirm orally that the written request represents his or her wishes. There are fatal flaws in this provision. First, it assumes that every patient making a request for physician assistance in dying will be capable of both oral and written communication. What of those conscious patients who cannot speak or write (e.g., a ventilator-dependent quadriplegic)? Shall these patients be denied access to physician assistance in dying because they cannot comply with this provision? Again, civil liberties organizations will have a

field day in the courts eliminating this provision, most likely by using the Citizens with Disabilities Act in federal court.

Second, it establishes an artificial waiting period that has no legal basis or medical significance. What of patients in immense pain who do not want to wait the full fifteen days? If the goal of the Act is to help patients avoid pain and suffering, what justifies allowing patients to suffer for two weeks? What is magical about a fifteen-day waiting period? Once again, civil liberties groups will challenge any waiting period, just as they have consistently done with abortion regulations that mandate waiting periods of twenty-four hours. How will the state convince the courts that a fifteen-day waiting period is not burdensome to the patient's right to die, when they consider a twenty-four-hour waiting period to be overly burdensome on a woman's right to an abortion?

3. *Oral requests are part of the process.* A third weakness is the acceptance of oral requests to physicians for assistance in dying. What counts as a valid oral request for assistance that starts the fifteen-day clock ticking? If a patient has an advance directive attached to his or her medical records, and that advance directive includes a statement about receiving assistance in dying, does this count as the original request for assistance under the Act? Does any mention of desiring physician assistance in dying by the patient satisfy the requirements of the Act? Would an oral request be considered invalid if the patient is in severe pain and moans that he or she wants the doctor to "do something"? The legal wrangling over this provision should prove interesting.

4. *Physician obligations are burdensome.* Physicians already bogged down by legal requirements and paperwork will not find any relief in the laws permitting assisted suicide. The passage of assisted suicide laws will necessarily require physicians to gain additional expertise in several areas. They will need further expertise in understanding patients' motivations for requesting physician-assisted suicide, assessing the mental status of patients, diagnosing and treating depression, acknowledging the presence of conditions that require professional counseling, maximizing palliative interventions, and evaluating the external pressures on patients who request assisted suicide. Doctors will not only be expected to accurately predict life expectancy, but also to predict the onset of functional and cognitive decline. They will need access to reliable information about effective medication and the dosages required to cause death.[1]

Under the Act, the attending physician must also be the one to determine that the patient's request is voluntary. How does he or she arrive at this conclusion? We may presume he or she will do so by asking the patient. However, is merely talking to the patient reliable? Do patients *always* tell doctors when they are being coerced by others or circumstances into accepting medical treatment? Do other individuals or circumstances ever influence physicians in their thinking about a particular patient? Yes, they do.

Another requirement to be fulfilled by the attending physician is that of judging the competency of the patient to make a life-ending decision. Surveys indicate that physicians themselves are not confident in their abilities to make such assessments. One such study of Oregon physicians who were not opposed to physician-assisted suicide revealed that more than half were not confident they could recognize depression in a terminally ill person. The Act requires the attending physician to refer the patient for counseling when it is suspected that the patient is experiencing depression or has other mitigating factors in his or her life. Yet, in the same study, more than 90 percent of Oregon's psychiatrists doubted their ability to determine in a single evaluation that a person seeking assisted suicide is mentally competent to make such a decision.[2]

As if these requirements did not place an enormous burden on the physician's shoulders, he or she must ensure that all steps have been rigorously carried out prior to writing a prescription for lethal medication. Considering that the average amount of time physicians spend with each patient is measured in minutes, not hours, how realistic is it to expect that physicians will be in a position to make such assurances?

5. *Insurance policies, annuities, etc., will be unaffected by decisions to obtain physician assistance in dying.* The Act prevents insurance companies from withholding or withdrawing coverage of an individual who makes a request for physician-aided suicide. In fact, both the Oregon law and the Michigan draft law stipulate that for insurance and inheritance purposes the death would be recorded as resulting from natural causes. When a person who dies with a doctor's assistance is by law considered a "natural death," the death is not subject to investigation. Thus, not only could the patient's heirs obtain the full life insurance death benefits, but they would be completely free to dispose of the body immediately without having an autopsy or medical examiner inquest. Consequently, even if the patient's death occurred under suspicious circumstances, the family could have the body cremated on the day of death and there would

be no way to perform a medical examination should anyone later challenge the circumstances of death.

It also means that insurance companies will be required to amend policy language related to suicide. Typically, life insurance policies do not pay death benefits in cases of suicide if the death occurs within a certain window of time from the policy's inception. It is doubtful that life insurance companies will be willing to pay death benefits for the suicides of their policyholders unless the company underwriting the policy also underwrites the patient's medical insurance.

PROBLEMS SUCH LAWS CREATE FOR DOCTORS

The Oregon "Death with Dignity" Act requires that two physicians (one attending and one consulting) must confirm the terminal nature of the patient's condition. The attending physician is responsible to ensure that all of the legal conditions are satisfied before writing a lethal prescription. The Act defines "attending physician" as the physician who has primary responsibility for the care of the patient and treatment of the patient's disease.

There is no requirement that an established doctor-patient relationship exist. Patients are allowed to request a lethal prescription the first time they see their new attending physician.

Both attending and consulting physicians must agree that the patient is terminally ill. A terminal condition is defined as an illness reasonably expected to cause death within a period of six months or less, with or without treatment.[3] It is important to note that such a definition of terminal illness has little medical significance. It is, at best, a guess, a speculation about the patient's life expectancy. The "six-month" criterion was initially used in the context of making decisions about chemotherapeutic regimens and was codified to define eligibility for Medicare hospice benefits.[4]

Although physicians are often called upon to make predictions about life expectancy, accurately predicting that a seriously ill person will die within six months is extremely difficult. A study of Oregon physicians in 1996 revealed that more than half worried they are not able to accurately judge when a patient has less than six months to live.[5] Making an accurate prognosis and communicating probabilities of life expectancy is a complex task that sometimes produces misleading results. Although the methods for estimating survival in critically ill patients are becoming increasingly sophisticated, relatively little data are available for predicting survival of patients who are not yet critically ill, but who have a disease that will become terminal with or without treatment.[6]

The first person in New York for whom a "right to die" petition was approved was Carrie Coons, eighty-six. She had been declared to be in an "irreversible" vegetative state. She neither spoke nor showed any signs of alertness. A computerized tomography scan (CT) and electroencephalogram (EEG) supported the clinical diagnosis of "persistent vegetative state." In January 1989, Mrs. Coons's sister obtained court permission to have her feeding tube removed, maintaining that her sister never wanted to be kept alive in this condition. The decision was also based in part on medical testimony that Coons's condition was "hopeless and irreversible." However, a state judge withdrew permission for the removal of her feeding tube after she began talking and eating on her own. When asked whether she would now want her food and water stopped if she were again in such a situation, she responded, "It would be a difficult decision." She died two-and-a-half years later.[7]

Of course, such cases are rare. But they are not unknown. Consider a few examples of instances where medical personnel were wrong about chances of recovery—or even about whether life was still present:

- The family of a fourteen-year-old girl was told she was "essentially brain dead" and asked to donate her organs. They refused. Two months later she was off life support, learning to walk again, and teasing her sisters.[8]
- A man who was declared dead after a traffic accident spent two days in a metal box in a mortuary. Eventually he became alert enough to yell for help.[9]
- Conley Holbrook, twenty-six, had been comatose since he was beaten with a log on November 27, 1982. On February 28, 1991, he awoke and said, "Momma." He then named the cousin and cousin's girlfriend who beat him. The recovery occurred while he was being treated for pneumonia at Lexington Memorial Hospital in North Carolina.[10]
- Jackie Cole, forty-four, was diagnosed in a "persistent vegetative state (PVS)" with chances for recovery as low as "one in a million" according to her doctor. A judge ruled that life support could be discontinued. When a friend came to pay his last respects, Jackie opened her eyes and smiled. She continues to give interviews.[11]

Obviously, doctors are not infallible. And predicting life expectancy for individuals with cancer, heart disease, and other degenerative diseases in the absence of acute symptoms requiring critical care is quite uncertain. Patients must be certified as terminally ill before being admitted to hospice care, but if a mistake is made and the patient lives longer than expected, little harm comes from it.

However, certifying that a patient is terminally ill for the purpose of providing a lethal prescription requires a higher degree of accuracy because any error in judgment is fatal. An error in judgment here robs the patient of the one thing that cannot be replaced —time. This should concern people who oppose the execution of convicted criminals because some may actually be innocent. Should we not be concerned about physicians incorrectly certifying patients as terminally ill for purposes of assisted suicide?

Under hospice certification guidelines, Alzheimer's patients can now be certified as terminally ill. Individuals with congestive heart failure, those who must undergo weekly kidney dialysis, as well as individuals with emphysema or other degenerative respiratory diseases may now be regarded as terminally ill. Significant problems arise when physicians try to diagnose a disease that will become terminal, but where no acute symptoms exist. Is an HIV-positive person who does not have any acute symptoms terminally ill? Patients may have conditions that weaken them to the point where a secondary condition overwhelms them (e.g., leukemia that leads to pneumonia), or they may have a combination of conditions, each of which makes the others incurable, thus forcing alterations in the patient's prognosis. All in all, physicians who certify patients as terminally ill for purposes of assisting suicide face a daunting assignment.

When hospice patients live longer than the six months, they need to be recertified in order for the hospice to continue providing care and be reimbursed under Medicare, Medicaid, and private insurance. Consequently, it is not uncommon for hospice personnel to exaggerate descriptions of a patient's symptoms in order to keep him or her certified under hospice guidelines and receive reimbursement. I am not arguing that this is unjustified, for these patients and their families need the care that a hospice provides. However, it is an illustration of how the "best interests" of the patient can be used to justify fudging a bit on certification requirements. If death is considered to be in a patient's "best interests," either by the patient, his or her family, or the physician, is it not likely that some physicians will equivocate about the patient's prognosis?

These regulations also undermine some of the main arguments used to justify assisted suicide in the first place. The principal arguments advanced to justify physician-assisted suicide are (1) the right of self-determination, (2) the obligation of physicians to alleviate pain and suffering for terminally ill persons, and (3) the absence of state authority to determine how much suffering a dying individual must endure. I believe these arguments make active involuntary euthanasia inescapable.

As argued in chapter 6, self-determination (autonomy) can be abused in several ways; therefore, the mere assertion of autonomy is insufficient to justify assisted suicide. Justifying assisted suicide on the basis of autonomy is an abuse of the principle. It is a logical contradiction to exercise autonomy in order to end autonomy.

POTENTIAL CONFLICTS OF INTEREST

It is dangerous that the patient's attending physician may both certify the terminal prognosis and prescribe the lethal medication. There appears to be ample room for conflicts of interest, something society seeks to avoid in other areas of medical practice. For example, when a physician declares a patient brain dead, he or she is not permitted to ask the family for organ donation, nor is he or she allowed to participate in organ retrieval. These regulations exist to prevent conflicts of interest.

IT IS NO SECRET THAT DEAD PATIENTS
COST LESS THAN LIVING ONES.

Yet no such barrier to conflicts of interest pertains to physician-assisted suicide. Although we scrupulously avoid conflicts of interest in the retrieval of organs from *dead* patients, we do not make every effort to avoid them with regard to potentially vulnerable *living* patients. Under the Act, the physician who certifies the patient's terminal illness is also allowed to provide the lethal prescription. In fact, if he or she is the attending physician, he or she must be the one to write the prescription. Other than the fact that a second physician must confirm the terminal prognosis, there is little protection against a conflict of interest.

What might be a conflict of interest between patient and physician? Certainly the fact that in this age of managed care, when physicians are called upon to be gatekeepers of medical resources, there is a possible conflict of interest between a physician's fiduciary responsibility to a patient and his managed care economic profile. When large sums of money are at stake, we should be alert to the potential for conflicts of interest. It is no secret that dead patients cost less than living ones.

Economic credentialing is already used by HMOs to screen which physicians coming out of residency will make "good" (meaning compliant) HMO physicians. Physicians will become more vulnerable to manipulation as managed care gains strength and economic credentialing becomes normative. As physician reimbursements are downsized by managed care organizations, there is a growing incentive to avoid patients who require expensive medical care. Those physicians whose patients tend to have high cost profiles will be deselected for inclusion in the managed care system. It will not take long for physicians to get the message.[12]

It is not just physicians who face potential conflicts of interest. Families do as well. Since voluntary physician-assisted suicide involves adults who likely have some sort of estate, there is the potential for families to encourage a seriously ill family member to end his or her life, or at least not make any effort to talk the person out of doing so, in order to secure the assets to be inherited by survivors.

It is not uncommon today for elderly people to put all of their assets into their children's names in order to qualify for certain types of government assistance, subsidized assisted living, or nursing home care. Since one of the main reasons people believe physician-assisted suicide should be legalized is the fear of becoming a burden to their family, we have good reason to believe that some families will urge patients to end their lives. We'll look at some of these problems in more detail in the next chapter.

NOTES

1. Margaret A. Drickamer, Melinda A. Lee, et al., "Practical Issues in Physician-Assisted Suicide," *Annals of Internal Medicine* (Vol. 126, 15 January 1997): 146–51.

2. Hilary Evans, "Pitfalls of Physician-Assisted Suicide," *Physician's News Digest*, 20 July 1998.

3. Hastings Center, *Guidelines for the Termination of Life-Sustaining Treatment and the Care of the Dying* (Briarcliff, N.Y.: Hastings Center, 1987).

4. Drickhamer, et al., "Practical Issues in Physician-Assisted Suicide," 150.

5. M. A. Lee, H. D. Nelson, et al., "Legalizing Assisted Suicide—Views of Physicians in Oregon," *New England Journal of Medicine* (Vol. 334, 1996): 310–15.

6. Current methods include those used in the Study to Understand Prognoses and Preferences for Outcomes and Risks of Treatments, and the Acute Physiology and Chronic Health Evaluation [APACHE III]. See W. A. Knaus, F. E. Harrell, et al., "The SUPPORT Prognostic Model: Objective Estimates of Survival for Seriously Ill Hospitalized Adults," *Annals of Internal Medicine* (Vol. 122, 1995): 191–203; and, W. A. Knaus, D. P. Wagner, et al., "The APACHE Prognostic Model: Risk Prediction for Critically Ill Hospitalized Adults," *Chest* (Vol. 100, 1991): 1619–36.

7. Jean Seligmann, "Whose Death Is It, Anyway?" *Newsweek,* 24 April 1989, 69.

8. *Isanti County* (MN) *News,* 7 January 1988.

9. *Minneapolis Star Tribune,* 22 March 1993, 2B.

10. "Coma Ended—Man Names His Attackers," *Boston Globe,* 6 March 1991, 11.

11. David Van Biema, "Ready to Pull the Plug—Jackie Cole Wakes Up," *People,* 13 October 1986, 43–44.

12. Lawrence R. Huntoon, "Managed Care, Medical Ethics, and the Killing of Patients for Profit," *Medical Sentinel* (Vol. 3, No. 1, January-February 1998): 33.

CHAPTER **8**

INESCAPABLE INVOLUNTARY EUTHANASIA:

The Future for a Society That Endorses Assisted Death

If states legalize the practice of physician-assisted suicide, will society one day accept the practice of active, involuntary euthanasia? Is there a "slippery slope" leading inevitably from *voluntary* physician-assisted suicide of terminally ill individuals to active, *involuntary* or *nonvoluntary* euthanasia of individuals who are not terminally ill?

THE SLIPPERY LOGIC OF SLIPPERY SLOPE ARGUMENTS

Slippery slope arguments (in formal logic, known as arguments by extension) are often overblown, and there is a tendency for these arguments to set up and attack "straw men"—imaginary, speculative scenarios that are set up just so they can be discredited. These types of arguments generally prove to be ineffective in changing people's minds about moral issues. Slippery slope arguments are based more on a particular view of human nature than on logic. There is no direct *logical* connection between voluntary assisted suicide and active involuntary euthanasia. To accept the first practice one does not logically require that the other be practiced. One does not necessarily follow from the other, which would need to be the case for slippery slope arguments to be logically valid.

For that reason, many people reject slippery slope arguments against physician-assisted suicide. Although they give the appearance of being logical, it is impossible to find a direct, logical, cause/effect relationship between the practice of assisted suicide and active involuntary euthanasia. However, although no direct logical connection exists, there are compelling reasons to believe that legalizing assisted suicide will inevitably lead to the legalization and practice of active involuntary euthanasia. There are forces and influences at work within the culture-shaping institutions of the United States that will make it impossible to prevent such a slide. I am not suggesting that some master conspiracy lurks in the shadows of American life to impose these practices on society. Rather, the move toward active euthanasia follows naturally from the dominant worldview in American culture.

A False View of Rights

Since the principal argument for supporting assisted suicide is the right of self-determination, there is no reason to believe physician-assisted suicide can be effectively regulated in a way that prevents a slide into active involuntary euthanasia. I'm not saying that active involuntary euthanasia is self-determination. I'm saying that if society continues to permit the doctrine of self-determination to preempt all other societal interests, there will be no effective way to regulate the practice of assisted suicide. First, it will be a right for conscious, competent terminally ill decision makers who request it. Then it will become the right of conscious, competent chronically ill (not terminally ill) decision makers. This restriction will eventually be challenged in court (just as the restrictions on abortion have been), and the right will be expanded to others under the doctrine of substituted judgment, something we already do with advance directives for health care.

Eventually, unconscious, incompetent persons will be given lethal prescriptions through the use of substituted judgment, which will give such decisions a veneer of respecting the person's right of self-determination. It is not much of a leap from here to conclude that a "reasonable person" would choose to die when faced with a diminished quality of life. All of this can be accomplished while maintaining that all we are doing is responding and adjusting to society's emerging understanding of how to apply the doctrine of self-determination. We'll be able to pretend that people really want us to kill them, that they would choose death if they were able to do so.

This is an inescapable conclusion drawn not from logic but from observation of three main forces within Western culture. First, a post-Christian culture that lacks a moral consensus among its members finds it very difficult to regulate personal behaviors that are justified by those who practice them with a radical notion of personal freedom. As Canadian newspaper columnist Andrew Coyne eloquently points out, "A society that believes in nothing can offer no argument even against death. A culture that has lost its faith in life cannot comprehend why it should be endured."[1]

We now look to the courts, not morality, to guide public policy. Laws that are not based on morality still have moral force, and the courts have taken the place once held by churches in speaking to public morality. Slogans, bumper stickers, and sound bites have replaced serious moral evaluation of contentious issues. An entire generation has been schooled in the banality of rhetoric touting "freedom of choice," as though merely making a choice is self-justifying.

However, the freedom to choose is not more important than the choice itself. The act of choosing is not of greater moral significance than the object of the choice. If I choose to rob a bank, is my action justified because I chose it freely? The morality of an action is to be found in its object, not in choosing it. By placing emphasis upon choosing, we detract from the moral significance of the choices themselves. Western post-Christian culture has exaggerated this in debates about issues like pornography. Rather than seriously debating the morality of commercial pornography, the focus has been on the freedom of individual choice. It isn't the thing being chosen that matters, but who makes the choice. We don't want the state telling us what we can or cannot look at in our own homes.

Pornographers frequently argue that they do not force anyone to purchase their merchandise. If we don't want to look at pornography, we can choose not to buy any. We're frequently told to just turn the channel if a particular television program offends us. If we don't want to see a particular film, listen to certain music, drink certain beverages, or engage in behaviors we find offensive, civil libertarians tell us to just avoid them. We're not being *forced* to do those things, and we're lectured not to impose our morality on others.

The problem is that while we personally choose to avoid those actions, we live in communities and neighborhoods with people who do practice them. Although I may choose not to attend or rent X-rated movies, my next door neighbor may. In a society where pornography is prevalent, I am likely to have to raise my children in a neighborhood where one or more of my neighbors is "entertained" by videos of women (or even children) treated as objects for male satisfaction. My children will then grow up around his children, who may adopt his perverse view of women and sexuality. Despite my choice to avoid pornography, and my rejection of the distorted notion of personal freedom that justifies being entertained by it, I find myself residing and raising my family among those who do use it. Invariably, I find myself in a position of having the immorality of others imposed on me.

When only a minority of the community choose to engage in a particular behavior, civil libertarians urge us to be "tolerant," to recognize the right of individuals to engage in it, to not impose our morality on them. However, as the number of people who choose to engage in it increases, the new majority has a tendency to become increasingly intolerant of the minority who still shuns it. Consequently, some that initially resisted may feel compelled to remain silent or in some way lend support to actions they morally resent. Even their silence is interpreted as consent.

WE ALL HAVE OBLIGATIONS TO OTHERS, EVEN IN THE MIDST OF TERMINAL ILLNESS.

An example of this can be seen in how public tolerance for pornography, homosexuality, and abortion has been achieved. How do popular culture (television, film, music, art, literature) and the secular press portray those who oppose pornography, homosexuality, and abortion? If one opposes the production and distribution of pornography, he or she is portrayed as puritanical, self-righteous, sexually repressed, and a book burner. To resist homosexuality makes one homophobic, a hate crime sympathizer, a bigot. Opposing abortion makes one anti-choice and anti-women. Not long ago, anyone who openly practiced or advocated these things was treated as a social pariah. Times have changed. To speak out against these practices today earns one membership in the "lunatic fringe" of society, a seat on the board of directors for the Flat Earth Society. Behaviors once believed to be detrimental to the stability of an ordered society have been normalized, and speaking out against them is now considered abnormal.

The immorality of pornography, homosexuality, and abortion has not changed, but the public perception of those who support such practices has changed. People who engage in them are merely exercising their freedom, and those who oppose this are the ones with the problem.

There is no way for an individual to engage in any of these practices without harming others. When individuals exercise these "freedoms" they force all of us to live with the consequences. When pornography is distributed by every available means, the nature of male-female relationships deteriorates for all of us, not just for the users of pornography. When homosexuality is embraced as just another lifestyle, we all must accept the results, including the social distortion of marriage and family. When abortion is socially supported, it affects all of us.

The loss of more than 35 million unborn children has affected every single person in America. Much of what politicians will fight over during the next few years will be shaped by the demographics of abortion. In a few years, 80 million retired baby boomers will need to be supported by the young, whose ranks have been depleted by 35 million individuals.[2] In addition, the ready access to abortion has changed the way we look at having babies; they are now something we choose to have (or not have) rather than a gift God gives us.

The proponents of physician-assisted suicide claim that society should not prevent competent terminally ill individuals from choosing death. They should be "free" to choose, as though their choice will have no impact on others. Yet, as in the case of abortion, such a notion of freedom undermines the very ideals of community. It exalts individualism to a status that harms the virtues of responsibility and obligation to others.

We all have obligations to others, even in the midst of terminal illness. We have an obligation to give and receive forgiveness, to give and receive love, to share wisdom, and to allow others to walk with us through the valley of the shadow of death. Because each of us is a unique human being made in God's image, death is not an exclusively personal experience. When our life on this earth ends, it is not just our personal loss, nor is it just a loss for our family and friends. Our death is a loss for the entire community; a generation has come to an end. Death is a shatterer of relationships. It cuts people off from those they love and with whom they share a common life. This threat is real and terrible, for human beings are created for community, not isolation. Human life is to be lived with others, and death makes its power felt when the dying are alienated from their everyday community of co-workers, friends, fellow church members, and family members.

Anna is dying. She sleeps much of the time and, at age ninety, her world has shrunk to the confines of the upstairs bedroom, hallway, and bathroom in her Berkeley, California, home. Hanging within arm's reach are items most familiar and precious to her, including a black-and-white photo of her son, now seventy-one. From her seat by a small square table, she can look out the curtained window upon the quiet hillside neighborhood she has known for years.

Some of her handiwork adorns the far wall. On the dresser is a stuffed teddy bear, a cassette player, and a stack of musical tapes. A TV table now functions as a storage site for toiletries, medical supplies, and diapers. A wheelchair stands ready to carry Anna down the hall to the bathroom. With the blessings of her son, who lives in Los Angeles and is coping with his wife's cancer and caring for his permanently disabled son, home care attendants and visiting nurses see to Anna's needs. Everyone works to ensure that her remaining days are spent in comfort and dignity.

In contrast to this love and care, eighty-two-year-old Alzheimer's patient John Kingery was abandoned at a dog racing track in Post Falls, Idaho. His daughter had checked him out of a Portland, Oregon, nursing home ten hours earlier. He was found sitting in a wheelchair, holding a bag of diapers.

If causing one's own death is determined to be a purely private act that the state must protect as a civil liberty, then we have given people tacit permission to dismiss obligations to others. We have seriously weakened the ability of society, through civil government, to protect human life. If choosing death is a civil liberty, under what circumstances and by what criteria can we ever justify intervening to prevent someone from ending his or her own life? When do we have an obligation to prevent death? How will I know that I am not imposing my morality on someone by preventing a suicide?

If this reasoning were not problematic for other reasons, remember that most people who attempt suicide do not really want to die. Attempted suicide is widely considered to be a cry for help. If we decide to be "nonjudgmental" and allow people to commit suicide, no questions asked, many who would rather live will instead die with the added despair that their loved ones did not care.

Once death is viewed as a highly private event that one may choose under medical auspices, it becomes increasingly difficult for society to "impose" life on those who do not want to live. If people choose to die, what right do any of us have to force them to live, especially if they are in pain or suffering? Having been tutored in the language of euthanasia, particularly the idea that there are fates worse than death (e.g., persistent vegetative states, so called "higher brain death," or the "injury of continued existence"), a public consensus will emerge wherein medically-assisted death is seen as a real solution, almost a duty, and there will be no other interests with sufficient public potency to resist it. A large number of people experience brief desires to die at some point during their lives. Are we going to offer counsel and love at those times, or will we glibly hand them the means to kill themselves?

A Desire for Unlimited Freedom

Second, it is a basic feature of fallen human nature to want more and more freedom. The right to die with physician assistance is especially pernicious because it, like abortion, is a full frontal attack on the sovereignty of God. All those involved in abortion take for themselves the freedom to decide whether or not a particular life is valuable or worthless, in direct contradiction to biblical teaching that all human life is a gift from God. One of the reasons euthanasia has been accepted in the Netherlands is attributable to the widespread rejection of Calvinist theology, especially its emphasis upon the sovereignty of God.[3] Recognizing a right to die with human assistance places the individual above both the state and God. Physician-assisted suicide and euthanasia makes one's death a completely private matter. Like abortion, it is a private concern between a physician and his or her patient. Once death is fully privatized, extending this "right" to formerly competent and never-competent individuals will merely be viewed as a logical, humane, and reasonable recognition of their privacy. Once autonomy is completely privatized, the law will be rendered utterly powerless to restrain the wishes of individuals lacking any moral restraint of their own and wanting to kill themselves, their ill family members, or their patients.

The Text of History

Third, history supports the prediction that voluntary physician-assisted suicide will inevitably lead to involuntary euthanasia. We are not limited to observing the social use of euthanasia in ancient Greece, Rome, and Nazi Germany, but we have a contemporary example in the Netherlands of how euthanasia is practiced in a democratic society. The Netherlands has been tolerant of assisted suicide for a long time. Only recently has the Dutch government taken steps to provide quasi-legal recognition for this practice, although government reports indicate that the medical community still practices it in secret, refusing to report deaths by physician assistance. Even more disturbing is how rapidly voluntary euthanasia moved into nonvoluntary euthanasia, where as many as five thousand deaths each year involve patients who were not consulted or who did not give consent to be killed.[4]

SLIDING TOWARD THE DEATH SOCIETY

All the evidence shows that the regulation of assisted suicide will prove socially ineffective and legally unenforceable. Despite the best intentions, these legal safeguards are little more than legislative papier-mâché—mere window dressing. They only provide an appearance of protection, just like the lofty language of the Supreme Court in *Roe v. Wade* purports to respect "potential human life." *Roe* allowed states, "in the interest of protecting potential human life," to prohibit late-term abortions. Yet, despite these words, the Congress of the United States has been unable to prohibit so-called partial birth abortion, a procedure performed exclusively in the later weeks of pregnancy. If legislators cannot find the resolve to outlaw one of the most barbaric acts imaginable, what gives anyone reason to think they will enact enforceable laws regulating assisted suicide that will survive inevitable legal assaults in the courts?

Even worse, these regulations will ultimately smooth the slide into active involuntary euthanasia because they will gradually supply physician-aided killing with a veneer of medical respectability that desensitizes society to what is really happening. Killing under medical auspices will not seem so much like killing.

Robert J. Lifton of Yale University has done a masterful work of exposing how the Nazis used physicians to provide a veneer of medical respectability to their genocidal practices. In his book *The Nazi Doctors*, Lifton exposes the complicity of the German medical community from the earliest days of the Third Reich.

When we think of the crimes of the Nazi doctors, what come to mind are their cruel and sometimes fatal human experiments. Those experiments, in their precise and absolute violation of the Hippocratic Oath, mock and subvert the very idea of the ethical physician, of the physician dedicated to the well-being of patients. . . . Yet when we turn to the Nazi doctor's role in Auschwitz, it was not the experiments that were most significant. Rather it was his participation in the killing process—indeed his supervision of Auschwitz mass murder from beginning to end. This aspect of the Nazi doctor behavior has escaped full recognition—even though we are familiar with photographs of Nazi doctors standing at the ramp and performing their notorious "selections" of arriving Jews. . . . Yet this medicalized killing had a logic that was not only deeply significant for Nazi theory and behavior but held for other expressions of genocide as well.[5]

Richard John Neuhaus tells how Dutch physicians heroically resisted the Nazis. During the Nazi occupation of the Netherlands, the Nazi Commissar ordered all Dutch physicians to turn over their patient records to the German Health Ministry. Knowing why the Nazis wanted these records, the Dutch doctors refused. They were then warned that if they did not turn over these records, the Commissar would revoke their medical licenses. En masse the Dutch doctors voluntarily turned in their medical licenses, closed their offices, and began seeing their patients secretly in homes. The Commissar then threatened to hang the Dutch doctors if they did not comply, and many were killed. Yet the Dutch doctors refused to cooperate with the most repressive regime in modern history.[6]

Tragically, some fifty years later, the Dutch doctors are doing what they heroically refused to do under the Nazis. The Dutch "vision" for end-of-life care of the elderly has been corrupted by the same vision that corrupted German doctors—*Lebensunwertes Leben*—"Life unworthy of life."

DEATH BY PROXY

It is dangerous to permit proxy decision-making that involves physician-assisted suicide, yet, as I have demonstrated, society will be forced to accept such decisions communicated through advance directives and proxy decision-makers. Some things in life require individuals to give direct, contemporaneous consent. We require individuals getting married to be personally present to take their marriage vows. We require voters to cast their own ballots. In neither case does the state recognize substituted judgment. Shouldn't a decision to end one's life face similar requirements if we are to recognize the existence of a right to die?

Substituted judgment is a necessary part of medical law because of the number of times complicated medical judgments must be made about the treatment of someone who is unconscious or unable to communicate his own wishes. It assumes that family members who know the patient well can communicate what he would want done in his particular medical condition. The courts view substituted judgment as an extension of a patient's right to self-determination.

In other words, just as the principle of self-determination provides the legal basis for a right to die, the doctrine of substituted judgment for health care decisions provides the legal mechanism for expanding physician-assisted suicide to those who are no longer conscious or competent to make their own decisions. It is quite likely that state assisted-suicide laws that restrict this "benefit" to those who are competent and conscious will be challenged on grounds that unconscious, incompetent individuals are being denied equal protection under the law, that they still have a right to die, a right that can be respected through the exercise of substituted judgment. Just as we show respect for patient autonomy by allowing close relatives to withdraw or withhold further medical treatment from loved ones who cannot make their own medical decisions, the elasticity of substituted judgment allows us to make a proxy decision to directly end the life of a patient.

The use of substituted judgment has been used in a number of instances involving abortion. For example, a pregnant New York woman was seriously injured in an automobile crash and remained in a coma for several weeks. Doctors advised her husband that "terminating her pregnancy" might improve her chances of recovery. Under *Doe v. Bolton,* the companion case of *Roe v. Wade* (1973), the U.S. Supreme Court ruled that a husband has no legal standing to interfere with his wife's right to an abortion. Since she was in a coma, doctors asked the husband for consent for an abortion under the doctrine of substituted judgment. However, had this woman awakened from the coma, the husband would have lost legal standing to make the decision.

To deprive an incompetent, unconscious woman of an abortion was considered a violation of her due process and equal protection rights under the Constitution. In a similar way, restricting physician-assisted suicide to conscious, competent terminally ill individuals might be seen as a violation of the due process/equal protection rights of unconscious, incompetent terminally ill individuals. These equal protection/due process rights can be "protected" through the use of substituted judgment.

Chief Justice William Rehnquist wrote the majority opinion in a landmark "right to die" case, *Cruzan v. Director, Missouri Rehabilitation Services* (1990). In this case, the majority ruled that although there is no explicit right to die in the Constitution, individual states may recognize one, and people who wish to exercise a state-recognized right to die can be required to say so in a clear and unmistakable way while they are competent. One way of providing this "clear and convincing evidence" is through the use of an advance directive (e.g., living will).

However, since the Patient Self-Determination Act of 1990 was implemented, the use of advance directives for health care decisions continues to be a problem. There seems to be just as much of a problem making treatment/nontreatment decisions at the end of life as there was before the Act was passed into law. Since 1990 there have been a number of studies on the use of advance directives for health care. These studies indicate that these documents have not had a significant impact on end-of-life care.[7]

Advance directives were intended to provide patients with a more effective way to avoid futile medical treatment and to assist physicians in knowing when to cease life-extending efforts. However, advance directives that specify treatment preferences for desperately ill patients have little impact on the type or cost of medical care patients receive in the final months of their life.[8] Likewise, the presence of an advance directive on a patient's chart does not guarantee that the patient's real preferences are known or that those preferences will be respected.

Such ambiguities often result in proxy decision-makers and physicians basing treatment decisions on their own concerns and needs, as opposed to those of the patient. They mistakenly assume themselves to be reasonable persons and surmise that if they would or would not want something done to them under similar circumstances, the patient would or would not want them either. Interestingly, a study of dialysis patients indicated that the majority did not want their advance directives strictly followed, that the vague language found in most advance directives, when strictly interpreted, does not necessarily reflect the preferences of the patient.[9] How, then, are we to rely on advance directives when they specify assisted suicide under certain conditions?

We would do well to remember that the advance directive is a model of decision-making developed *by* competent persons *for* competent persons, who understandably are preoccupied by the threats that future, unwanted treatment may pose to their interests as presently conceived. However, this does not take into account the substantial changes in interests that could accompany the onset of incompetence or impaired mental status.

Rebecca Dresser and Peter J. Whitehouse correctly observe, "We ought to be aware of the dangers arising whenever healthy persons try to assign qualitative value to the life experiences of impaired individuals. Once we move away from relying on the patients themselves for answers about the treatment they should receive, we risk unjustifiably undervaluing the lives of these vulnerable individuals who impose such substantial emotional and financial burdens on others."[10] Using advance directives in the context of assisted suicide would be extremely dangerous.

Wayne Cockfield, forty-eight, is a Vietnam veteran from Florence, South Carolina, who lost both legs and the use of one arm after stepping on a land mine. "People who advocate euthanasia are sincere," he says. "They even think they are doing us a favor—but they're wrong. Disabled people do not want to die.

"If you and I walked into the hospital together wanting to commit suicide, you would get suicide prevention therapy and I would get suicide assistance because I'm disabled. People look at me and wonder, 'Who would want to live like this?' If you had told me when I was fifteen that I would live most of my life with disabilities, I would have said I would rather be dead. That's because I was on the outside looking in." Cockfield spent more than two years in hospitals, enduring twenty-nine surgeries. Today, he is the director of South Carolina Right to Life. "The trouble with people who support euthanasia is that they're telling the disabled that the only way to have dignity is to die in a way that society has decided is appropriate for them."[11]

People often rescind their advance directives once medical treatment actually begins. One reason for this is that living wills fail to convey precise instructions about treatment, leaving physicians and family members to interpret the patient's intentions. When a document requests nontreatment when "there is no reasonable expectation for recovery from extreme physical or mental disability," most people think they have some idea what that statement means. However, words like "reasonable," and "extreme" are subjective terms, ones that often elude precise definition. And does nontreatment include ventilators, food, and liquids, or just invasive surgeries, medications, or therapies? Is it wise to craft a public policy of physician-assisted suicide using autonomy as justification when the patient's true wishes are unknown?

The Uniform Rights of the Terminally Ill Act provides for the revocation of advance directives "at any time and in any manner, without regard to the declarant's mental or physical condition." This language has carried over into legislation legalizing assisted suicide (e.g., Oregon's "Death with Dignity" Act). Yet, just exactly how a conscious, incompetent patient would revoke an advance directive remains unclear. How are we to gain access to the consciousness of another human being whose cognitive capacities elude us? Frequently, such patients cannot communicate using language. We are left to rely on behavioral and other physiological factors in our attempts to understand how an incompetent person experiences life.[12] Serious difficulties arise when competent persons impute to incompetent persons the interests and desires characteristic of competent individuals.

Steven Weighman of Stanwood, Michigan, was seven when he was thrown from a horse that had been struck by a car. In seconds, Steven was transformed from a fun-loving kid into a blind paraplegic. The earliest prognosis was dismal. He would never have cognitive brain function. He would never breathe nor eat on his own. His parents were told Steven would never be able to be part of their family again. "It's only fair to your other sons that he not go home," the doctors told Steven's parents, Gene and Ellen.

But they took Steven home anyway, despite the doctors labeling Steven a "vegetable." Gene Weighman says, "I told them they didn't know their vegetables. He's still breathing, isn't he?" Not only was Steven breathing—he later attended Ferris State University in Big Rapids, Michigan.

Steven, now forty-six, has written a book about his life, using special equipment that allows him to use a special keyboard to tap his thoughts into words with Morse Code, which his computer recognizes and transforms into text.

Not only does he tell uplifting stories about going to a summer dance with a beautiful young lady, but horrific stories of his abuse at the hands of an aide: being served nothing to eat but eggs for days on end . . . having drapes closed on him so he couldn't keep track of days and nights . . . being abandoned in a bathroom to sit in his own urine and contemplate suicide.[13]

RELIEVING PAIN AND SUFFERING

A second reason assisted suicide will slide into active nonvoluntary euthanasia relates to the perception that physicians have an obligation to relieve pain and suffering. If this obligation justifies physician-assisted suicide for competent individuals who choose it, terminal illness is itself an arbitrary boundary. If alleviating pain and suffering is sufficient grounds to justify assisted suicide, what justification can be given for restricting the practice to the terminally ill? Are the terminally ill the only patients who experience severe pain? What of chronically ill patients who often experience immense pain? What prevents them from claiming they are being denied equal protection under the law if assisted suicide is a "benefit" restricted to the terminally ill?

If society can justify extending the right of assisted suicide to include the chronically ill, what prevents society from including the handicapped, especially those deemed to have a low "quality of life"? Jack Kevorkian readily acknowledges this hypocrisy. Many of his "patients" have not been terminally ill. In some instances (e.g., Marjorie Wantz), they do not have a confirmed medical diagnosis of any chronic illness.

WHATEVER "SAFEGUARDS" WE ESTABLISH
WILL PROVIDE LITTLE OR NO PROTECTION
FOR EXTREMELY VULNERABLE PEOPLE.

As long as the claim to physician-assisted suicide hinges on individual autonomy and subjective notions of pain and suffering, we will be unable to contain its practice. Neither pain nor suffering can be truly measured by objective criteria, nor are they subject to the kinds of dispassionate judgment needed to construct a consistent, workable public policy, especially one that must meet the equal protection purposes of the Fourteenth Amendment.[14] Society may, through legislation and/or judicial fiat, impose arbitrary restrictions on physician-assisted suicide, but that is a path fraught with hazard.

Physician-assisted suicide is not a singular act absent of other consequences. Once litigation by "right to die" organizations expands the notion of equal protection to include the right of nonterminally ill, unconscious, and/or incompetent individuals to assisted suicide, we will see how morally and legally flimsy the notion of "self-deliverance" really is. Patients who are neither conscious nor competent cannot effect "self-deliverance." Someone other than the patient must control the means and timing of death, which moves us well beyond assisted death and directly into the realm of active nonvoluntary euthanasia. Nonvoluntary euthanasia is just a short distance away from involuntary euthanasia.

One-hundred-and-two-year-old Olga M. (not her real name) resided in an upscale nursing home in Michigan. Her only daughter, now in her seventies, lives in Florida and Northern Michigan, yet insisted on being consulted for even the most routine treatment of her mother. When Olga's hearing worsened, she became disoriented and confused. Nursing home personnel suggested to the daughter that an inexpensive hearing enhancement device could be purchased from Radio Shack that would alleviate the problem. They would be happy to get one. The daughter refused. A few weeks later, Olga developed an infection on one toe. Staff requested permission to give Olga a standard antibiotic to treat the infection. She refused to authorize it. The infection developed into gangrene, which began to cause vital organs to malfunction as it spread. Doctors requested permission from the daughter to amputate her foot to prevent the gangrene from spreading further. The daughter again refused to give permission. Olga died two months after her daughter refused to permit surgery.[15]

If we accept the arguments offered in support of legalized assisted suicide, whatever "safeguards" we establish will provide little or no protection for extremely vulnerable people. Since there is little consensus now on the issues surrounding life and death, it will not be possible to articulate consistent public safeguards against nonvoluntary euthanasia. Over time, as society comes to accept assisted suicide (as it has abortion), such safeguards will be increasingly difficult to defend. The outright rejection or covert evasion (as in the Netherlands) of these safeguards is likely.[16]

VOLUNTARY CHOICE IN EUTHANASIA AND ASSISTED SUICIDE

The social policy of legalized abortion provides a good laboratory for determining physician competence to ensure that patients are

acting voluntarily. How many of the 1.5 million abortions performed each year are truly voluntary, and how many of the doctors
performing them actually take steps to find out if a patient has voluntarily sought an abortion?

Testimonies from postabortive women reveal that doctors who
perform most abortions rarely talk to their "patients." They simply do
not ask about a woman's motivations for obtaining an abortion. Abortionists generally rely on their staff to counsel the patient and obtain
consent. If anyone is going to be in a position to know what a woman
is really thinking it will be a staff member, not the physician. Yet there
is ample evidence that at no point in the events leading up to an abortion is it actually confirmed that a woman is acting voluntarily.

In 1988, a nineteen-year-old idealistic Venezuelan young woman
came to the U.S. on a visa with high hopes of getting married and
raising a family. Soon after arriving, she met a handsome Marine.
They dated for ten months, with every date chaperoned, as is customary in Latin-American families. In June 1989, they were married, shortly before her visa was to expire.

Anxious to fulfill her dream of having a "dream house, family
and children," she deliberately became pregnant in the spring of
1990. She did not tell her husband right away. When she was several months pregnant, she bought a tiny baby's bib, waited for a private moment together, and gently laid the bib upon his chest,
offering him the gift of their child. She expected him to share her ex-
citement since in her family a child was the greatest gift a woman
could give her husband.

Instead of being happy, he erupted in anger, cursing at her and
insisting that she would have an abortion. She pleaded, but he refused to budge. She would abort. He threatened to leave her. She
told her employer, who let her know that another employee was also
pregnant and she could not keep two pregnant employees through
their maternity leaves. Lacking support and torn between her love
for her child and her duty to her husband, she gave in. On June 15,
1990, when she would otherwise have been preparing for their first
wedding anniversary, she had an abortion. To ensure that she went
through with it, her husband accompanied her to the clinic and sat
in the room while the doctor performed the abortion. Clinic staff indicate that he taunted and laughed at her during the procedure. Although it was clear she did not want the abortion, the clinic staff did
nothing to help her.

The abortion was a tremendous blow to her self-esteem, idealism, and dream of having a family. Aborting was against her conscience. "I couldn't eat," she later stated. "I feel like nothing—like life is over." Meanwhile, her husband acted oblivious to her feelings. He told her she would get over it.

But the abortion began to affect several areas of their marriage. She became sexually distant from him. He began to see other women. They purchased a house, which she says he made her pay for with money she earned, while he spent his as he pleased. Allegedly, the financial pressure led her to start stealing from her employer: She allegedly stole $7,200 in cash over a period of time, and she shoplifted clothing.[17]

After the abortion, their fights became more frequent and increasingly more violent. Police were called on several occasions, and formal complaints were filed. Yet they seemingly always "made up." But the fighting continued, and the violence escalated until one Tuesday evening he forced her to have sex with him. He fell asleep soon after, while she went to the kitchen. As she sat at the table, her eyes came to rest on a knife. She began to have a flashback experience in which she remembered the abortion, her fear of the syringes, the insults he had hurled at her while her child was torn from her body. She took the knife back into the bedroom, pulled back the covers . . . and Lorena Bobbit would soon become a household name. All Lorena wanted was a husband, children, and a life in America. At her trial, psychiatric experts testified that the emasculation of John Bobbit was inextricably tied to his having forced Lorena to abort her child.[18]

As with abortion, no one will really know if an assisted suicide is voluntary. No one seriously believes that every surgery performed in America is totally voluntary. There are times when families place pressure on their members to accept medical treatment, often out of justified concern for the well-being of their loved one. In some instances, they even argue that the individual has a duty to get treatment.

Institutionalized abortion has now educated an entire generation of women that there are circumstances when obtaining an abortion is virtually their duty (e.g., cases of severe fetal deformity). As Americans age, the rhetoric of self-determination, death with dignity, and quality of life, combined with the ethically dubious cost-cutting medical practice under managed care, will seriously undermine notions of informed consent.

KILLING AND THE STATE

Many question how the state can force individuals to experience ongoing agony when death is inevitable.[19] This is a valid question, but perhaps we should put the question differently. What role does the state have in controlling how individuals end their lives? What right does the state have to determine how dead bodies shall be handled? What right does the state have to regulate death in any way? What grounds the state's interest in protecting vulnerable human beings?

Victor Rosenblum asks an equally valid question in response: "What business does the state have in deciding that some lives are less worthy of the law's protection than others, and in suggesting through legalization of assisted suicide that this is a 'rational' way for people to end their lives?"[20] Proponents of assisted suicide are willing to use the power of the state when it suits their purposes, but not when the state prevents them from doing what they wish. They cannot have it both ways.

It is folly to think that legalized assisted suicide will only involve a small number of exceptional cases, but not affect society as a whole.[21] Although Oregon has recorded only a handful of physician-assisted suicides since its law went into effect in 1997, it is ludicrous to suggest that assisted suicide will be practiced in only rare cases. It will not take long for the educational effect of assisted suicide to infect our thinking about the kind of care individuals should seek and receive at the end of life. It will not take long for doctors to understand their new dual roles: as lifesavers in one arena and as death-dealers in another.

How long will it be before the goal of eliminating the suffering of patients is transformed into eliminating the "suffering" of the families who must provide care, pay the medical bills, and gradually see their inheritance slip away into the pockets of nervous physicians and an impersonal medical bureaucracy?

The temptation to "just get it over" will prove too great for some families, and the ability to obtain relief from the obligation to care under medical auspices will gradually be converted into a virtue. We may even come to see family members' actions as understandable. However, mitigating circumstances do not by themselves exonerate people from the moral or legal implications of their actions.

Yet once a society excuses an action on grounds that it was driven by mitigating circumstances, it becomes harder the next time to muster a strong opposition to the action itself. Once one form of killing (e.g., abortion) is legitimized by society, it becomes harder to call it killing, and having done it millions of times, it becomes something else altogether—a mere medical procedure perhaps.

NOTES

1. Andrew Coyne, "The Slippery Slope That Leads to Death," *Globe and Mail* (Toronto), 21 November 1994.

2. David Mastio, "Abortion Altered America's Future," *USA Today*, 21 January 1998, 15A.

3. Herbert Hendin, *Seduced by Death: Doctors, Patients and the Dutch Cure* (New York: Norton, 1997), 136.

4. L. Pijnenborg, P. J. van der Maas, J. J. M. van Delden, and C. W. N. Loonan, "Life-Terminating Acts Without Explicit Consent of the Patients," *Lancet* (Vol. 341, 1993): 1196–1200.

5. Robert J. Lifton, *The Nazi Doctors: Medical Killing and the Psychology of Genocide* (New York: Basic Books, 1986), 4.

6. Richard J. Neuhaus, "The Return of Eugenics," *Commentary*, April 1988: 15–26.

7. Ezekiel J. Emmanuel, David S. Weinberg, et al., "How Is the Patient Self-Determination Act Working?" *American Journal of Medicine* (vol. 95, 1993), 619–28. Also Susan M. Wolf, Philip Boyle, Daniel Callahan, et al., "Sources of Concern About the Patient Self-Determination Act," *New England Journal of Medicine* (Vol. 325, 1991), 1666–71.

8. Lawrence J. Schniederman, et al., "Impact of Advance Directives on End-of-Life Care," *Annals of Internal Medicine*, October 1992.

9. Ashwini Sehgal, Alison Galbraith, et al., "How Strictly Do Dialysis Patients Want Their Advance Directives Followed?" *Journal of the American Medical Association* (Vol. 267, No. 1, 1 January 1992): 59–63.

10. Rebecca Dresser and Peter J. Whitehouse, "The Incompetent Patient on the Slippery Slope," *Hastings Center Report*, July-August 1994: 6.

11. "Disabled Fear Trend Toward a Need to Die," *Washington Times*, 11 December 1997.

12. Rebecca Dresser and Peter J. Whitehouse, "The Incompetent Patient," 8.

13. Steven Weighman, *Don't Count Me Out* (Stanwood, Mich.: Blue Spruce Publishing, 1998), also Tom Rademacher, "Triumph of Book Partially in Its Writing," *Grand Rapids Press*, 18 October 1998, B1.

14. Victor Rosenblum, "Compassion and 'Quill,'" in Michael M. Uhlmann, ed., *Last Rights: Assisted Suicide and Euthanasia Debated* (Grand Rapids: Eerdmans, 1998), 547.

15. This story was told by a nurse at the facility, and it was confirmed by the director of health services. Sources requested anonymity. Interview by author, 29 September 1998.

16. Daniel Callahan, *The Troubled Dream of Life* (New York: Simon and Schuster, 1993), 107.

17. David Reardon, "The John and Lorena Bobbitt Mystery Unraveled," *Post Abortion Review* (Spring/Summer 1996), 3.

18. Ibid., 5.

19. Friends of Merian, the group who placed physician-assisted suicide on the Michigan ballot in November 1998, published campaign literature that raised this point. They framed the issue as pitting the rights of suffering, dying individuals against the state, who wanted to dictate how much and how long people must suffer before they die. The image this creates in the average citizen's mind is so powerful that the state is seen as the villain.

20. Rosenblum, "Compassion and 'Quill,'" 548.

21. Ibid., 548.

CHAPTER 9

THE ROLE OF PHYSICIANS AT THE END OF LIFE:

Should Doctors Be Killers?

It is 1943 in Auschwitz, the day after Christmas. The German physician has returned to camp after spending three days with his family. Snow falls softly as he walks briskly to the showers. To-day, like so many days before, he will meet several hundred "guests" of the Reich—Jews brought to the camp by train. As always, he will use his most soothing manner with the women and children in re-questing that they disrobe and shower before a physical examina-tion. It amazes him how easily they comply, duped into believing that the same Nazis who stuffed them into locked cattle cars have suddenly become humane. He sees in their eyes the faint hope that the water will be hot and steamy enough to wash away the grimy despair of the trip.

The doctor steps into the control room to activate the showers. He knows that the pipes fill not with water, but with Zyklon-B poi-sonous gas. German law requires that a physician be the one to turn the nozzle. His job is not finished until he has made his examina-tion, ensuring that the deadly gas has done its job. Indeed, the bod-ies of the women and children, lying as they fell, now pave the shower floor. After falsifying the death certificates, he is satisfied his work is completed. It is now time for lunch. All in a day's work . . .

History records that millions of Jews under the Third Reich died at the hands of physicians. The Nazis were scrupulous about ensuring that physicians attended the exterminations of Jews. Vulnerable people die today at the hands of physicians, not from Zyklon-B gas poisoning, but from surreptitious euthanasia. Many will complain that equating the Holocaust with giving a patient "aid in dying" is inaccurate, even misleading. They will argue that the Nazis were motivated by racism and hatred, while those who practice euthanasia today are motivated out of humanitarianism. I disagree.

While we must be careful not to make facile analogies to the Holocaust, there are ominous parallels between the practice of euthanasia under the Third Reich and the euthanasia movement in the U.S. The process that so corrupts physician attitudes that they embrace the practice of euthanasia as morally acceptable within the larger practice of medicine is similar to that which infected German physicians even before the Holocaust.

LESSONS FROM AUSCHWITZ: EUTHANASIA'S SMALL BEGINNINGS

Leo Alexander, the chief psychiatric consultant to the Allies during the Nuremberg War Crimes Tribunal following World War II, conducted an extensive study of the German medical community's participation in the Holocaust. In a 1949 article published in the *New England Journal of Medicine* entitled "Medicine Under Dictatorship," Alexander wrote:

> Whatever proportions these crimes finally assumed, it became evident to all who investigated them that they had started from small beginnings. The beginnings at first were merely a subtle shift in emphasis in the basic attitude of physicians. It started with the acceptance of the attitude, basic to the euthanasia movement, that there is such a thing as life not worthy to be lived. This attitude in its early stages concerned itself merely with the severely and chronically sick. Gradually the sphere of those to be included in this category was enlarged to encompass the socially unproductive, the ideologically unwanted, the racially unwanted and finally all non-Germans. But it is important to realize that the infinitely small wedged-in lever from which this entire trend of mind received its impetus was the attitude toward the non-rehabilitable sick.[1]

It might be argued that the passions of World War II influenced Alexander's views about the participation of the German medical community in the Nazi scheme. But Robert J. Lifton, writing more than four decades later in his masterful work *The Nazi Doctors,* draws the same conclusion as Alexander, detailing how the notion of a "life unworthy of life" (*Lebensunwertes Leben*) corrupted physician respect for human life across the board, even before the Holocaust began. The belief in *Lebensunwertes Leben* was held by many German physicians long before Hitler's rise to power. Writes Lifton:

> Of the five identifiable steps by which the Nazis carried out the principle of "life unworthy of life," coercive sterilization was the first. There followed the killing of "impaired" children in hospitals; and then the killing of "impaired" adults, mostly collected from mental hospitals, in centers especially equipped with carbon monoxide gas. This project was extended to "impaired" inmates of concentration and extermination camps and, finally, to mass killings, mostly the Jews, in the extermination camps themselves.[2]

Lifton also details how the Reich leaders insisted on physicians "selecting" the individuals to receive "special treatments," operating the gas chambers, performing the postmortem examinations, falsifying the death certificates to resemble natural causes, and in many other ways conspiring with the Reich to maintain a medical facade for genocide. This did not happen overnight. The genesis of Nazi genocide began in the attitudes of individual German physicians who succumbed to the nefarious notion that some lives are not worth living.

Who taught them this? What aspects of German society led to this mind-set among the doctors? The seeds that would give rise to the Holocaust were sown with the passage of laws such as the Law for the Prevention of the Congenitally Ill Progeny on July 14, 1933. This law authorized the involuntary sterilization of those considered harmful to the nation's "racial health." "Hereditary health courts" enforced laws such as this. Medical personnel, especially medical students, were trained in *rassenhygiene*—race hygiene.[3]

Israeli film director Nitzan Aviram produced a Holocaust documentary entitled *Healing by Killing*, which made its debut at the New York Film Forum in April 1998. It is a documentary about the role physicians played in Hitler's "Final Solution." Aviram's focus is not so much on the Holocaust itself, but on its first victims—the mentally and physically disabled—and how leading German psychiatrists and others laid the theoretical groundwork for genocide before anyone had heard of Hitler.

When asked why he made such a film he answered, "When I was growing up I heard stories about the Holocaust and I couldn't understand why there were so many doctors in places where people were getting killed. But the presence of a doctor was undeniable, like on the selection ramp, where physicians made instantaneous 'diagnoses' of who should go directly to the gas."[4]

Aviram tracks the beginnings of euthanasia to the health and fitness craze among Germans early in the twentieth century. Germans came to despise sickness, disease, and disability. He documents how during the Weimar era, German doctors carried out sterilizations and "mercy killings" of the mentally and physically disabled, genuinely believing that they were doing what was best for the individuals and society.[5]

In the film, a former Auschwitz doctor, Hans Munch, looks directly into the camera to tell precisely how he certified that the gassed corpses were really dead. Later, he ruefully admits, "Auschwitz was a medical operation." The film traces the career of Irmfried Eberl, who ran the first medical killing center, and played a central role in expanding the euthanasia campaign, which slaughtered between 70,000 and 100,000 disabled people before turning to the Jews, using Eberl's methods.

The film also examines attitudes among Germany's current medical students. In one scene, a student is asked if ethics should be taught in medical school. "I don't think so," he replies. "We already have so many subjects to study." Aviram is currently touring U.S. medical schools, and he says American medical students laugh and identify with that part. Perhaps the most chilling aspect of Aviram's film is how much of Jack Kevorkian's rhetoric is similar to that used by pre-Hitler physicians.

The president of the New York Academy of Medicine, Jeremiah Barondess, notes that there already exist troubling attitudes among physicians toward certain types of patients. In U.S. emergency rooms, blacks with bone fractures are much less likely to receive pain medication than whites. "Do Not Resuscitate" orders are more common for blacks, women, and people who are incontinent.

Maria Matzik uses a ventilator to breathe. She works with the Access Center for Independent Living in Dayton, Ohio. She tells of her battles with nurses during a 1993 hospital stay. "The nurses kept asking me to sign a 'do not resuscitate' order. They said that meant nothing drastic would be done if I had a cardiac arrest. When I said I wouldn't sign the DNR order, they said it didn't matter. Since I use a ventilator, nothing would be done if I had a cardiac arrest."[6]

Perhaps the late novelist Walker Percy, who was also a medical doctor, said it best. Although he did not argue that America's friend-liness to abortion and euthanasia means the nation is on the verge of becoming another Nazi Germany, he said that "once the line is crossed, once the principle [of lives not worthy to be lived] gains ac-ceptance—judicially, medically, socially—innocent human life can be destroyed for whatever reason, for the most admirable socioeco-nomic, medical or social reasons—then it does not take a prophet to predict what will happen next, or if not next, then sooner or later. At any rate, a warning is in order."[7]

DOCTORS MUST NOT KILL

From the time of Hippocrates, codes of professional medical ethics have prohibited killing by physicians, even when undertaken for presumably merciful reasons. These codes express three essential beliefs concerning physicians. First, the moral arguments that could be made to permit physicians to kill certain patients are logically in-adequate. Second, killing by physicians perverts the healing relation-ship and distorts the concept of what constitutes a treatment (death is not a medical treatment), and third, the enormous social conse-quences attached to killing by physicians is morally prohibitive.[8]

LEGALIZING PHYSICIAN-ASSISTED SUICIDE IRREVOCABLY UNDERMINES THE DOCTOR-PATIENT RELATIONSHIP.

The current status of medical practice notwithstanding, physi-cians have been among the most trusted professionals for centuries. This has been particularly true at the end of life. The physician is considered to be a central figure in managing the dying process, alle-viating pain, and making patients as comfortable as possible. Trust is essential between a physician and a patient because the doctor-pa-tient relationship is, for the most part, an unbalanced one, with the physician wielding far more power than the patient. Daniel Calla-han and Margot White observe:

The general prestige [of physicians] as professionals whose training and experience are widely thought to enable them to understand matters of life and death better than the rest of us, and their capacity to give or withhold lethal drugs, already establish the power differential between them and their patients. . . . The fact that most of Dr. Kevorkian's patients . . . were perfectly capable physically of committing suicide by themselves, including most obviously the one physician he helped die, suggests that the desire to medicalize PAS [physician-assisted suicide] already bespeaks the power and legitimation conferred by medical approval of it.[9]

Legalizing physician-assisted suicide irrevocably undermines the doctor-patient relationship. It does not and cannot strengthen it. Protecting human life has been viewed as the central purpose of medicine. Social sanctioning of physician-assisted suicide dismantles this tradition, giving physicians greater power over patients and undermining society's ability to protect them. Despite the fact that initially it will be patients directly requesting that physicians assist them with a lethal prescription, it defies all that is rational to think that relations with patients who do not request a lethal prescription will not be affected. Can physicians kill patients upon request and return unaffected to the care of patients whose conditions are similar, but who choose not to die? How will the cancer patient who desires to live as long as possible view the physician who returns from a conference on the latest euthanasia techniques? A recent survey of cancer patients revealed that a majority would not only lose trust in their physician if he or she raised the issue of assisted suicide with them, but they would also change doctors if they learned he or she had helped another patient die.[10]

The concept of physician-assisted suicide as an appropriate treatment option for dying patients depends substantially on what one considers to be the purpose of medicine. Daniel Callahan states, "I would note at the very outset that a physician who participates in another person's suicide already abuses medicine. Are we to 'medicalize' suicide, turning judgments about its value and worth into one more clinical issue?"[11] Callahan raises an important point. Are doctors now to be given the moral authority to make judgments about the kinds of life worth living and to withhold their blessing from those deemed to fall below the threshold? What competencies will doctors claim for themselves in order to play such a role?

Within a biblical worldview, the root cause of illness and mortality is theological, not medical. Sickness, disease, and death have both theological and biological components. If the question relates to the physiological causes of illness and physical death, then medicine, as a scientific discipline, has a proper role. However, when we consider death within the general context of the meaning of life, we have moved beyond the limited scope of medicine.

Doctors as doctors have no conceivable way of evaluating the value and meaning of life for a particular patient exclusively within the confines of science and medicine. Callahan says, "It is not medicine's place to lift from us the burden of that suffering which turns on the meaning we assign to the decay of the body and its eventual death. It is not medicine's place to determine when lives are not worth living or when the burden of life is too great to be borne."[12]

Historically, modern science and technology have their roots in a distinctly Christian worldview.[13] The assumption that the world has a rational, intelligible order is rooted in the biblical doctrine of God and creation. The assumption of modern science that human beings can discover order because they are rational beings is also rooted in a biblical worldview.[14]

Kevorkian asserts that medical judgments should be based on "common sense," not "revelation," but he does not address the question of what counts as common sense, nor does he give any rational account for rejecting revelation out of hand. For that matter, Kevorkian does not give any rational account of how he or anyone else is to arrive at a moral judgment, or what counts as knowledge. How will we know when our actions are in accord with common sense—when they correspond with what he deems appropriate?

According to Kevorkian, religious restraints have been imposed on medicine from the outside. He fails to comprehend that religion influences the rational and ethical basis for medicine because it shapes the person who practices it. He does not grasp that most people's "common sense" leads them to believe there is a connection between their belief in God and how the world is, how the human body works, and the motivation people have for providing a high quality of medical care. Kevorkian is stacking the debate toward his own viewpoint by insisting that even those who believe in God should practice medicine without factoring in God and ultimate truth.

The Judeo-Christian foundation of medicine in the U.S. is the principal reason our medical care is the envy of the world. It is not only the sophistication of our medical technology that attracts the rest of the world, but the manner in which those technologies are delivered to patients. Quality medical care requires much more than good equipment and well-trained practitioners. There is the human side of medical care—the bedside manner—that contributes to this. The quality of medical care improves whenever "paganized medicine" is replaced by medical practice rooted in a Judeo-Christian ethic. The practice of medicine flourished and gained respectability when physicians came to be seen as healers exclusively, when spiritual care was taken to be a standard part of good medical care.

REGARDLESS OF THE EUPHEMISMS USED TO MASK ITS REALITY, ASSISTED SUICIDE INVOLVES KILLING HUMAN BEINGS.

Christianity has had a major influence upon the development and proliferation of medical care throughout the world. Countless hospitals and other facilities have been established by Christians, driven largely by the belief that human beings are created in God's image and are worthy of being treated with respect. The Judeo-Christian ethic is grounded mainly in a supernatural view of the world, which believes that there is a direct relationship between human beings and their Creator.

PHYSICIAN ATTITUDES TOWARD ASSISTED SUICIDE AND EUTHANASIA

Regardless of the euphemisms used to mask its reality, assisted suicide involves killing human beings. How do physicians feel about this? The answer takes us to the heart of what physicians believe is the purpose of medicine.

Recent surveys of physicians' attitudes toward assisted suicide and euthanasia reveal a disturbing trend. There is a subtle but perceptible shift in the direction of accepting the notion that giving "aid in dying" to patients is morally appropriate medical care. A 1997 survey of physicians that was reported in the *New England Journal of Medicine* indicates that a substantial proportion of physicians in the United States receive requests for physician-assisted suicide and euthanasia, and a disturbing number of them have complied.[15] Sixteen percent of the respondents reported that they had written at least one prescription to be used to hasten death, and nearly 5 percent said they had administered a lethal injection.

It is enlightening to consider the attitudes of physicians toward assisted suicide and euthanasia in a state where active efforts have been taken to legalize the practice. In 1994, voters in the state of Washington narrowly rejected a ballot initiative to legalize physician-assisted suicide. Prior to the vote, a statewide survey of Washington physicians revealed 53 percent believed assisted suicide should be legal in some instances, and 40 percent would be willing to provide assistance if asked. Interestingly, hematologists and oncologists were most likely to oppose assisted suicide and euthanasia, while psychiatrists were most likely to support the practice.[16]

A troubling study published in the *Journal of the American Medical Association* revealed that those doctors who helped patients end their lives frequently fail to consult other physicians and sometimes do not even involve the patient in the decision. In 15.3 percent of the cases reported, the patients were not involved in the decision. Rather, families had asked the physician to end the life of the patient.[17]

THE ROLE OF THE PHYSICIAN
IN RELIEVING PAIN AND SUFFERING

Those who wish to make physician-assisted suicide legal commonly speak of "pain and suffering" in the same sentence, which suggests that the two are synonyms or that they always occur together. In reality, one is a cause (pain) and the other a result (suffering). Pain may cause suffering, but it is not identical to suffering. Pain ordinarily refers to a highly distressful, undesirable sensation or experience ordinarily associated with a physical cause.[18]

Suffering ordinarily refers to a person's psychological or spiritual state, and it is characteristically marked by a sense of anguish, dread, foreboding, futility, meaninglessness, or a range of other emotions associated with the loss of meaning, control, or both. Not all pain results in suffering, nor is all suffering attended by severe physical pain.[19]

Scripture calls upon believers to bear one another's burdens (Galatians 6:2). Life in a fallen world is filled with burdens, pain and suffering among them. Some of the worst sufferings an individual can experience are those times when intense physical pain drives us to wish for its end at nearly any cost. Such pain threatens us by its intensity and its longevity. Most people cannot bear to watch others suffer in this way.

As a pastor, I visited many people in the throes of incredible pain. One individual lay dying from bone cancer, perhaps the most painful form of cancer. It was not possible to touch a single hair on his arm without inflicting enormous pain. Increased dosages of painkilling medication did not seem to help much. He died after a lengthy and painful period lasting several months. Unfortunately, his dying occurred at a time when little was known about hospice and palliative care. I suspect his experience would have been entirely different today using current pain therapies.

There are times when we can do little more than suffer *with* someone, when all we can offer is a comforting presence that assures we will go through the valley of the shadow of death with him. Such valleys are brutal reminders that this earth is not our home, that life in this earthly body is transient and temporary and especially vulnerable. In these valleys people need to be reminded that God is still good. But in the midst of intense pain, amid great suffering, there is a strong temptation to question God's goodness. People who are suffering want to scream out, "Does God know what He is doing?" More often than not, it takes a sizable decision of faith to discipline the emotions and hold fast to the belief that He does.

Many are willing to put greater trust in physicians than in God, especially when God seems to fail them. However, physicians are not as knowledgeable about caring for people at the end of life as many believe. Relatively few physicians have received special training in pain management. A recent report from the U.S. Department of Health and Human Service's Agency for Health Care Policy and Research stated, "Pain control in people with cancer remains a significant problem in health care even though cancer pain can be managed effectively in up to 90 percent of patients. Recognition of the widespread undertreatment of cancer pain has prompted recent corrective efforts from health care disciplines, professional and consumer organizations."[20]

The report cited several reasons for this discrepancy in physician practice, including inadequate training of physicians in pain management. If physicians are not well-trained in pain management, what makes us believe they can effectively supply a lethal prescription that will guarantee a "good" death?

Mark Stucky, an anesthesiologist and pain management specialist at the University of Minnesota School of Medicine, expresses alarm at

Kevorkian's proposal that physician-assisted suicide be carried out by those most familiar with the procedure of induced coma. Part of his alarm stems from the fact that it is anesthesiologists who have this expertise. "If physician-assisted suicide is legalized I will look for another line of work," says Stucky.[21]

Like the moon, there is a dark side to modern medical technology because it can leave some patients worse off, not better. Although the vital organs of the body continue to function vigorously, the personality known to family and friends is no longer exhibited. This is a fate virtually everyone fears. This patient has become the symbol of our failed technological efforts to control the life continuum. Such patients are convenient, gut-wrenching symbols for euthanasia advocates. If society is to successfully resist the temptation to solve this patient's dilemma by appropriating death as a "cure," we will have to make some hard decisions about the current expansion of life-extending technology. We will need to openly discuss whether pain and suffering are the only experiences we should take into account when we consider medical treatment at the end of life.

It is important to note that the patients Kevorkian and Derek Humphry believe would "benefit" from assisted suicide are not the unconscious, incompetent "vegetables," but the conscious patient who is not imminently dying and who fears experiencing an unacceptable quality of life. The physical suffering is not so much at issue as is the emotional, psychic suffering brought about by disability and dependence upon others.

Yet are a person's dignity and value dependent upon the quality of life? Is killing a valid function of true compassion and mercy? These virtues of compassion and mercy are best illustrated by the life of the Lord Jesus Christ. He personifies love, yet He was also the One who sweated drops of blood in the Garden of Gethsemane. He was the One who endured the beatings of Roman soldiers, the assaults of the Jewish mobs, and, ultimately, the enormous pain and indignity of crucifixion. Clearly, God's view of mercy and compassion allows for the presence of pain and suffering. Suffering need not rob people of the intrinsic dignity they possess as divine-image bearers.

In the midst of His suffering and in anticipation of His death, Jesus cried out to God, "My God, my God, why have you forsaken me?" (Matthew 27:46 NIV). In the Garden, He prayed, "Father, if thou be willing, remove this cup from me: nevertheless not my will, but thine, be done" (Luke 22:42). In both instances the heavens were like brass. His suffering continued until His death. Yet, from this suffering has come all of the hope that resides in the hearts of Christians. The problem of evil is resolved by the death of Christ. Out of His death, burial, and resurrection have come every victory we will ever experience over death. One need only read 1 Corinthians 15 or 2 Corinthians 5:1–10 to understand the significance of these events.

WHO DECIDES?

Death is not a blessing to be sought to avoid the dying process itself. They go together. Joys, doubts, fears, pain, and tender memories combine in one's final days. Nobody should know that better than those who work with dying people, which includes doctors. Nothing is more menacing to a society than the participation of physicians in ending the lives of patients, whether by knowingly providing the means of death or by engaging in direct acts of killing. No matter how technological or commercial the modern physician may have become, he or she is still supposed to be a healer. When the physician crosses the line from healing to killing, he abandons a tradition that all civilized cultures revere and depend on for the protection of the vulnerable.

Despite the claim that assisted suicide is grounded in patient autonomy, that it should be the patient's choice alone, there is compelling evidence from the practice of Dutch physicians that doctors retain the preeminent position in the delicate balance of power between doctor and patient. Doctors decide who "qualifies." Doctors control the lethal prescriptions. In both the Oregon and Michigan legislation, family members need not be notified of a loved one's intent to obtain a lethal prescription from a physician. The doctor alone retains the power to decide whether to provide assistance. A physician can recommend it, refuse it, or even dismiss a patient's ambivalence and help him make a decision.

Herbert Hendin illustrates this from a conversation with Professor Joost Schudel, chairman of the Royal Dutch Medical Association's (KNMG) subcommittee on medical decisions at the end of life.

Who should decide whether a patient who cannot speak for himself should live or die? Professor Schudel . . . declared unambiguously, "The doctor decides." Professor Schudel explained that the cardinal principle that a doctor should follow with such patients is to ask himself if he would accept life if he were in the patient's position. I asked if the relatives of such a patient could decide they wished the patient to be kept alive and Schudel repeated "no, the doctor decides." . . . To bring the conversation down to earth, I asked Schudel about my mother, who was then ninety-two. She was unable to communicate intelligibly, but was in relatively good health and in no evident physical or emotional distress. I told him that since my mother had never given me instructions that she would not want to live in such a situation, I felt some responsibility for her well-being. I had read that in the Netherlands and under KNMG guidelines, doctors would not treat demented patients for infectious diseases. A leading Dutch advocate of euthanasia frequently cites the remark "pneumonia is an old person's best friend." Schudel did not answer directly at first, but told me that KNMG policies do not include operating on demented people. . . . He seemed reluctant, at first, perhaps out of consideration for my feelings, to state what Dutch policy would be in treating pneumonia in a person like my mother. . . . Finally he said that such patients would be given symptomatic relief for difficulties in breathing, but the underlying infection would not be treated, since one had to ask what quality of life the patient would be returned to. . . . I thought, but did not say that it sounded as though pneumonia provided an excuse to get rid of someone who doctors decided did not have a life of sufficient quality to preserve.[22]

No matter how one tries to argue differently, the doctor remains the person most in control of the situation at the end of life. He or she is the one who maintains the most power, including the power to impose strong paternalism on patients. In the Netherlands, between the time records started being kept and 1991, 25,000 deaths by lethal injection or lethal medication involved patients who had not been consulted, and in 20,000 of those cases doctors cited the patient's impaired ability to communicate as justification for not seeking explicit consent.[23] Disturbingly, there is evidence of this same practice among U.S. physicians who admit assisting in the deaths of patients.[24] If doctors will euthanize patients without their consent when the practice is technically illegal even with consent, what might they do when it is both legal and socially supported?

If physician-assisted suicide is legalized, who will protect patients from the kind of nonvoluntary death that apparently occurs in the Netherlands? If these acts are private ones between a patient and physician, who other than the doctor will really know the facts once the patient is dead? Hendin is correct when he says:

In practice, it is still the doctor who decides whether to perform euthanasia. He can suggest it, not give patients obvious alternatives, ignore patients' ambivalence, and even put to death patients who have not requested it. Euthanasia enhances the power and control of doctors, not patients. If the Dutch experience teaches us anything it is that euthanasia brings out the worst rather than the best in medicine. In the name of an illusory and self-righteous compassion for the patient, the decisive role of the physician's needs and values in the decision for euthanasia remains concealed.[25]

NOTES

1. Leo Alexander, "Medical Science Under Dictatorship," *New England Journal of Medicine* 241 (1949): 39–47.

2. Robert J. Lifton, *The Nazi Doctors: Medical Killing and the Psychology of Genocide* (New York: Basic Books, 1986), 1.

3. Tom Neven, "It Can't Happen Here—Or Can It?" *Physician,* May/June, 1998: 21.

4. Mark Schoofs, "First, Do Harm: How Doctors Set the Stage for the Holocaust," *Village Voice,* 15 April 1998.

5. "From Auschwitz to Kevorkian," *New York Post,* 27 April 1998.

6. Kathi Wolfe, "Disabled Activists Fight Assisted Suicide," *The Progressive,* September 1996, 16.

7. Nigel Cameron, *The New Medicine: Life and Death After Hippocrates* (Wheaton, Ill.: Crossway, 1992).

8. Edmund D. Pellegrino, "Doctors Must Not Kill," *Journal of Clinical Ethics* (Vol. 3, No. 2, Summer 1992): 95.

9. Daniel Callahan and Margot White, "The Legalization of Physician-Assisted Suicide: Creating a Potemkin Village," in Michael M. Uhlmann, ed. *Last Rights: Assisted Suicide and Euthanasia Debated* (Grand Rapids: Eerdmans, 1998), 577.

10. "Attitudes Toward Euthanasia Sharply Divide, Survey Finds," *Reuters,* 29 June 1996.

11. Daniel Callahan, "When Autonomy Runs Amok," *Hastings Center Report* 22 (March/April 1992): 55.

12. Ibid., 54.

13. For an extended discussion of this, see Nancy R. Pearcy and Charles B. Thaxton, *The Soul of Science: Christian Faith and Natural Philosophy* (Wheaton, Ill.: Crossway, 1994), chapter 1.

14. Nancy R. Pearcy, "Technology, History, and Worldview," in John F. Kilner and Frank E. Young, *Genetic Ethics: Do the Ends Justify the Genes?* (Grand Rapids: Eerdmans, 1997), 41.

15. Diane E. Meier, Carol-Ann Emmons, et al., "A National Survey of Physician-Assisted Suicide and Euthanasia in the United States," *New England Journal of Medicine* Vol. 338, No. 17, 23 April 1998.

16. Jonathan S. Cohen, Stephan D. Fihn, et al., "Attitudes Toward Assisted Suicide and Euthanasia Among Physicians in Washington State," *New England Journal of Medicine* Vol. 331, No. 2, 14 July 1994.

17. *Journal of the American Medical Association,* 12 August 1998.

18. Eric J. Cassell, *The Nature of Suffering and the Goals of Medicine* (New York: Oxford Univ. Press, 1991), 34–37; see also David B. Morris, *The Culture of Pain* (Berkeley: Univ. of California Press, 1991).

19. Daniel Callahan, *The Troubled Dream of Life* (New York: Simon & Schuster, 1993), 95.

20. U.S. Department of Health and Human Services, *Management of Cancer Pain: Clinical Practice Guideline No. 9,* Public Health Service, Agency for Health Care Policy and Research, March 1994, 1.

21. Personal conversation with Mark Stucky, April 1995.

22. Herbert Hendin, *Seduced by Death: Doctors, Patients and the Dutch Cure* (New York: Norton, 1997), 80.

23. P. J. van der Maas, J. J. M. van Delden, and L. Pijnenborg, *Euthanasia and Other Medical Decisions Concerning End of Life* (New York: Elsevier, 1992), 134, cited in Hendin, *Seduced by Death,* 76.

24. *Journal of the American Medical Association,* August 1998.

25. Hendin, *Seduced by Death,* 214.

CHAPTER 10

MEDICAL ISSUES
AT THE
END OF LIFE:

Hard Questions
on Euthanasia and
Medical Futility

It is important to address some of the central medical issues related to the end of life. They are significant factors in shaping our perceptions about the quality of life a person experiences, whether physicians and other caregivers believe continued medical intervention is beneficial or morally obligatory, and what sorts of nonmedical assessments and assistance may be brought to bear on the needs of a seriously ill individual.

ARTIFICIAL LIFE SUPPORT/
HEROIC MEDICAL TREATMENT

Over the past three decades, medical research has given us exceptional abilities to intervene in helping people avoid death a little longer. Numerous methods are used every day, and they no longer seem remarkable to us: Pacemakers are routinely used to maintain a steady heartbeat, kidney dialysis is routine for those experiencing kidney disease and/or failure, and ventilators are commonly employed for individuals in need of breathing assistance. Feeding tubes can be inserted to provide nutrition and fluids to those unable to receive them by mouth.

However, there are situations when these technologies do not work as well as we hope, when they succeed at maintaining physical functions but not mental ones. People know that machines have limitations. Yet they appear to harbor unrealistic expectations about what medical therapies and machines can do. People who have a loved one dying of an incurable disease hope for a miracle, expecting that machines will keep the person alive long enough for a cure to be found. Consequently, some find themselves facing tough decisions about the use of technology to extend life. They are confronted with the dual evils of the modern age: being undertreated and thereby dying prematurely, or being overtreated and living under daunting and unwelcome circumstances. I suspect people fear the latter far more than they fear the former, probably because we are more likely to have that be our actual experience.

It is common to hear people say that under certain circumstances they would not want to be kept alive by "artificial medical treatment" or "artificial life support." What exactly do these terms mean? Is artificial medical treatment the opposite of natural medical treatment? Is any medical therapy truly "natural," or are they all man-made? I am not trying to be facetious, nor am I trying to undermine the legitimate concerns people express. I am interested in helping people come to a better understanding of what lies behind the terminology they use.

THE IDEA THAT MEDICAL EQUIPMENT
CAN KEEP A DEAD PERSON
ALIVE INDEFINITELY IS FICTIONAL.

Similar questions can be asked concerning supposedly "heroic" or "extraordinary" medical treatment. What counts as "heroic" or "extraordinary" medical treatment? Is the opposite of it "nonheroic," "ordinary" treatment? Even textbooks on medical ethics use such terminology, as do most advance directives in use today. Rather than clarifying things for us, these terms tend to confuse them.

Most people apply these terms to medical equipment such as ventilators, kidney dialysis machines, and heart-lung pumps, or techniques like cardiopulmonary resuscitation, defibrillation, etc. However, the use of these tools is quite normal or "ordinary" in most circumstances. Ventilators do nothing more than "breathe" for people who cannot breathe on their own. This is normal, ordinary use for a ventilator. We don't use ventilators with people who can breathe adequately without them.

A ventilator may be used in an intensive care setting where the patient is recovering from major surgery, a serious injury, or respiratory paralysis caused by a spinal virus or injury. Regardless of the circumstances, the basic nature and function of the ventilator remains the same—it pushes air into the patient's lungs. Likewise, a kidney dialysis machine cleanses blood, and a defibrillation machine shocks the heart back into a regular rhythm. There is nothing about the function of a particular medical machine that makes it heroic or extraordinary. It is *circumstances* that lend themselves to the label "extraordinary" or "heroic" because circumstances can change, whereas the nature and purpose of medical equipment does not.

If ventilators are neither ordinary nor extraordinary, are individuals morally obligated to use them? Certainly no one is morally obligated to use a ventilator just because it exists. The invention of a new technology does not make use of that technology morally mandatory. At the same time, there are many situations in which ventilators come in handy, such as during or after routine surgery. Generally speaking, people should be careful about making an unqualified statement such as "I never want to be hooked up to a ventilator." It is not the equipment that is morally special, but the circumstances wherein one may find himself or herself.

Perhaps it is better to describe situations governing the use of life support as beneficial versus burdensome medical treatment. Decisions about withdrawing or withholding medical treatment should be based on the overall physical condition of the patient, the probability of the treatment's contributing to his recovery or comfort, and the patient's life expectancy, not on the nature of the medical equipment available. Medical treatments are removed from patients all the time if they don't work or they produce side effects that are worse than what is being treated. If a certain course of medical treatment does not produce the intended results, there should be no moral dilemma over its withdrawal. If there is little expectation of direct benefit to the patient from a given medical procedure, one ought not expect doctors to perform it.

The idea that medical equipment can keep a dead person alive indefinitely is fictional. Life depends on the spontaneous, integrated function of key organ systems. No one survives for long without sufficient oxygen flow into the bloodstream. (This is why it is crucial to remove organs as quickly as possible for organ donation.) Thus, a ventilator may perform its function by getting oxygen into the lungs, but if the lungs no longer transfer oxygen into the bloodstream, the heart and other tissues of the body will begin to deteriorate.

Physicians have available to them various tests to determine how well the lungs are functioning and whether they are functioning sufficiently to sustain the major organ systems. When they are not working well, and the ventilator is no longer benefiting the patient, there is no reason to agonize over withdrawing the ventilator. If the lung malfunction is due to a lethal underlying condition that will take the patient's life whether a ventilator is used or not, withdrawing the ventilator is not what ends the patient's life. Rather, the patient dies from his or her underlying condition.

Likewise, if in the best available medical judgment a particular therapy is not expected to provide physiological benefit to a terminally ill patient for more than a few days, there is no moral obligation on the physician to recommend it, nor on the patient to accept it.[1]

This is not to say that doctors are justified in ignoring requests by patients or families to provide seemingly futile, burdensome therapies. Sometimes treatments such as ventilators, chemotherapy, or a feeding tube extend life long enough for a distant loved one to travel to the dying patient's bedside, or they comfort the family by ensuring they did everything possible for their loved one. Using such treatments, though futile, can have a beneficial, nontherapeutic effect by psychologically helping families as they go through the period of bereavement after the patient dies. Using medical technologies to accomplish these ends can be morally appropriate, though not morally obligatory.

Prior to his death from cancer, the late Christian philosopher/ theologian Francis Schaeffer asked his doctors to cease chemotherapy and treat him with steroids in order to give him the strength to conduct a speaking tour with his son, Frank. Although the steroids provided no curative benefit, they allowed Schaeffer to accomplish what he desired.[2] Some patients choose surgery to remove a tumor as a means of improving pain control, knowing that it will not cure them.

Some might argue that to continue nonbeneficial medical treatment is poor stewardship of resources, that the moneys spent to accomplish these ends could be better spent elsewhere. However, there are good ends to be achieved other than accountants balancing their spreadsheets. A compassionate and caring society, particularly one as affluent as America, should accept that providing a good quality of care at the end of life may involve the expenditure of financial and medical resources that might otherwise be used someplace else, but this is a small price to pay. A society that supports speculative space programs, interesting but virtually useless scientific experiments, experimental educational programs, and expensive congressional pensions should have little complaint over providing medical care of dubious physiological benefit.

WITHDRAWAL AND WITHHOLDING OF TREATMENT

Some have come to the morally confusing conclusion that withdrawing or withholding medical treatment from a dying patient is tantamount to euthanasia. They consider it immoral to refrain from using whatever technologies are available to prevent death, and they deem it equally immoral to withdraw a treatment once it has been started. According to this line of thinking, nearly every instance of withholding or withdrawing medical treatment that results in death is an act of euthanasia.

This type of thinking reflects confusion about the nature of medical intervention, the moral status of medical technologies, and the realities of human mortality. It makes no distinction between killing and allowing death; no distinction between taking action with the intent of causing death and refraining from taking action to allow an unavoidable death to occur—letting nature take its course.[3]

IS THERE A DIFFERENCE BETWEEN
KILLING A PERSON AND ALLOWING
DEATH TO OCCUR? YES.

In most cases, people are clearly in the process of dying before doctors begin talking with patients or families about foregoing medical treatment. An exception to this are those patients who experience catastrophic injuries or illnesses that are life-threatening. Even here, however, the person's condition must be quite serious before a discussion ensues concerning treatment versus nontreatment. There are life-threatening circumstances present or anticipated when these discussions occur. The patient who has just been told by his physician that a primary cancer has spread to other parts of his body may consider whether or not to proceed with additional chemotherapy regimens. Parents of a newborn with a severely herniated diaphragm, a condition that usually prevents the lungs from fully developing, may decide against surgery. In either case, the decision to forego further medical treatment (treatment that in itself is ordinary) and permit nature to takes its course is quite different from euthanasia since the condition that will inevitably cause death already exists.

Must all effort be made to extend a human being's life for whatever length of time? No. Is there a difference between killing a person and allowing death to occur? Yes. Few disagree with the idea that medical treatment should cease when it becomes futile. No one really thinks doctors are required to attempt aggressive cures on a person who is dying and cannot possibly benefit from the treatment. But how should futility be measured? How do doctors know when a medical treatment is futile?

While making a precise judgment about the futility of a specific medical treatment remains difficult, it is generally accepted that curative medical treatment may be stopped when doctors can no longer halt (for more than a few days or weeks) a downward, deteriorating course they fully expect to result in death. Care for the patient at this point should be redirected toward symptom relief and comfort care. Comfort care may include surgeries or medications whose aim is to reduce pain or alleviate other disease symptoms. This type of care is known as palliative care.

Thus, we may find ourselves providing medical treatment to a terminally ill patient with the goal of making him or her more comfortable, without any illusion of curing the person. A decision to forego life-extending and life-sustaining medical treatment does not automatically mean a decision has been made to forego all medical treatment. This is the basic nature of hospice care.

There seem to be two extremes represented in modern medicine. At one end of the spectrum is aggressive medical intervention with little or no consideration of the financial or familial costs. At the other end is the complete abandonment of the patient. It seems we either want to deploy our complete arsenal of medical expertise and technology in the war against death, or nothing at all. Such an either/or approach is hard on patients, families, and caregivers.

Daniel Callahan points out one persistent illusion embraced by society is that, aided by the right laws and medical practices, we'll be able to recognize the exact, appropriate moment to halt medical intervention, allowing death to occur.[4] However, clinical experience does not offer such precision. In most cases doctors and nurses manage the process of dying quite well, but in others they do not. There can be a number of reasons why dying is not managed well in some instances, but the lack of caring is not usually one of them. Doctors and nurses care deeply about their patients, with rare exceptions. Some of the failures can be attributed to inadequate training in palliative care, personal biases concerning death and dying, notions of quality of life projected onto the patient, etc.

Killing Versus "Letting Die"

Many people equate the failure to use all available technology to extend the life of a dying patient with murder. In other words, if we can intervene, then we must by all means do so. This suggests that we should apply the same sense of moral obligation to medical technologies that we apply to human beings. Under this framework, technologies kill just as people do.[5] But this is silly. Technologies can't do anything by themselves. They are useless until people use them.

Attaching a sense of moral obligation to medical technologies is wrongheaded and fraught with hazard because we are always developing new ones. There will always be one more treatment to try, one more surgery, one more round of experimental chemotherapy. The result is often longer lives lived by sicker people. Some families will bankrupt themselves to pay for futile medical treatments, perhaps because they believe this is what is expected of them, or to avoid feeling guilty for not doing more after their loved one dies. Families should talk about these matters before faced with a real-life situation.

Cheryl and Bob were preparing for the Christmas holiday when Cheryl experienced pain in her groin. A quick visit to her doctor turned into immediate hospitalization, where she was diagnosed with a fast-growing cervical cancer that had already spread to her kidneys and liver. Through a mutual friend, I was called to visit them in Cheryl's hospital room to discuss how hard they should fight the cancer. During my visit with them, it became apparent that they believed the only "Christian" option was to fight the cancer tooth and nail—spending themselves into bankruptcy if necessary. After a lengthy discussion about the sanctity of human life and how this principle should be applied in their situation, Cheryl decided to forego any aggressive medical treatment and accept a palliative care approach. I urged them to consider contacting a local hospice organization to coordinate her care and to provide help for Bob. They later agreed to this approach. Cheryl died just three weeks later. However, the family's finances were spared an unnecessary ransacking.

If it is true that the failure to use all available technology is tantamount to killing a person, then it is not the disease that killed the person, but us. It is as though death can be rejected outright, as though nature has been subdued and there remains no room for natural causes of death. Every death that is not sudden, or too distant from the hospital, becomes a preventable contingency. If failing to use all existing technologies to resist death is the same as killing someone, then the failure to invent more lifesaving technologies also kills. Such thinking binds us to a limitless technological search for immortality. It also puts technology in the place of God. There is no logical place to stop.

If we are morally obligated to use every technological means possible, we will not know when to cease attempts to extend life. There can be no difference between killing and letting someone die a natural death.[6] The fact that death has not been completely conquered can only be viewed as a defeat and a motivation for the development of more technology whose aim is the extension of life. Every death must be seen as a human failure. Leland Kaiser, a medical futurist, says, "By the year 2500, death will be a voluntary event."[7]

If one accepts that withdrawing medical treatment from a dying person (e.g., a person dying from metastatic cancer) is euthanasia, then one would also have to accept the conclusion that the physician who ceases cardiopulmonary resuscitation (CPR) on a patient in cardiac arrest is engaging in euthanasia. If the failure to always perform CPR "hastens death" and is morally blameworthy (not to mention legally culpable) behavior, patients who refuse CPR are committing suicide. The doctors who write "Do Not Resuscitate" orders are guilty of assisting suicides.

Professor George Annas is correct on this point. "The failure to distinguish real causes of death from the existence of various medical tools and techniques that may temporarily substitute for particular bodily functions is a fatal one."[8] Most deaths occur in hospitals, and many of those deaths come after some medical intervention is refused or deemed useless. Are we to conclude that there is an epidemic of suicide and homicide in the nation's hospitals?

For some, letting people die sounds very much like passive euthanasia. Is that what "letting die" really means? Not at all. Euthanasia, whether we call it passive or active, is quite different from letting someone die when death cannot be avoided. Euthanasia involves an intention to cause or hasten death. Despite alleged humanitarian motivations for euthanasia and assisted suicide, these practices are murderous.

Euthanasia is an act that involves an intention to produce death. In a medical context, euthanasia can be effected by either a direct act (e.g., lethal injection of poison, a bullet in the head, suffocation with a pillow) that produces death immediately or a deliberate neglect (e.g., withdrawing medication, withholding food and water) that creates the conditions by which death occurs after a period of time. An essential component of euthanasia is the intention behind either an action or a refusal to act to knowingly bring about a person's death. Another important component is the fact that euthanasia occurs when the action or neglect produces the conditions by which death occurs. Killing not only involves the means by which death occurs, but the intention that death occur; it involves not only causality, but culpability. Not only does the person bring about death, but he or she intends to bring about death.

For example, James Guthrie Jr. of La Mirada, California, clearly intended to produce death when he gave his seventy-nine-year-old cancer-ridden mother a massive dosage of drugs, which failed to end her life. He then took a lead pipe he had wrapped in tape and a sock, stood behind her as she sat up in bed, and hit her on the back of the head. It took several blows to the head and three days for her to die. Guthrie was charged and convicted of manslaughter and sentenced to ten months in prison for the deed. Clearly, Guthrie intended to kill his mother, albeit perhaps for merciful reasons. He clearly used lethal means that created the conditions under which death occurred.[9]

Had death occurred because his mother decided to forego further medical treatment and let "nature take its course," Guthrie would not be in prison. His mother would have died from a lethal condition he did not create and could not prevent. However, because he took matters into his own hands and chose to create the conditions by which his mother died, his actions were both causal and culpable.

Assisted suicide is self-murder involving a second party. Although the patient kills himself, he is helped by someone else. The point is that both euthanasia and assisted suicide differ in terms of intention and culpability from letting someone die.

Both cancer and guns kill people. Cancer kills "naturally," while gunshots require human agency. There is a difference between what nature does to us, what others do to us, and what we do to ourselves. Letting someone die is only possible if there is an underlying condition causing death. If I am placed on a ventilator while perfectly healthy, I won't die if it is turned off because my lungs are healthy. It is quite a different matter, however, for a physician to inject me with a drug that paralyzes my lungs. In order to "allow death" there must be an underlying sickness; killing creates its own pathology.[10]

All it takes for death to occur is time. The issue is the limitations of medical intervention and the reality of human mortality. Murder requires an intentional act by a human agent, whereas allowing a terminally ill person to die when death cannot be prevented merely acknowledges the inevitable. If firemen give up trying to extinguish a fire that totally engulfs my home in flames, does this mean they intended to have my house burn down? If I give up shoveling my driveway during a heavy snowstorm, does this mean I intended to let my driveway fill up with snow? It simply means that the firemen and I have recognized our limitations in the face of overwhelming, uncontrollable circumstances.[11]

Allowing death to occur is similar. For the most part, nature kills us with events, illnesses, and diseases that are not controllable by human interventions. Many times, our best medical efforts are an exchange of one disease process for another. Since death is biologically inevitable sooner or later, we can hardly be said to intend death because we admit we can no longer stop it. At some point, medical treatment will be incapable of holding it at bay and we will die. It may be possible for a physician to extend life a few days, weeks, or even months, but it can hardly be said that he intends death by honoring a terminal patient's request to cease useless treatment.

Sometimes treatment may extend life, and it may not. For example, chemotherapy and organ transplants require a risk/benefit analysis by both the physician and patient. One is usually called upon to make decisions regarding the use of these therapies as a last resort. Neither is provided unless there is a direct threat to life. The progression of the disease that threatens the person's life makes a difference in the effectiveness of the proposed therapy, and usually there is a considerable body of previously gathered data to inform patients about the efficacy of the therapy in their particular circumstances. Efficacy is determined according to the expectation of five-year survival.

Withholding Versus Withdrawing Treatment

If it is morally acceptable for physicians to honor a patient's request to withhold a medical treatment, is it equally acceptable to withdraw one? Is there a moral difference between not starting a medical treatment and withdrawing one that has been started?[12] Some argue there is a difference, that withholding treatment is morally acceptable, but once treatment begins there is no way to morally justify its removal. I disagree.

Whatever conditions morally justify withholding treatment also justify withdrawing treatment. In both cases, the belief that a particular treatment will not be or is not a benefit to a patient is a valid justification. In the case of withholding treatment, a judgment is made about the probability of the therapy's improving the patient's physiological condition. When considering withdrawal of a treatment, the same issues are present, only we have some evidence for the judgment that a treatment is no longer beneficial. We know whether the treatment produced the desired ends or not, whether the burden of the treatment was greater than the benefit. In both instances, the decision to either withhold or withdraw a treatment is grounded in the concept of beneficence, one of the standard principles of medical ethics.

A patient with metastatic-to-bone cancer may decide to forego further chemotherapy treatments because there is little or no hope of deriving any benefit from them. The patient is going to die with or without treatment, and his physician may suggest that the remaining time he has to live will be better served without the rigors of chemotherapy. The patient's care may be reoriented from curative care to providing comfort care. This is an example of withdrawing a treatment.

An example of withholding treatment may be found in the circumstances of the same patient. Just as the continued use of chemotherapy may be withdrawn because it does not offer any reasonable hope of benefit, surgery to remove cancerous tissue may be withheld for the same reasons.

What often complicates treatment/nontreatment decisions is when nonmedical, nonphysiological criteria are added to the notion of beneficence. For example, if, in order to deem it beneficial, we expect a treatment to be miraculous, to restore brain function to a person diagnosed as permanently and irreversibly brain damaged, then we have added a dimension to our notion of medical beneficence that transcends the scientific purposes of medicine. God can perform a miracle, but that is outside the scope of a medical treatment.

I am not saying that all treatment/nontreatment decision-making must be completely based on a conception of medical beneficence. In fact, beneficence can be defined in two ways: physiologically (dealing with the physical aspects of life) and ontologically (dealing with the nature of life).[13] The preceding argument provides my description of physiological beneficence. Generally, it is a minimalist position since it is limited to discerning whether or not a particular treatment is or will be effective in alleviating specific physical symptoms, or symptoms that have a physiologic basis.

By contrast, ontological beneficence addresses issues beyond the restoration of physiological functions—issues related to what some call "quality of life." From the perspective of physiological beneficence, a proposed medical treatment may yield direct physical benefit by eliminating symptoms related to a specific condition (e.g., antibiotics to treat the respiratory infection of a bedridden Alzheimer's patient with dementia), but it may not produce an ontological benefit (e.g., restoring the person to full mental capacity).

Many want to make medical decisions strictly on the basis of physiological beneficence, with no regard to the quality of life (ontological beneficence). However, this is nearly impossible. Like other areas of life, many, if not most, medical decisions are made with at least some consideration of the quality of life to be derived from treatment or nontreatment. Who accepts a painful, invasive medical procedure without considering the improvement it will make to his or her quality of life? In the normal course of events, improving the quality of life influences most of our decisions, whether improving our health, pursuing a particular vocation, purchasing a home, or deciding to drive a certain model of automobile.

When death is imminent and continuing ventilator support is futile, there is no moral problem with taking a person off the ventilator if that is what he would want done. However, when a person can continue living with partial or complete ventilator-assisted breathing, is quality of life a valid consideration? Jack Kevorkian challenges us to consider such a circumstance: "Let my critics consider the quality of life of a high quad who's dependent on a ventilator."[14] Mark O'Brien, a high quad who spends all but one or two hours a week on a ventilator, took up Kevorkian's challenge when he wrote:

> I am such a high quad, high quad being medical jargon for a person who has suffered an injury high up on the spinal chord. As a high quad, I cannot move my arms or legs, hands or feet. This is so with most high quads. I need a ventilator, that is, a respirator to help me breathe. I ask you to consider the quality of my life. I live in a pleasant new apartment in Berkeley, California, one of the most interesting cities in the world. I write articles for newspapers and magazines, and commentaries for radio. My poetry has been published. I have tons of books, an alarming collection of cassettes and CDs, a girlfriend, a web site, a documentary film about me and a proclamation from the city of Berkeley declaring Mark O'Brien Day. Who could ask for anything more?
>
> Now I ask you to consider Dr. Kevorkian's quality of life. His main interest, nay, his obsession is killing disabled people or people who say they are disabled. This mostly cashes out to mean depressed, middle-aged women. They come to Dr. Kevorkian seeking release through death. Occasionally, Dr. Kevorkian is put on trial for murder. This gives him a chance to pose as the humane martyr to the laws passed by insensitive politicians. He has never been convicted. The jurors say afterwards, O yes, they would rather be dead than be, horrible shudder, confined to a wheelchair.
>
> Well, how do they know? Have they ever been disabled? Have they ever had a serious discussion with a disabled person? Has the prosecution had the sense to call a disabled person to the witness stand to testify that many factors beside medical condition affect a person's quality of life? . . . Dr. Kevorkian's quality of life doesn't sound so hot to me. A serial killer who has the intelligence to pick on a despised minority doesn't sound like he has much to live for.[15]

Interestingly, although 86 percent of spinal cord injured high-level quadriplegics rate their quality of life as average or better than average, only 17 percent of their ER doctors, nurses, and technicians think they would have an average or better quality of life if they became quadriplegics themselves.[16]

Jeanette Tette is another ventilator-dependent person who rejects the notion that her quality of life is so dismal that death is preferable. The fifty-year-old wife, mother, and grandmother has thought more about death than most people since a rare lung disease took away her independence and the ability to breathe on her own more than two years ago. Tette recalls how she seriously thought about giving up and just going home to die. Instead, she entered a special unit in a Michigan hospital for ventilator-dependent patients, where she is surrounded by stuffed animals, a butterfly mobile, a row of books, and pictures of her family. "I felt I was going to die," says Tette. Then she looked into the eyes of her husband, Paul, and her grandchildren, and she decided she had to live. "I will fight to the very end."[17]

Using quality of life considerations to make medical decisions does not justify making such decisions exclusively on the basis of quality of life criteria. They represent one facet of the decision-making process, not the entire process. There is a difference between anticipating what a given treatment may mean for a person's quality of life in light of other factors and judging solely on the basis of the person's quality of life to cease or withhold treatment. The impulse that shows respect for the quality of life should be guarded, for without care and vigilance, it can become transformed into a distorted effort of quality control.[18]

Withholding/Withdrawing Food and Fluids

Withholding or withdrawing medications, dialysis machines, or ventilators is one thing, but is it ever morally justified to withhold or withdraw food and fluids from a person? The idea of death by starvation and dehydration is repugnant, and deliberately withdrawing or withholding food and fluids from people in order to hasten their deaths is active euthanasia. To withhold or withdraw food and fluids seems to fly in the face of what we consider normative in caring for dying people. However, as we will see later, there can be instances of withholding or withdrawing food and fluids that are not euthanasia.

Yet it is no trivial matter to begin tampering with basic treatments like providing food and fluids. As Daniel Callahan observes, "[These traditions] were cultivated to provide as solid a fortress as morality can offer against a human propensity—seen time and again with the elderly—to neglect, abuse, or kill the powerless, the burdensome, and the inconvenient. . . . It is one thing to make an occasional exception to the general rule to provide food and water as part of minimal nursing care, and still another to make it a routine way to help death along."[19]

Are food and fluids like other medical treatments we can withhold or withdraw, or is there special moral significance attached to them? There exists no universal agreement on this issue. Several state courts have ruled that food and fluids, when supplied with the aid of medical equipment, are the same as medical treatment.[20] Thus, they may be withheld or withdrawn on the same basis as other treatments, and patients may refuse food and fluids just as they may refuse any other medical treatment.

Others consider food and fluids to be morally special, believing they do not fall into the same category as medical treatments. Unlike medical therapies that have specific applications to specific medical conditions, food and fluids are necessary for existence to occur at any level. Although it is possible for a person to live without taking an analgesic for pain, no one, regardless of how healthy he or she may be, can live for long without food and fluids. For this reason, I do not regard food and fluids supplied under medical auspices to be the same as other medical treatments.

Advanced disease or a degenerating chronic condition, including advanced aging, can diminish one's appetite or render one unable to assimilate the nutritional benefits of food. A person may lose his or her appetite as a disease progresses or as aging deteriorates the body. At some point, an individual may lose the ability to swallow as well. When this occurs, is it a symptom of a terminal condition, an indication that the body is shutting down, or a medical emergency requiring the use of a feeding tube?

Complicating this picture is the medical and moral significance of the feeding tube. Although there is evidence that primitive feeding tubes were used in the nineteenth century, in modern medicine the first use was as a post-operative bridge following certain kinds of surgery. However, since about 1970, the feeding tube has come to be regarded as morally required treatment for individuals who cannot receive food and fluids orally. Thus, for some, removing tube feeding from a person who cannot swallow represents a form of killing. However, before 1970, the long-term inability to receive food and fluids orally was considered a symptom of an underlying terminal condition. When death occurred, it was the underlying condition that caused it, not starvation or dehydration. The terminal condition prevented the intake of food and fluids, or it dulled the appetite. Strokes occur as blood vessels weaken and burst, sometimes eliminating several functions at once. Among the lost functions can be the ability to swallow. That circumstance was never, until recently, considered to be "starving the person to death." The inability to receive nourishment orally helped bring on the final, usually gentle, coma, which led to a relatively nonviolent death.[21] Whether we like it or not, and whether or not we choose to accept it, some people actually die from the complications of old age.

Once again, we are faced with a situation wherein technology redefines what constitutes dying, thereby dictating to us what counts as moral obligation at the end of life. Are we obligated to force-feed an imminently dying person, on the grounds that the person will die of starvation and dehydration if we don't?[22] Is it a violation of the sanctity of life principle if we do not feed by tube a terminally ill person who cannot swallow?

Does the fact that feeding tubes now exist constitute an obligation to use them? If it does, we have imputed moral obligation to a technological invention, in some way imputing morality to inanimate machines, tubes, etc. Technologies are not moral entities; people are. Physicians have moral obligations; machines don't.

The physician is not obligated to use every piece of technology available to him or her, but to make judgments about the appropriate use of that technology. The doctor's first responsibility is to avoid harming patients. But even here the physician is required to make distinctions. Is it harming a patient to perform invasive, painful procedures on him or her? Perhaps, if the procedures are unlikely to produce a beneficial result.

When a patient's metabolism slows, whether because of advancing age or illness, and there is a corresponding loss of appetite, coupled with the inability or difficulty to receive food and fluids orally, it is difficult to see how the sanctity of human life principle can be construed to require forced tube feeding. Although the sanctity of life principle is a life-enhancing perspective, God does not demand that people stay alive as long as possible.

Sometimes lost functions return, and therapies may help a patient regain the ability to swallow and digest food, or restore appetite, but a sanctity of human life ethic does not require medical personnel to impose food and fluids on patients when death is clearly approaching. This process of dying is not abnormal. Someone advanced in age, whose condition may be described as "overwhelming," who exhibits no appetite and/or makes no request for nourishment, and who cannot swallow, should not be regarded as starving to death because he or she refuses food and fluids.

This does not mean society should establish policies requiring the withholding or withdrawal of food and fluids from people on the basis of age. Nor should society adopt hard-and-fast rules about the insertion or withdrawal of feeding tubes. Some nursing homes virtually force patients and their families to make decisions about tube feeding before they are admitted. Such regulation may cause more problems than it solves. Generally, our policy should be to supply food and fluids unless:

1. The patient's condition makes it impossible to supply food and fluids.
2. The patient's death is judged to be imminent beyond a reasonable doubt.
3. The patient's body cannot assimilate the nutritional benefit from food or fluids.
4. Food and/or fluids would exacerbate the patient's pain and discomfort.
5. The patient verbally or physically rejects food and fluids, or there is clear and convincing evidence that the patient would not want them (e.g., advance directive, consultation with family members).

For the person who is unconscious and/or incapable of participating in his or her own decision-making, we ought to presume it is in his best interest to provide food and fluids. Exceptions to this would be those situations in which a formerly competent, conscious (now unconscious, incompetent) adult has provided clear instructions concerning the withholding or withdrawal of food and fluids, either through an advance directive or prior conversations with family members and caregivers.[23]

WE SHOULD ERR ON THE SIDE OF LIFE.

Despite the general assumption that providing food and fluids is in a person's best interest, there are situations when continued provision of food and fluids actually harms a person more than it helps. For example, fluids may accumulate in the lungs (pulmonary edema), making respiration difficult and causing the patient to be restless, delirious, or anguished. A person in the end stages of colon cancer may experience greater pain if food is provided. In either case, the cessation of food and fluids can be viewed as an appropriate palliative response to the symptoms of a terminal condition, allowing a patient to live out the final hours or days of his or her life in greater comfort. Caregivers can apply comfort care measures to alleviate the problems associated with the lack of fluids.

What of withholding food and fluids from someone who is not imminently dying? Is this a form of euthanasia? Although it is difficult to know what someone's real intentions are, if food and fluids are withdrawn because the person is not dying fast enough, such an act should be regarded as euthanasia. This act alone will create the conditions under which death can occur. It is only appropriate to consider withdrawing or withholding food and fluids when other life-threatening factors are present and irreversible. However, when there is an inability to take food orally due to an underlying condition, and that condition is expected to take the patient's life with or without treatment, the sanctity of life principle does not require the use of a feeding tube.

For individuals diagnosed as permanently unconscious, the provision of food and fluids should be regarded as customary comfort care. A feeding tube is not expensive, nor is it unduly burdensome. As in the case of Nancy Cruzan, some individuals are capable of taking nourishment orally, although there is the risk of inhaling solids or fluid into the lungs, which can lead to infection and possible respiratory failure.[24]

Consequently, feeding tubes are used to avoid such a development. I believe this is an appropriate use of a feeding tube. A feeding tube should only be withheld or withdrawn when there is clear and convincing evidence that the patient does not want it, or when the patient's terminal condition warrants removal or withholding. Otherwise, we should err on the side of life.

Some will suggest that permitting the withholding or withdrawal of feeding tubes from anyone, even in the most extreme circumstances, is to step onto the slippery slope of active euthanasia. If it is permissible to withhold or withdraw a feeding tube because it is beneficial for the person, then we will inevitably come to regard hastening death as beneficial. It may be argued that there can be no other purpose for withholding or withdrawing a feeding tube from an individual than to hasten death. Therefore, such an action, if not euthanasia itself, is at least friendly to it.

Once again, we must return to the distinctions made earlier between killing and letting die. Killing creates its own conditions, whereas letting someone die is possible only when an underlying lethal condition exists. Other than in some routine postoperative situations, a person must be seriously ill to require a feeding tube. If the gag reflex is absent, the patient exhibits an inability to swallow, or there is a loss of appetite (or all three), then an underlying condition exists that threatens the life of the patient. Other than routine use of feeding tubes postoperatively, unusual conditions must exist before we seriously consider using one.

BRAIN DEATH AND PERMANENT STATES OF UNCONSCIOUSNESS

Special medical, moral, and legal problems arise when individuals are deemed to have experienced a catastrophic loss of higher brain function, or so-called "brain death," or are diagnosed as being in a permanent unconscious condition (frequently called persistent vegetative state).[25] Although relatively few people experience such a fate, there is a widespread perception among the general population that such a life is not really life at all, that no reasonable person would want to live under these circumstances.

Among those functions people describe as essential to meaningful existence is brain function. When one loses the ability to perceive events, people, and circumstances, the result is a diminished quality of life, a loss many find unacceptable. Losing the capacity to participate in the human community through communication, interpersonal relations, and meaningful activities is one of our greatest fears.

For some, the loss of cognitive brain function is sufficient to justify euthanasia, on grounds that being permanently unconscious is a fate worse than death, and thus causing death is an act of caring—a benefit rendered. To most people, once one loses the functions we associate with humanness, there no longer exists the conditions to make life meaningful. People often focus on such a person's diminished quality of life, questioning the value of continued existence.

It is common for people to describe such a patient as a "vegetable." However, this is an extremely pejorative term that dehumanizes the individual. Referring to a seriously ill individual as a "vegetable" not only offends that person's intrinsic value and dignity, but it is a negative term formulated on weak philosophical grounds. The absence of higher brain functions does not diminish that person's value, because value is not based on function. Our value is intrinsic to who we are—beings made in God's own image. Using demeaning terms to describe a person while talking of compassion is contradictory, and believers should avoid such talk.

As I argue throughout this book, a case may be made that causing death under such circumstances may be compassionate, but it is not caring, and we should not confuse the two. Caring implies an acceptance of the burdens and inconveniences associated with the problem of lost brain function. The loss of cognitive brain function is a significant loss, and generally we view such an event as grievous. However, causing death, even under the most compassionate of conditions, is a repudiation of burdens and inconveniences, which are still our responsibility to the person.

The person who is permanently and irreversibly brain damaged represents a challenge to both sides of the euthanasia question. For the proponents of euthanasia, a permanently unconscious individual who is not imminently dying and whose major organs function completely without mechanical assistance personifies undignified existence, yet he or she is still a human being with a beating heart and a heaving chest. In order to bring about the cessation of those functions deliberate actions must be taken, and it is hard to describe such actions as anything other than killing. For those who hold a sanctity of life position, it is difficult to interpret the meaning of a life characterized by permanent unconsciousness. It seems foolish to many to argue that such a life is anything other than tragic and futile.

A great deal of mystery surrounds patients who remain physically alive yet unconscious and/or unaware for ten or more years. Do they ever understand what others are talking about in their presence? Do they experience pain? Do they hear or see? God alone knows their true state. One thing we do know—patients in a permanent noncognitive state are not dead according to current criteria for the determination of death. Although the higher brain may be destroyed, the integrated function of the major organs continues, often without mechanical assistance. Society ought not regard those without higher brain functions as dead. Dying, perhaps, but not dead.

MEDICAL FUTILITY AND RESUSCITATION

Since death is inevitable, there will come a time when medical intervention will be futile, when efforts to sustain or extend life will fail. Futile medical intervention may be defined as care that does not lead to improvement in the patient's prognosis, comfort, well-being, or general state of health.[26] There are instances when medical treatments are obligatory to make a person comfortable in the remaining hours or days of life, a distinction between sustaining life and extending life.

Sustaining life simply means that efforts are made to support existing physiological functions and provide comfort care, while taking no steps to curatively treat the patient's underlying terminal condition. For example, providing ventilator support to a person in the end stages of lung cancer is life sustaining, but it is not life extending since a ventilator does nothing to cure or directly treat lung cancer.

Extending life implies that measures are taken with the expectation that a person's life can be lengthened by weeks, months, or years. There is some expectation that curative efforts will produce beneficial results. Surgeries, organ transplants, chemotherapy, radiation, and medications are examples of life-extending treatments. When doctors have clear and convincing evidence that such curative measures will not extend a patient's life, when death is expected regardless of what measures are employed, further medical intervention may be deemed futile. It is certainly appropriate to refrain from resuscitating patients whose lives cannot be extended by more than a few hours or days.

In the natural course of events, sustaining life by technological intervention reaches its limits. It is not a contradiction nor an insult to God for an individual to both pray fervently for a miracle and decide to forego further medical treatment.

What of resuscitating a person from a heart attack, stroke, or respiratory failure? Are believers obligated to undergo resuscitation? Does faithfulness to the sanctity of life principle mean submitting to bone-breaking CPR, direct injections of drugs to the heart, electrical shocks, or internal heart massage? Is it a form of suicide to refuse resuscitation efforts? Must we resuscitate everyone, regardless of mitigating circumstances that suggest such efforts are futile?

We have little choice but to leave the decision about resuscitation to individuals or those they may designate to make such decisions on their behalf. I find it difficult to justify forcing terminally ill or elderly individuals to submit to resuscitation efforts against their wishes. The sanctity of human life ethic does not require a person to be resuscitated following cardiac arrest or respiratory failure. Such interventions may be warranted on prudential grounds, but not necessarily on principle grounds. However, the sanctity of human life principle does presume that people want to live whenever possible.

In most prehospital settings, resuscitation should be viewed as beneficial medical intervention. When someone suffers a heart attack while shoveling snow or falls out of a boat and apparently drowns, we assume the person would want to be resuscitated. The amount of time that elapses between the catastrophic, life-threatening event and the commencement of resuscitation efforts is crucial to the success of these efforts in restoring him or her to life. If help arrives an hour after the event, resuscitation is likely to be futile. If only a few minutes have passed, there is reason to expect that resuscitation will be beneficial. These are difficult judgment calls, often requiring the wisdom of Solomon to assess.

Nursing homes and hospital intensive care units present a different set of problems. Advanced age, chronic degenerative diseases, or previous cardiac/pulmonary events can make resuscitation efforts less likely to succeed. Even when resuscitation succeeds in restoring cardiac and respiratory functions, there can be other mitigating factors that make future resuscitation efforts unwise and unnecessary. Cardiac arrest often damages the heart, diminishing its function, which means that if a person has another arrest, resuscitation may be futile. Persons in these settings may rightly decide against any resuscitation.

Similarly, persons in advanced stages of terminal illnesses (e.g., cancer) may request that no resuscitation efforts be undertaken on their behalf. They may decide against maintenance of an airway (intubation and ventilator support), or even against the further use of antibiotics to eradicate infection. If treatment cannot be curative, there is no moral obligation to receive it. However, a decision to forego resuscitation in the event of a major cardiac arrest or respiratory failure should not be construed as a decision against any and all medical treatment. Although a treatment may not be curative, it may in fact provide comfort to the patient (i.e., pain medication, antibiotics, respiratory therapy). "Do not resuscitate" does not mean do not treat.

NOTES

1. By "best available medical judgment" we mean that the patient or family has secured from at least two independent physicians the diagnosis that further use of a medical therapy is not physiologically beneficial to the patient.
2. Frank Schaeffer, speech at the annual banquet for Lake County Women's Center, Merrillville, Indiana—September 1991.

3. By using the phrase "allowing to die," I am not implying that people must give permission for others to die. I use it only as a means of distinguishing between killing, obligations to prevent death, and recognizing death as imminent and unavoidable.

4. Daniel Callahan, *The Troubled Dream of Life* (New York: Simon & Schuster, 1993), 37.

5. A similar argument is often made concerning guns. The focus of gun control is on the weapons themselves more than it is on the people who use them. Guns, like medical technologies, do not have being, therefore, they cannot be treated as rational agents. Guns don't decide to kill people. Neither do medical technologies.

6. I mean by "natural death" one that occurs through the demise of natural, physiological functions due to age, illness, or disease.

7. Medical Futurist Symposium (Grand Rapids: Butterworth Hospital, June 1989).

8. George Annas, "The 'Right to Die' in America: Sloganeering from Quinlan and Cruzan to Quill and Kevorkian," *Dusquene Law Review*, vol. 34, 875, 895 (1996).

9. Dana Parsons, "A Life Sentence Inside for 'Mercy Killers,'" *Los Angeles Times*, 26 April 1998.

10. Callahan, *The Troubled Dream of Life*, 76–82.

11. Ibid., 82.

12. "Withholding" treatment does not mean refusing to treat a patient. It simply means not using a medical treatment with a particular patient, either because the patient or patient's family requests that it not be used, or because a physician determines that it is not appropriate for a patient under the present circumstances. "Withdrawing" simply means removing a medical treatment because it no longer provides its intended benefit and/or there is no expectation that it will provide it.

13. Ontology is a branch of metaphysics dealing with the nature of being, of personal existence.

14. Mark O'Brien, "A High Quad Defends Quality of Life—Kevorkian Argues I Would Be Better Off Dead Than Alive," *Pacific News Service*, 450 Mission Street, Room 204, San Francisco, CA 94105, 20 February 1996. Used by permission of author.

15. Ibid.

16. K. A. Gerhart, et al., *Annals of Emergency Medicine* (Vol. 23, 1994): 807–12.

17. Ted Roelofs, "Controversial Proposal is a Matter of Life and Death," *Grand Rapids Press*, 25 October 1998, A1.

18. Brent Waters, *Dying and Death: A Resource for Christian Reflection* (Cleveland, Ohio: United Church Press, 1996), 88.

19. Daniel Callahan, *Setting Limits: Medical Goals in an Aging Society* (New York: Simon & Schuster, 1987), 188.

20. *Brophy v. New England Sinai Hospital* (Massachusetts, 1985); *Conroy* (New Jersey, 1985); *Cruzan v. Harmon* (Missouri, 1988).

21. Callahan, *The Troubled Dream of Life*, 81.

22. Imminent death is defined as a death which is anticipated to occur within mere hours or a few days at best, with or without the provision of food and fluids.

23. In the case of *Cruzan v. Director, Missouri Rehabilitation Services,* the U.S. Supreme Court ruled that food and fluids may be withheld or removed from incompetent patients when there exists "clear and convincing evidence" they would want it withheld or withdrawn.

24. During a circuit court trial in Missouri, a suit brought by the parents of Nancy Cruzan seeking court permission to remove Nancy's feeding tube, several of Cruzan's nurses testified that she was able to receive food and fluids orally, but to prevent aspiration into her lungs and to expedite caregiving by the staff, a feeding tube was inserted. See *Cruzan v. Harmon,* 760 S.W.2nd 408 (1988) and Alan Meisel, *The Right to Die* (New York: Wiley Law Publications, 1989), 124.

25. Due to the fact that the term "persistent vegetative state" suggests an individual is something less than human (some colloquially refer to such a person as a "vegetable"), I prefer to use the term permanent state of unconsciousness or unawareness. Despite the loss of the higher brain, the part of the brain that controls thought, emotion, and consciousness, such individuals are still human beings to be treated with dignity and respect.

26. L. J. Schneiderman, N. S. Jecker, et al., "Medical Futility: Its Meaning and Ethical Implications," *Annals of Internal Medicine* (Vol. 112, 1990): 949–54.

CHAPTER 11

LOVING
INDIVIDUALS
IN FINAL
TRANSITION:

How to Help
Dying People

A hospice organization in Michigan offers this succinct explanation for its existence: "When people enter the world they are surrounded by love, comfort, and care. Shouldn't they receive love, comfort, and care when they leave?"[1] Our intuitive response is yes, people should receive love, comfort, and care as they leave this world. However, in actual practice there are often significant deficiencies in the care dying people receive. It is easier to recruit caregivers for babies than it is for terminally ill individuals.

Consider the McCaughey family in Iowa. Kenny and Bobbi McCaughey made history when Bobbi gave birth to seven live babies, a feat even the medical community considered a miracle. Despite the odds against Bobbi's carrying these babies far enough to give them a good chance at survival, the world's first septuplets were born. When word got out, their little town of Carlisle, Iowa, was overrun with media from around the world. Instantly, the McCaughey babies became the world's babies. All of the major American television networks did special programs on the babies. Gifts of clothing, furniture, toys, and money poured in. Kenny's employer gave the family a new van. Neighbors began building the family a new house. Many weeks after their birth, the first of the seven babies came home from the hospital. By mid-1998, all seven were home in Carlisle. Seven babies for one couple to handle!

A remarkable thing happened. Not only did the McCaugheys' church organize to help them, but the entire town of Carlisle rallied behind them as well. People not only gave of their substance to help these babies, they gave the most precious commodity in modern life—time. People altered their lives in order to give the McCaughey babies the care they needed. Farmers took time away from their chores to hold the tiny babies. The McCaughey household became a busy place, with people working in shifts around the clock.

MORE THAN ANYONE ELSE,

CHRISTIANS HAVE A MAJOR STAKE IN WHAT

HAPPENS TO PEOPLE AT THE END OF LIFE.

Why would so many people give so much of themselves to one family? Babies project hope. They give us a sense that the world might be a better place because they are here. It's easy to anticipate the future with a baby in your arms (especially one who is asleep with a fresh diaper). As you look into a baby's eyes, you wonder what will become of him or her. What contribution to the world will this child make?

However, when people are dying, when they are coming to the end of life and there is little more than death to anticipate, it is harder to generate the same level of anticipation and involvement in their care. The smells and minor inconveniences we endure with babies seem harder to endure when they involve adults. With the aroma of death comes a sense of hopelessness. Babies are easier, perhaps, because we know that in the normal course of events they will grow out of their complete dependence upon us. Caring for dying adults is not like that.

More than anyone else, Christians have a major stake in what happens to people at the end of life. Such a large stake provides a powerful incentive to improve care at the end of life. Like birth, dying is a uniquely important time in a person's life, even though the individual may not be aware of all that is happening around him. Death is the final stage of a person's earthly existence, the concluding chapter of human mortality. For this reason, the end of life can be a meaningful time for dying persons and their loved ones. It is imperative that Christians be in attendance to provide care, counsel, and encouragement. Since Christians have hope, it is essential that they exhibit a presence in the face of death in order to project that hope.

This sounds simple, but it seldom is. Although death may be a natural process in a fallen world, it is rarely easy. The dying process requires a specialized kind of support, the kind that is centered not only in the challenges unique to each individual, but on the special challenge of identifying and ministering to the person's spiritual needs at a time when physiological hardships are frequently overwhelming. Every person is different, and the quality of care is not just a question of the technical skills performed by caregivers. Rather, the quality of care will be dictated by the unique emotional and spiritual stability of caregivers. Not everyone can work effectively with dying people.

Those models of end-of-life care that focus primarily on meeting medical needs frequently do not deal very well with the special needs of dying patients. Medical needs must be met, but that is not all there is to the end of life. Dying individuals need people around them who know them well. In the past, this need was met by immediate and extended family members—spouse, siblings, children, cousins, aunts, etc. These extended, multigenerational families shared together the realities of life and death. The entire life cycle was played out for all to see. People were born at home, and they frequently died at home. Although medical care was far less sophisticated and could not promise complete relief from pain, at least the family was there to offer whatever comfort and caring they could.

The growth of organized medicine and the development of modern medical systems changed all that. The pace of modern life quickened as social mobility, economic prosperity, two-career marriages, and rising divorce rates became commonplace. In the process, many Americans grew increasingly isolated from their families, either geographically, emotionally, or both. The responsibility to care for people at the end of life gradually shifted to physicians, and personal dramas of serious illness became hidden behind the walls of hospitals and nursing homes. Here the medical staff often depends on emotional detachment to protect themselves from their own grief over the deaths of patients. It is not unusual for terminal patients to be moved into a single unit or to be moved to the end of the ward, farthest from the nurses' station, where they will not be a constant reminder of the system's "failure."

The reintroduction of hospice care, first used in medieval times, began to change the "medicalization" of death, providing an alternative to dying in a hospital surrounded mostly by strangers. The modern hospice movement has retained much of the original hospice focus—supplying spiritual care, listening, and providing respite for families—while using modern techniques of pain relief, symptom management, and grief support for the terminally ill and their families. More than any other aspect of medicine, it was the hospice movement that demonstrated what holistic care means, integrating medicine, psychosocial needs, and spiritual care.[2] In this respect, hospice is perhaps the most patient-driven form of care available.

Where possible, dying at home is the best option for most patients and their families. Debbie Abitia's ninety-seven-year-old grandmother, Agnes Campana, lives in the family room of Abitia's Pinole, California, home. Though largely confined to her bed, Campana is seldom alone. Abitia, her four children, and her husband are always around. They can visit with her while watching television or using the computer near Campana's bed. "From the kitchen we can see her through the dining room," says Abitia, "and from the upstairs bedroom we can hear her." She is part of the family. The Abitias consider caring for Campana as the opportunity to give her one final gift.[3]

By providing a quality of holistic care to chronically and terminally ill individuals and their families, hospice illustrates for us the best of modern professional caregiving. Its effective use of both salaried and volunteer personnel demonstrates that individuals and families need not face serious illness alone.

Curiously missing in much of this has been the evangelical church. If anyone should have an interest in how people die, it is the church. If there exists any group of people a dying person should be able to count on to walk with him through the valley of the shadow of death, it is those who claim to belong to the Good Shepherd (Psalm 23). If anyone can speak with authority about life after death, it is those who know the One who is the Resurrection and the Life (John 11:25). If anyone can comfort, it is those who themselves are indwelt by the Comforter (John 14:16–17), who can comfort others because they have been comforted by God (2 Corinthians 1:3–11).

From its inception on the Day of Pentecost, the church has been marked by its ministry of compassion to the less fortunate and the vulnerable. Throughout church history, Christians have led the way in responding to the physical and spiritual needs of people. Only in this century has the body of Christ seemingly moved away from caring for the physical needs of people, permitting by default the intrusion of non-Christian organizations and institutions into the most intimate areas of life. In some cases, this retreat paved the way for policies and practices that are decidedly unbiblical, as the current battle over assisted suicide and euthanasia illustrates.

People live in fear of the worst happening to them at the end of life. But where is the clear voice of the church speaking not with rhetoric, but with action that proves such fear is unjustified? Moral leadership does not lead by its rhetoric, but by its compassionate competence. Moral leadership leads with actions, not just with words.

The hospice movement and the patients it serves would benefit enormously from an influx of local churches willing to take on the responsibility of caring for their members and their families when serious illness strikes. There is little that hospice does for a dying individual or a family that believers in a local church cannot be trained to do. Apart from the medical aspects of end-of-life care, the vast majority of needs can be met by laypeople trained by experienced hospice personnel.

The current situation necessitates that Christians become proactive in providing alternatives to assisted suicide and euthanasia, in much the same manner as the Christian community now provides alternatives to abortion through pregnancy care ministries.

THREE PROMISES TO THE TERMINALLY ILL PERSON

All terminally ill persons should be given assurance that they will have their needs met to the best of our abilities. Christians cannot accept a passive role in this, merely standing aside while disease ravages loved ones. In the Introduction and chapter 1, I stated that every terminally ill person should be given three promises:

> To the best of our ability, we will not allow you to die in pain.
> We will not allow you to die alone.
> You will not be a burden to anyone.

These promises represent the basic necessities of a Christian approach to end-of-life care. These promises should be recited by the church every time we are confronted with the needs of a terminally ill individual. That is what loving individuals in final transition requires. These promises embody what it means to "bear ye one another's burdens" (Galatians 6:2).

BOTH HOSPICES AND CHURCHES
BENEFIT BY COLLABORATION.

We can be grateful for the groundbreaking work of the hospice movement in addressing the special needs of terminally ill individuals and their families. Those who work in hospices represent the very best qualities human beings are capable of offering one another. Hospices have shown that care at the end of life can be geared to the patient's specific needs, that care need not succumb to the intricacies of medical bureaucracy, and that the valley of the shadow of death need not be devoid of joy and happiness.

However, being patient-driven, there is a potential downside within the hospice philosophy. States that provide legal endorsement of assisted suicide (e.g., Oregon) make it likely that hospices will have to accept patients who intend to seek assistance in dying, and there is nothing inherent in the hospice philosophy to resist such a drift toward euthanasia.

A hospice philosophy is single-minded in its focus on the terminally ill patient, and most hospice programs vigorously avoid giving the appearance of imposing any moral or religious views on patients. Consequently, if physician-assisted suicide is legal, it will be up to those hospices whose operating philosophy is explicitly opposed to such practices to provide alternatives. Thus, both hospices and churches benefit by collaboration.

A PROGRAM OF CHRISTIAN HOSPICE CARE

LIFT® (Loving Individuals in Final Transition) is a program of Christian hospice care, grounded by a commitment to the doctrines of historic biblical Christianity and a strong belief in the responsibility of local congregations to care for its members.[4] LIFT is designed to be "franchised" to local congregations that desire to provide their members with the skills needed to provide high-quality care to terminally ill individuals and their families. In this sense, LIFT is not only a protest against assisted suicide and euthanasia; it is an expression of the Christian commitment to the sanctity of human life.

I have been developing LIFT for the last three years, not as a replacement for existing hospice programs, but as an enhancement of their services. Many believers today do not avail themselves of hospice care, either because they are not aware of its existence in their community or because of misconceptions about the nature of hospice. For example, I asked a group of pastors what word came to mind when I mentioned the word *hospice.* Most of these pastors said "New Age." They seriously believed hospice is some New Age fringe organization. It is tragic that so many believers would not receive excellent end-of-life care because of such misconceptions.

By implementing LIFT in the local church, patients and their families receive the best possible care. From a hospice they receive excellent patient-driven care, including needed medical services. From LIFT, they receive a distinctive Christian approach to spiritual care.

MISSION AND PURPOSE

LIFT can be organized within a single congregation or as a cooperative between two or more congregations. LIFT services are primarily nonmedical in nature and are provided in the home of the terminally ill person or his family, although the mission of LIFT is to provide services wherever needed. LIFT is staffed by members of the sponsoring local church, who volunteer their time and services on an "as available/as needed" basis.

The ministry is administered by a Care Coordinator appointed by the church. This individual will usually be an experienced caregiver (e.g., nursing, home health aide). The Care Coordinator serves as a liaison between the patient, the patient's family, and the local congregation. In this sense, the Care Coordinator anchors a team of caregivers.

Caregiving teams provide an effective way to respond to the complexities of end-of-life care because their interdisciplinary nature brings a wide range of expertise to bear on the needs of the patient and his or her family. The team approach provides a continuum of care, accomplishing goals that a lone caregiver could not. Most of the services needed by terminally ill individuals and their families involve the types of things laypeople can provide. Below are some examples of services a congregation can provide to a terminally ill person:

Style or cut the patient's hair.
Do the laundry.
Redecorate the patient's room.
Take out the trash.
Dust.
Cook a meal.
Take the patient for a drive.
Feed the pets.
Give the patient's child a birthday party.
Drive children to or from school.
Adjust clocks to the correct time.
Return books to the library.
Water plants.
Rake or mow the lawn.
Buy a cheery new bedspread.
Find someone to do the patient's taxes.
Help with a shower or bath.
Take the patient away for the weekend.
Put up new curtains in the bathroom.
Do the ironing.
Vacuum the house.
Get the newspaper.
Bake a cake.
Give a back rub.
Walk the dog.
Shovel snow from the driveway.
Take pictures at a special event.
Make a collage of family photos.
Clean the birdcage.
Assist with filling out insurance forms.
Deliver/pick up items from the dry cleaners.
Clean the bathroom.
Get an eyeglass prescription filled.
Take a son or daughter to camp.
Clean out a closet.
Take the patient to a doctor's appointment.
Find a podiatrist who will make house calls.
Help the patient put on makeup.

Watch sports with the patient.
Program the VCR.
Play some soothing music.
Send the patient's husband off on a weekend fishing trip.
Purchase some thank-you notes and stamps.

When we accept the challenge of caring for the dying, we are not merely performing a duty. We are committing ourselves to more than easing pain and suffering, more than sitting sadly by the bedside. We are dedicating ourselves to putting Christ's love in action—ready to receive as much as we give, prepared to learn and even change, ready to ponder anew what we mean by dignity and honesty, and ready to ensure that the one we love will live out his/her days to the glory of God, leaving us and the world a little better.

LIFT volunteers are not restricted to providing assistance in a person's home. Care can be provided wherever the patient is, whether in a hospital, a nursing home, assisted living facilities, or a private residence. The focus is the patient, not his or her surroundings. LIFT is committed to serving families as well as patients. The goal is to provide practical assistance as well as emotional and spiritual support. While LIFT personnel cannot treat a person's underlying disease, we do work with medical personnel to treat all of the patient's symptoms.

GUIDING PRINCIPLES OF LIFT

- *The first priority of LIFT is to affirm the intrinsic God-given worth of each individual, regardless of physical, mental, or spiritual condition. Therefore, we are committed to treating every person with respect and dignity as one created in the image of God (Genesis 1:26–28; 9:6). Our commitment is to obey the command to "love your neighbor."*

- *Relief of pain is a top priority and we will seek to ensure that each person receives adequate pain relief. We will serve as advocates of individuals to medical providers to ensure that adequate measures are taken to alleviate pain and control other physiological symptoms of terminal illness (breathing difficulties, nausea).*

- *We are committed to cooperating with each person's personal physician and other medical caregivers (nurses, physical thera-*

pists, etc.) to ensure holistic and appropriate care is provided. We will cooperate with other agencies that provide assistance to terminally ill individuals and their families as much as our Christian commitment will allow.

- *We oppose all forms of euthanasia and assisted suicide on grounds that these practices are contrary to biblical teaching.*

- *We will provide participants with assistance in drafting and implementing biblically-appropriate advance directives when such assistance is requested.*

- *LIFT is a service ministry operating under the authority of a sponsoring local church. All volunteers are ultimately accountable to the pastors and congregations of the sponsoring church(es).*

A NETWORK OF LIFT® CHURCHES

Beyond the impact of LIFT upon a single congregation is the value of establishing a nationwide network of local congregations trained to provide hospice-type services. Geographic distances that separate individuals from their immediate family present a special set of problems when a serious illness occurs. The children of aging parents often find themselves struggling to care for a loved one from a distance, which usually means hiring caregivers to do what they cannot do for themselves. In some cases, this means that the quality of care a loved one receives falls below the standards we would want for ourselves.

CARING IS THE NATURAL OUTGROWTH

OF BEING A REDEEMED PERSON.

LIFT offers at least a partial solution to this problem. Since the LIFT training is standardized in its scope, even the person who lives some distance from family members can be cared for in a manner consistent with biblical principles and family values. By establishing a network of cooperating churches and publishing a directory, believers nationwide can obtain help during a time of serious illness.

Invariably, loving individuals in final transition requires us to restore some of the social connectedness that an overemphasis upon individualism undermines. Competitiveness and striving for prominence have overshadowed a biblical social ethic and a commitment to nurturing a caring community. This individualistic stance does not stand on a solid theological foundation, and it leaves us vulnerable to a godless culture encroaching upon areas of human life that rightly belong only to God. Tragically, local church autonomy is used to excuse a lack of cooperation and mutual caring between like-minded churches. This creates an atmosphere ripe for exploitation by social forces whose objective is to culturally marginalize the church.

More than any other institution, the church must be committed to fostering structural changes in society that will lead to more caring, others-oriented patterns of behavior. Rather than fostering the view that personal caring for the dying is peripheral to the mission of the church (i.e., proclaiming the Gospel of personal redemption), we should set ourselves about the task of showing that caring is the natural outgrowth of being a redeemed person (John 13:35). Making these changes may seem a formidable task. But the failure to try to make these changes represents a far more formidable failure—a failure to be obedient to God.

NOTES

1. Hospice of Michigan promotional brochure, September 1998. Used by permission.
2. The term "holistic" is used here to describe an approach to care that considers the person in his or her totality—physically, emotionally, socially, and spiritually.
3. Liz Harris, "Home, Home at Last," *San Francisco Examiner*, 9 July 1997, ZA1.
4. For additional information about LIFT, contact Mark Blocher, 7750 Henry Ave., Jenison, MI (616) 457-2797.

CONCLUSION

Instead of orienting believers to seek out the latest medical wizardry to extend their earthly lives, we should orient them toward cultivating a familial and church social context that cherishes and respects the elderly. Recognizing the debilitating effects of advancing age prepares us to accept the deaths of loved ones and ourselves. We need to get beyond asking physicians to deliver what they cannot give—immortality.

When there were fewer methods for extending human life, the attitude toward death was different than it is today. For one thing, many people dying today are not dealing with God and family but with doctors and nurses. Previously, once certain symptoms appeared, the only attitude to the approach of death was to let it happen. People strove to die "at peace with God." Today, we live in a medical culture that does not teach the art of dying, but the art of saving lives, and the dilemmas associated with this art (not science) are never ending. Except for hospice, we do not really attempt to manage the process of dying. Rather, we rescue, or we abandon when rescue becomes impossible.

Some of this is due to how modern culture worships youth. Commercials feature the young and the beautiful, not the old and the gray. Mandatory retirement policies, senior citizen discounts, nursing homes, and declining health remind us that there is little to look forward to in old age. Technological medicine necessarily embraces the temporal value of youthfulness—physical and mental vitality. It does so because these are relatively tangible and measurable.

Like the Greeks, we worship man. When this world is all there is and man is the chief being in that world, and when rationality and functionality are necessary to be capable of "meaningful life," all effort must be expended toward shoring up the functions of our youth. People are not permitted to die of old age.

Therefore, we find the elderly today dying in hospitals surrounded by strangers rather than in their homes surrounded by loving family and friends. "Modern medicine means modern dying in a modern hospital, where death can be hidden, cleansed of its organic blight and finally packaged for modern burial."[1] Nursing homes have grown in number as we have watched the dismantling of the family. Our affluent economy and the comforts of materialism have allowed us to travel far and wide seeking our fortune. It is not unusual for people to have family members living from coast to coast. The demographics of family life today mean the elderly, who become less mobile with age, usually have their needs met by someone other than their family.

WE NEED TO RESURRECT THE CONCEPT OF "DYING WELL" IN CHRISTIAN THINKING.

We need a revival of the concept of extended family, which could be helped considerably if Christians would have larger families. If more of us raised our children with daily connections to grandparents, aunts, uncles, etc., old age as a prelude to death would not be so foreign to many of us. Unfortunately, many Christians choose to effectively sever these relationships for a paycheck in another state.

I grew up within walking distance of both sets of grandparents. Most of my aunts and uncles also lived close to our home. I observed my grandparents aging and my parents as they dealt with it. I experienced firsthand the frustration of caring for my grandfather as he slipped into the dark abyss of senility and, ultimately, a permanently unconscious state that lasted six years. I visited my grandmother in her later years as she suffered with Hodgkin's disease, yet she maintained a sweetness toward her family and a spiritual vitality I can only hope to duplicate.

But physical deterioration is what happens to us with age, and it is useless vanity to think that if we only develop more gadgets and pills, potions and lotions we can fend off the physical certainties of our fallen condition. There are some evident limits to our earthly bodily existence, and we could save ourselves considerable frustration if we would recognize this.

Some will respond with the accusation that I sound like the advocates of euthanasia, that it is dangerous to propose "giving up" on extending the lives of the elderly. This is not what I am suggesting. What I am suggesting is that believers take a posture toward medical technology that recognizes that all of this life is a stewardship given to us by God. We need not cling to earthly bodily existence at all costs.

We need to resurrect the concept of "dying well" in Christian thinking. Learning to live well as Christians means that we learn the balance between not struggling too long or giving up too soon. When we mourn the loss of a loved one, we should mourn the loss of the person's presence and love, not experience guilt that we did something wrong or think that if we had only spent more money things would have turned out differently.

We already have sown the seeds of a public policy that would suggest the elderly have a "duty to die." I am not endorsing this specious concept. The educational effect of legalized abortion has begun to reduce official barriers to killing. The failure of Michigan authorities to prosecute Jack Kevorkian sends a chilling message that there are some people who not only have a right to die but who should die. Instead of conveying to the elderly, terminally ill, and other dependent persons that we want them around and are willing to care for them, the presence of a Kevorkian suggests that we would not mind getting rid of them. This is clearly the wrong message.

Sickness is a reminder that we are not gods. The demand for health and the resistance to the death that is inevitable must not be permitted to impose nearly ruinous burdens on others. However, interposing euthanasia as a means of avoiding these burdens, or any other burdens, creates an atmosphere wherein a "duty to die" may be fashioned. That is, if it is my right to have life peacefully ended by a physician and I choose to remain alive, am I now forced to justify my continued existence? If physician-assisted suicide is a properly competent and moral response to pain and suffering, on what grounds would remaining alive to endure pain and suffering be considered competent and moral?

Attempts to legalize physician-assisted suicide have moved into high gear. My goal is to provide the reader with arguments of sufficient public potency to abate this momentum. In a violent society, where managed care models of medicine demonstrate all of the caring of a rush-hour traffic jam, it is a dangerous proposal to remove sanctions from acts intended to cause the death of human beings. A second issue is whether or not medicine and death can be reconciled. Can the two coexist, or must physicians continue to wage a "no holds barred" war against death?

Theologically, no death can be considered a "good death." Death is a judgment from God against sin. In this sense, there really is no acceptable way to die, and there certainly can be no such thing as "death with dignity." Death is an affront to dignity. But how are people to die if there are no acceptable ways to die?

DYING IS NOT MERELY A BIOLOGICAL MATTER —IT IS A MORAL AND THEOLOGICAL MATTER.

Death is a certainty. Health is clearly a losing proposition. In this sense, any death is expected. However, modern technological brinkmanship engages in a "tooth and nail" battle all the way up to imminent death. There is a refusal to accept the reality and inevitability of death. It is ironic then, that when death becomes inevitable, we often seek to hasten it.

Physician participation in legalized abortion has contributed to the "institutionalization" of the practice. The American College of Gynecologists and Obstetricians has adopted abortion as the "treatment" for anencephalic preborns and other preborn children with serious anomalies.[2] When such a procedure is endorsed by such a respected professional association, it seems less like killing. The educational effect of legal abortion should help us understand how physician-assisted suicide and, ultimately, active euthanasia will make these practices seem less like actual killing.

Likewise, advocates contend if assisted suicide is legalized, even physicians who do not participate in it will be freed from the fear of legal jeopardy when they aggressively provide palliative care to terminally ill patients. They believe this will lessen patients' fear of overtreatment with medical technology. But will it lessen patients' fear of medicine itself? An unmistakable educational effect will occur among physicians when the law allows them to write lethal prescriptions for patients. What further corruptions of the medical profession might we be forced to tolerate when medicalized killing is expanded?

Christians must strike a balance between making too much of human bodily existence and maximizing their earthly lives for God's glory. If dying is part of the human condition (Hebrews 9:27), then dying is not merely a biological matter—it is a moral and theological matter. Death must not be seen as a purely biological event, defined solely in medical terminology. The Bible speaks to the event of death in remarkably nonbiological terminology. According to Scripture, death is not annihilation, but separation (2 Corinthians 5:1–10; 1 Corinthians 15). The death of a person is not just the loss to the human community of a biological being, but the loss of a person made in God's image—a person with God-given talents and abilities. Likewise, the dying process involves more than physiological concerns. How a person dies—how a person views death and what lies beyond its doors—is the ultimate personal manifesto of values and beliefs.

Legalizing physician-assisted suicide not only invites additional forms of medical killing but guarantees that medicalized killing will ultimately extend to people beyond the conscious, competent person who requests "aid in dying." Arguments by extension are valid when there is clear evidence to support them, and the Netherlands' experience is clear and convincing. The Netherlands is not a backward, unsophisticated, nonreligious nation. Its people are well educated, and Dutch medicine is among the best in the world. It is a nation with a distinctive spiritual history. Despite this, active involuntary euthanasia is a growing problem.

The Dutch government report on euthanasia in the Netherlands reveals a disturbing trend as tolerance for the practice has grown over the last few years. As many as 40 percent of euthanasias are not even reported, and only 29 percent of physicians who admitted performing euthanasias filled out death certificates honestly. This occurs despite the fact that the Dutch government instituted a law in 1994 stipulating that a physician who performs voluntary euthanasia will not be prosecuted.[3]

THE REALITY IS THAT PHYSICIAN-ASSISTED SUICIDE CONSTITUTES UNJUSTIFIABLE KILLING OF HUMAN BEINGS.

My hope is that this book will convince the reader of the unbiblical and immoral nature of suicide altogether, whether "assisted" by a physician or undertaken by an individual. The rising suicide rate among teens and the elderly suggests that this form of killing is becoming socially acceptable. Syndicated columnist Charles Krauthammer writes, "Ours is a society with 31,000 suicides a year, a rate 30 percent higher than the homicide rate about which people are in such a panic today. Our problem is not the difficulty of committing suicide, but the ease."[4]

On strictly theological grounds, physician-assisted suicide is not an option for Christians since it is a violation of the sixth commandment—"Thou shalt not kill."[5] The prohibition of killing human beings (Genesis 9:6) encompasses all "private killing." It encompasses not only homicide (killing someone else) but suicide (self-murder). The Bible, particularly the Old Testament, makes it quite clear killing a human being is only justified by direct divine command, such as approximately twelve capital offenses recorded in the Law of Moses, and in instances of accidental killing. Nowhere does the Bible sanction private arrangements between two individuals for one person to kill another.

Despite the humanitarian rationale presented by ethicists who contend that giving "aid in dying" is a compassionate and loving act, and despite the vigorous, well-intentioned appeals to "freedom of choice" by modern moral philosophers, the reality is that physician-assisted suicide constitutes unjustifiable killing of human beings.

Despite scrupulous "safeguards," specialized medical training, and widespread public education, physician-assisted suicide will not remain a "safe, legal" procedure managed by compassionate, professional physicians, but, like abortion, will devolve into a form of medical and social corruption, even extortion, carried out by misrepresentation, deceit, coercion, and the manipulation of those who are the most vulnerable.

Physician-assisted suicide, like abortion, will inevitably become the domain of a few practitioners who function largely outside of the medical mainstream. Like abortionists, they will operate largely in unregulated facilities, protected by the aggressive, litigious actions of civil liberties organizations who will use the courts to expand the categories of persons who should be able to exercise their "right to die." Suicide "providers" (a term abortionists also prefer) will hide behind the Constitution, recruit legislators to write protective legislation for their lethal activities, hire lawyers who will "judge shop" for sympathetic jurists to enforce the laws, and engage in influential public relations efforts to portray themselves as compassionate, caring individuals.

The temptation for the Christian community will be getting sidetracked into partisan political battles while not working to improve care for the dying. Passing and enforcing laws is merely one part of a total strategy.

The bulk of the Christian strategy must be focused on improving care at the end of life and advancing the moral arguments against euthanasia in a winsome and compassionate manner. The face of Christianity must be the face of caring and compassion. That is a face Christians have not always worn in the heat of partisan political contests. The church must be seen as a place of healing, a place of refuge and shelter when the messenger of misery stops at one's doorstep.

NOTES

1. Sherwin B. Nuland, *How We Die: Reflections on Life's Final Chapter* (New York: Vintage Books, 1995), 1.

2. The American College of Obstetricians and Gynecologists has consistently called for increased training in abortion procedures by medical schools and residency programs (ACOG Press Release, 26 October 1998). Its official position regarding abortion is that it is a legitimate, legal medical service. Although ACOG respects a physician's conscience against abortion, the association maintains that its standards of care obligate member physicians to inform pregnant women of the availability of prenatal testing and the

option of abortion for a negative diagnosis. Physicians who oppose abortion for religious or other reasons must refer women who desire abortions to physicians who will perform them.

3. Herbert Hendin, *Seduced by Death: Doctors, Patients and the Dutch Cure* (New York: Norton, 1997), 49.

4. Charles Krauthammer, "Make Dr. Kevorkian a Test Case—Then Throw the Book at Him," *Pittsburgh Post-Gazette*, 6 December 1993, 1B.

5. Exodus 20:13.

APPENDIX:

Some Relevant
Legal Issues and Cases

Although the first "right-to-die" case was not decided until 1975 (*In re Quinlan*), the legal forerunners of the present conception of a right to die were historically recognized principles. One principle relates to the issue of battery, one that protects individuals from unwanted, nonconsensual bodily contact, which the law recognizes as including unauthorized medical procedures. Under battery laws, individuals may not be medically treated without informed consent, which implies a right to refuse medical treatment. Thus, the right to die is an aspect of the right to refuse medical treatment generally. Its origins are in the same constitutional and common-law doctrines as the right to refuse medical treatment that will not lead to the patient's death.[1] The body of case law prior to *Quinlan* shows a significant reluctance to permit patients to refuse medical treatment when that refusal would likely lead to the person's death. After *Quinlan*, the right to refuse even life-saving medical treatment gradually came to be recognized by virtually every state.

Quinlan (137 N.J. Super. 227, 348 A.2d 801 (1975) rev'd, 70 N.J. 10, 355 A.2d 647 (1976)

Details of Karen Quinlan's case are provided on page 93. *Quinlan,* as the first "right-to-die" case in the U.S., established a legal precedent in New Jersey that it is permissible to withdraw treatment from incompetent patients when that treatment will keep patients alive but not restore them to health. Furthermore, it established the right of incompetent patients to refuse life-sustaining medical treatment through the exercise of substituted judgment by a proxy (parents).

Superintendent of Belchertown State School v. Saikewicz (373 Mass. 728, 370 N.E. 2d 417 (1977)

This case was the first major court decision extending the *Quinlan* principle beyond New Jersey. Joseph Saikewicz was a sixty-seven-year-old resident of a state institution for handicapped persons. He had been a resident of that facility for more than fifty years. Profoundly mentally retarded, Saikewicz communicated only through grunts and gestures, yet was mobile and physically healthy until April 1976, when he was stricken with a fatal form of leukemia. The central medical issue in *Saikewicz* centered on whether to administer chemotherapy. The superintendent of the Massachusetts institution sought court guidance about providing chemotherapy to Saikewicz. A lower court ruled in May 1976 that treatment for leukemia was not in his interest, a decision upheld by the Massachusetts Supreme Court in July 1976. Saikewicz died in September 1976.

Satz v. Perlmutter (362 So. 2d 160 (1978), aff'd 379 So. 2d 359 Florida 1980)

This case involved Abe Perlmutter, a seventy-three-year-old man suffering from amyotrophic lateral sclerosis (ALS or Lou Gehrig's disease), whose condition had deteriorated to the point where he was immobile, speech was a great strain, and breathing was maintained by a ventilator. The patient was mentally competent and sought removal of the ventilator, resulting in death within an hour. Describing Perlmutter's condition as "never ending physical torture," a lower court authorized removal of the ventilator. The Florida Court of Appeals upheld this ruling on the basis of a terminally ill patient's purported constitutional right to discontinue "extraordinary" treatment.[2]

Bouvia v. County of Riverside (No. 159780 California Superior Court, Dec. 16 1983; *Bouvia v. Superior Court*-Glenchur 179 Cal

App. 3d 1127, 225 Cal Rptr. 297 (1986) *Bouvia v. County of Los Angeles*, 195 Cal. Appl 3d 1075, 241 Cal. Rptr. 239 1987)

Elizabeth Bouvia, a twenty-six-year-old quadriplegic with cerebral palsy, checked into a California hospital with the intention of resisting all nourishment and starving to death because she perceived her condition as distasteful and humiliating. She sought the hospital's cooperation in providing painkillers and hygienic care to ease the dying process. The hospital objected to Bouvia's plan and obtained a court order in its favor. Nutrition was forcibly administered through a nasogastric tube until Bouvia checked out of the hospital on April 9, 1984. The superior court ruled that Bouvia's request was tantamount to suicide and warranted state intervention as long as she remained in a government (county) hospital. Bouvia later sued a county-owned nursing facility where she resided for the right to refuse hydration and nutrition, when supplied through a nasogastric tube inserted against her wishes or through spoon feeding.[3]

Cruzan v. Director, Missouri Department of Health (497 U.S. 261 1990)

Details of Nancy Cruzan's case are supplied on page 93. This case involved the request of Cruzan's parents to have their adult daughter's feeding tube removed. Virtually every reported right-to-die case involving the issue of foregoing artificial hydration and nutrition before Cruzan held artificial nutrition and hydration to be a medical procedure, and held that it may be forgone under appropriate circumstances, as any other medical procedure, provided that the patient is in such a condition that life-sustaining treatment in general might be forgone. At issue in the Cruzan case was whether there was "clear and convincing evidence" that Nancy would not want to have her life sustained by "artificial medical treatment." Both the Missouri Supreme Court and U.S. Supreme Court ruled that "clear and convincing evidence" did not exist that she would not want continued hydration and nutrition. Cruzan's parents returned to Missouri and later petitioned a probate court for removal of the feeding tube by presenting new witnesses. This court permitted the feeding tube to be removed, and Nancy died on December 26, 1990.

Washington v. Glucksberg; Vacco v. Quill (No. 95-1858, 117 S. Ct. 1997)

These companion cases were brought to the U.S. Supreme Court in 1997 from the Second and Ninth Federal Courts of Appeals, courts that cover the states of Washington and New York. At issue in both cases was the constitutional question of physician-assisted suicide. Both cases involved challenges to state laws (Washington and New York) that make causing or aiding a suicide a felony. *Glucksberg* and *Vacco* involved the petition of physicians who claimed they would assist dying patients to take their own lives were it not for their respective states' statutes making it a felony to do so. The physicians argued that such a statute was unconstitutional inasmuch as it violated patients' Fourteenth Amendment "liberty interests." The Second and Ninth Courts of Appeals agreed, which led each of the states' attorneys general to appeal the matter to the U.S. Supreme Court.

A liberty interest, while not specifically mentioned in the Fourteenth Amendment, is one of the penumbras (shadows) previous Supreme Courts have "discovered" in ruling that women have a constitutional right to birth control (*Griswold v. Connecticut*, 1965) and abortion (*Roe v. Wade*, 1973). This liberty interest is viewed by the courts as an aspect of the right to privacy, an important principle in what the drafters of the Constitution called "ordered liberty." The liberty interest was important in crafting the right of competent adults to refuse medical treatment. The Court found that while an individual has a right to refuse medical treatment intended to save his or her life, there is no constitutional right to commit suicide with or without another person's assistance. However, the Court did leave the door open for states to craft their own laws related to assisted suicide.[4]

NOTES

1. Alan Meisel, *The Right to Die* (New York: John Wiley and Sons, 1989), 43.
2. Norman L. Canto, *Legal Frontiers of Death and Dying* (Bloomington, In.: Indiana University Press, 1987), 2.
3. Alan Meisel, *The Right to Die*, 126.
4. For additional analysis see Alexander Morgan Capron, "Death and the Court," *Hastings Center Report*, September-October 1997, 25–36.

Moody Press, a ministry of Moody Bible Institute,
is designed for education, evangelization, and edification.
If we may assist you in knowing more about Christ
and the Christian life, please write us without obligation:
Moody Press, c/o MLM, Chicago, Illinois 60610.